THE SEARCH FOR THE PICTURESQUE

John Plaw, *Rural Architecture* (1794), frontispiece.
Victoria and Albert Museum, London

# The Search for the Picturesque

*Landscape Aesthetics and Tourism*

*in Britain, 1760-1800*

MALCOLM ANDREWS

*Stanford University Press*

STANFORD, CALIFORNIA

Stanford University Press
Stanford, California
© 1989 Malcolm Andrews
Originating publisher: Scolar Press,
    Gower Publishing Co., Ltd., Aldershot
First published in the U.S.A. by
    Stanford University Press, 1989
Printed in Great Britain
Cloth ISBN 0-8047-1402-9
Paper ISBN 0-8047-1834-2
LC 86-63668
Paperback printing 1990

# Contents

———

Preface, vii
Acknowledgements, x
List of illustrations, xi
List of maps, xvi

# Preface

When we describe something as 'picturesque' we usually have very little sense of how that adjective differs from 'beautiful', 'pretty' or 'quaint'. A rich sunset, a Caribbean beach, a ruined Greek temple, a thatched cottage, a gnarled fisherman mending his net, a morris dance: these have little in common except that, in different ways, each is visually attractive and enriched with sentimental associations. However, the travel-brochure writer would not hesitate to call each one 'picturesque'. The word is a valuable coin in the currency of tourism. It means 'like a picture' and implies that each scene fills some pictorial prescription in terms of subject-matter or composition. The travel-brochure writer is trading on his company's being able to offer access to the living originals of the pictorial stereotypes with which we have long been familiar, and which are reproduced again and again on television commercials, calendar photos and chocolate box lids. The firsthand experience of such scenes is greatly enhanced by the recognition that their type has for long been familiar in pictures: the postcard home will record that specific pleasure by describing the scenery as picturesque. It may be beautiful or quaint or colourfully old-fashioned; but if it is also *picturesque* it is established immediately as compatible with all one's fond preconceptions. The same mode of appraisal is there in the phrase 'pretty as a picture'. We hardly bother to ask *'what* picture?' We just accept that the scene has been accorded a high aesthetic status, since it evidently conforms with standard pictorial representations of beauty.

There is a peculiar circularity in the tourist's experience. He values the kind of scenery which has been aesthetically validated in paintings, postcards and advertisements; he appraises it with the word 'picturesque'; and then he takes a photograph of it to confirm its pictorial value. Scenery valued in this way becomes a commodity, as the modern tourist industry is well aware. But it is a source of pleasure not necessarily debased because of its commercial exploitation: indeed it existed long before commercialised tourism. 'We find the Works of Nature still more pleasant, the more they resemble those of Art', wrote Joseph Addison in *The Spectator* in 1712. The term 'picturesque', used in a commendatory sense, conveys exactly the kind of pleasure described by Addison. Though Addison does not actually use the term, it was coming into vogue in the early eighteenth century as an anglicisation of the French *pittoresque* or Italian *pittoresco*. Initially it carried no particular reference to landscape but meant the kind of scenery or human activity proper for a painting. Even William Gilpin, whose published journals of his tours around Britain in the late eighteenth century established the vogue for picturesque tourism, did not commit the term exclusively to landscape aesthetics. As he wrote to the illustrious Joshua Reynolds in 1791: 'With regard to the term *picturesque*, I have always myself used it merely to denote *such objects, as are proper subjects for painting*: so that according to *my definition*, one of the cartoons [of Raphael], and a flower piece are equally picturesque'. Three years later Uvedale Price's *An Essay on the Picturesque* added the definite article and elevated an unassuming adjective into an aesthetic concept of bewildering contentiousness. I shall hereafter distinguish with a capital 'P' eighteenth-century Picturesque from the modern vernacular usage of the term.

Most modern discussions of the Picturesque, from Christopher Hussey's classic study *The Picturesque* (1927) to John Dixon Hunt's recent essays, have stressed its importance in relation to developments in the history of taste in the eighteenth century. Hussey remarked that 'the picturesque interregnum between classic and romantic art was necessary in order to enable the imagination to form the habit of feeling through the eyes': 'it occurred at the point when an art shifted its appeal from the reason to the imagination'.[1] Hunt has described the complex 'movement from a learned and universally translatable picturesque to one much more hospitable to the language of forms and to the vague, the local, the sentimental, and the subjective'.[2] An example of the shift might be taken from the changing attitudes towards ruined castles. The 'classic', 'learned' response would see the ruin primarily as a moral emblem of mutability: the later response would be less inclined to *interpret* than to indulge random melancholic associations or admire the rugged contours of broken masonry and the mixed tints of lichen and moss. The present 'search' for the Picturesque has two senses. In tracing movements such as those described by Hussey and Hunt, it investigates the evolution of Picturesque tastes in the eighteenth century, in poetry, painting and aesthetic theory, and emphasises the ways in which the various pressures of nationalism in Britain promote the value of British scenery for the poets, painters and tourists. Part II has a more documentary, anecdotal function: it follows in the footsteps or carriage-wheel ruts of the first tourists, who went off to remote regions of Britain in search of landscapes which approximated to those described by the poets and painters, and which were thus Picturesque. In other words, it shifts attention from the professional connoisseurs of the Picturesque to the amateur enthusiasts of fine scenery who, in the last two decades of the eighteenth century, 'discovered' North Wales, the Lakes and the Scottish Highlands.

Modern studies of the subject began a little over half a century ago with Elizabeth Manwaring's *Italian Landscape in Eighteenth Century England* (1925) and Hussey's *The Picturesque*. Their research remains invaluable, even if some of their judgements now seem unsatisfactory. The subject of the history of British tourism (not specifically Picturesque tourism) has been ably treated in Esther Moir's *The Discovery of Britain* (1964), and her very extensive bibliography has greatly helped to launch my own research. Like so many others working in this field, I must acknowledge the pervasive influence of E. H. Gombrich's *Art and Illusion* (1960). Picturesque practice might be the tailor-made illustration of his thesis on the artist's and writer's need for an inherited vocabulary before each can 'copy' reality. Studies of the Picturesque have, over the last ten years or so, been greatly invigorated by what amounts to a school of criticism which exposes the political ideologies underlying and informing the landscape art of the eighteenth century: this approach is particularly evident in the work of John Barrell, Michael Rosenthal and David Solkin.[3]

Several friends have, often unwittingly, stimulated ideas developed in the book. Joe Engbeck's great good sense and sensitivity to nature as process rather than picture has been most helpful in my efforts not to lose the larger perspective. I have been very fortunate in the shared teaching of a course on landscape in painting and poetry at the University of Kent with three colleagues, Mary Anne Stevens, Graham Clarke and Robert Williams, each of whom has read and commented on early drafts. I would also like to acknowledge the help of Tony Hozier, with whose conversation over many years and companionship on quasi-Picturesque excursions I happily associate much of what has gone into this study. None of these should be inculpated in the book's shortcomings, but each must share any credit that comes its way.

Visits to libraries up and down the country have, without exception, been remarkable for the pleasantness and cooperation of librarians and archivists. This aspect of the 'search' has been a great pleasure. So too, of course, have my various retracings of the Tours themselves. In both kinds of research I have been generously helped by an award from the Small Grants Research Fund in the Humanities from the British Academy and by some research grants from the University of Kent. The typescript was prepared by the secretaries of Eliot College under the supervision of Ros Webb: their patience, efficiency and expeditiousness are much appreciated. So, too, is the editorial help given by Martin Bailey. The maps for the tours were drawn by Robert Williams.

My fullest debt of gratitude must go to Kristin, my wife, who has given so much support throughout the book's development. By a delightful coincidence, she has an ancestor in the General Wade who superintended the making of the great roads into the Scottish Highlands after the 1715 uprising and who subsequently earned the gratitude of the later tourists. In every important sense but the literal, Kristin has paved the way for my own search for the Picturesque.

M.Y.A.

# Acknowledgements

---

The illustrations in this book are reproduced by kind permission of the following (numbers refer to figure numbers):

Abbot Hall Art Gallery, Kendal (65); Sir Francis Beaumont (14); City of Birmingham Museums and Art Gallery (40); Bodleian Library, Oxford (17, 36, 63, 76); British Library, London (9, 25, 27, 34, 42, 46, 47, 52, 57, 60, 64, 66, 74, 75, 78); Trustees of the British Museum (7, 38, 39); Courtauld Institute of Art (3, 35, 44); Derby Art Gallery (56); Trustees of Dove Cottage, Grasmere (51, 59); Fitzwilliam Museum, Cambridge (23); Fry Gallery, London (11a & b); Kings College, Cambridge (61, 62); Lady Lever Art Gallery, Port Sunlight (82); Historic Buildings and Monuments Commission, Marble Hill House, Twickenham (1); National Gallery, London (4); National Galleries of Scotland (67, 69, 70, 80); National Library of Scotland (15); National Library of Wales (5, 16, 18, 22, 26, 31, 32, 33, 43, 48, 72, 73); National Museum of Wales (13, 28); Royal Academy of Arts (41); Science Museum (12); Tate Gallery (8, 45); Toledo Museum of Art, Ohio (2); Victoria and Albert Museum (frontispiece, 6a & b, 20, 24, 37, 49, 53, 55, 58); Walker Art Gallery, Liverpool (81); Yale Centre for British Art, Paul Mellon Collection (19, 29, 30, 50, 54, 68, endpapers); Private Collection (21).

The author and publisher would also like to thank the following for allowing quotation from manuscript material in their possession (citation of the copyright owner accompanies each reference for such quotations in the Notes and References):

The British Library Board; The Syndics of Cambridge University Library; Central Library, Cardiff, County of South Glamorgan Libraries; The Feoffees of the Chetham Library, Manchester; Edinburgh City Libraries; the librarian of Glasgow University Library; The John Rylands University Library of Manchester; The Mitchell Library, Glasgow; The Trustees of the National Library of Scotland; The National Library of Wales; The Wigan Record Office, Leigh, Lancashire.

# List of Illustrations

# List of maps

―――――

FOR KRISTIN

# PART I

# The Rise of the Picturesque

# I

# Poetry and the discovery of British landscape

At the heart of Picturesque tourism is a set of paradoxes. Two can be introduced here at the start. Firstly, the tourist wants to discover Nature untouched by man; and yet, when he finds it, he cannot resist the impulse, if only in the imagination, to 'improve' it. Secondly, the tourist travelling through the Lakes or North Wales will loudly acclaim the *native* beauties of British landscape by invoking idealized *foreign* models – Roman pastoral poetry or the seventeenth-century paintings of Claude and Salvator Rosa. The second is related to the first in that the impulse to 'improve' is usually inspired by an educated awareness of what constitutes an ideal landscape. The paradoxical nature of these responses seldom seems to have perplexed the tourist for whom the experience of natural scenery was simply enhanced by this habitual exercise of comparison and association. Thus a Welsh valley acquired a higher aesthetic value if it looked like a Gaspard Dughet painting. The first sight of a Cumberland shepherd climbing the fells with his flock became more thrilling the more it approximated to a literary prototype: Virgil's *Eclogues* suddenly loomed into the space between the tourist and shepherd. Even scenes of an industrialised landscape could be transformed imaginatively, as when a clergyman tourist at Tintern saw through the window of his inn the blazing iron-works on the river bank: 'We saw Virgil's description realized, and the interior of Etna, the forges of the Cyclops, and their fearful employment, immediately occurred to us'.[1] Again, a poetically-minded tourist in the early 1770s confronts some coal-pits near Manchester:

> This novel station to my mem'ry brought
> The classic fables we're so early taught;
> The old mythology we learn at school
> Old CHARON'S ferry and the STYGIAN pool.[2]

A literary education thus functioned as an extra, expensive piece of intellectual equipment to take into the field. It developed what Archibald Alison described as 'a new sense' for the appreciation of landscape:

. . . it is probable most men will recollect, that the time when nature began to appear to them in another view, was, when they were engaged in the study of classical literature. In most men, at least, the first appearance of poetical imagination is at school, when their

3

imaginations begin to be warmed by the descriptions of ancient poetry, and when they have acquired a new sense as it were, with which they can behold the face of nature.[3]

Given this, the Picturesque tourist is aesthetically more privileged than the illiterate spectator. As Richard Payne Knight remarked in 1805, 'a person conversant with the writings of Theocritus and Virgil will relish pastoral scenery more than one unacquainted with such poetry'.[4] Essentially the same point could be made by substituting Claude and Salvator Rosa for the classical poets. The Picturesque tourist – at least in the first generation of Picturesque tourism – is a connoisseur, trained in classical literature and familiar with the work of Claude, Dughet and Rosa. In that peculiarly restricted eighteenth-century sense of the phrase, he is a 'man of taste'. Here is the phrase employed by John Clare, whose own social background was very different from that which produced the connoisseur elite described above, but who uses the same vocabulary of discrimination:

I always feel delighted when an object in nature brings up in ones mind an image of poetry that describes it from some favourite author . . . a clown may say he loves the morning but a man of taste feels it in a higher degree by bringing up in his mind that beautiful line of Thomsons 'The meek eyd morn appears mother of dews'.[5]

The 'man of taste' and the 'clown': such distinctions exemplify the elitism of the Picturesque. There must have been many occasions on the tours when these two were brought into vivid confrontation: a Lakeland shepherd stands stupefied by the sight of a dapper tourist crouching in a stream with sketch-pad and pencil, trying to find the correct angle on some waterfall which 'savage Rosa' might have envied. A comparable encounter, expressed in allegorical terms, can be seen in the aquatint frontispiece to John Plaw's *Rural Architecture* (1794) (frontispiece). On the banks of Windermere, the elegantly dressed figure of Taste is introducing Rural Simplicity to the artificial embellishments of the natural landscape, the new classical villa (designed by Plaw) on Windermere's Belle Isle. Rural Simplicity's inscrutable expression is presumably meant to convey gratification.

In this chapter on landscape poetry I have two purposes. The first is to suggest what the 'man of taste' would be expected to know in imaginative literature: the poetry of country life, largely inherited from the Roman poets, which provided idealized models for the tourist's assessment of rural life and scenery in Britain. The second purpose is to indicate, through a few well-known texts, how these classical models were repudiated or naturalised by British poets as the century advanced. This had important consequences for what I have called the 'discovery' of British landscape. The beginnings of Picturesque tourism in Britain in the middle decades of the eighteenth century coincided with strong challenges to the cultural authority of Greek and Roman literature, with attempts to give an English vernacular flavour to classical genres of poetry, and with experiments in alternative, native traditions, such as those exemplified in Gothic and Celtic revivalism. In many respects, Picturesque tourism self-consciously functioned as the continuation of this process of cultural self-definition.

When I am become bankrupt, and have exhausted my little stock of sentiment, remark, or description, I draw upon the poets, for a fresh, and indeed, a far richer supply . . . In short, with respect to this spot [on a Highlands tour] nothing is wanting but an Amintas, to make me imagine myself in Arcadia.[6]

This whimsical reflection, from the 1775 travel journal of Mary Anne Hanway, is typical of the sort of general invocation to Pastoral by tourists who find themselves in a promising landscape and who wish to heighten their pleasure by associating the scenery with idyllic images recalled from the poets, and in particular, the Roman Augustan poets, Virgil and Horace. The use of the term 'Augustan' to describe British literature of the early eighteenth century is a way of distinguishing writers like Pope who consciously modelled their work on those Latin poets who flourished during the emperorship of Caesar Augustus in the first century B.C. The latter-day Augustan pastoral poets were fully aware of the artificiality of their genre. They knew that contemporary shepherds bore little resemblance to their idealized literary counterparts, and that they themselves were well insulated from the shepherd's world. Charles Jenner neatly illustrated the incongruity of the two worlds in his satirical *Town Eclogues* (1723) when he called to mind the leading pastoralists of his day, Pope, Ambrose Philips and John Gay:

> On Thames' smooth banks, they fram'd the rural song,
> And wander'd free, the tufted groves among;
> Cull'd every flow'r the fragrant mead affords,
> And wrote in solitude, and din'd with lords.

Pastoral was a means of escaping imaginatively from the pressures of urban or courtly life into a simpler world, or, one should say, into a world which had been deliberately simplified as a contrast to the social complexities of the city. If those late-eighteenth-century travellers set off on their tours to North Wales or the Lakes in much the same spirit, what could be more natural than that they should, like Mary Anne Hanway, frame their expectations according to the conventions of Pastoral? Even if they were not, in Payne Knight's words, specifically 'conversant with the writings of Theocritus and Virgil', they would certainly know an assortment of anglicised versions of the classics, anything from Dryden's verse translations of Virgil to a range of British pastorals, or simply vivid glimpses of a pastoral world in the works of James Thomson, Goldsmith and others. Such glimpses were sufficient if they afforded, in Pope's words, 'an image of what they call the golden age',[7] that mythical time set in an eternal spring when man lived in harmony within his society and with the natural environment.

The longing to discover a Golden Age harmony surviving in remote corners of Britain encouraged the tourists to overlook the realities of pastoral life. An example of one such scene could be found in Glencroe, the pass to the west of Loch Lomond. Both William Gilpin and Dorothy Wordsworth were captivated by the spot. Here is Gilpin's description:

In the middle of the vale stands a lonely cottage, sheltered with a few trees, and adorned with it's little orchard, and other appendages. We might call it a seat of empire. Here resides the hind, who manages, and overlooks the cattle, which in numerous herds, grazes this fertile vale: and if peace, and quietness inhabit not his humble mansion, it does not harmonize with the scene, to which it belongs.[8]

Without any further enquiry, Gilpin passes on, delighted with his pastoral idyll. Nearly thirty years later another tourist took a closer inspection of this same cottage. Its area was about twenty-seven by fifteen feet and it was divided into two rooms, the larger for the cattle and the other for the family. The cowherd had to support himself and his family on about £15 *per annum*. The tourist, reminded by contrast of one of the best-known pastoral lyrics, Marlowe's 'Passionate Shepheard', was horrified by the mother's cadaverous appearance:

... everything around her afforded substantial proof, if indeed proof were necessary, that the pastoral life, notwithstanding all the pleasures

> 'That hills and vallies, dale and field,
> And all the craggy mountains yield'

is wholly destitute of those Arcadian delights which have been ascribed to it by the wanton imaginations and 'seething brains' of the poets.[9]

The Golden Age idyll served both nostalgic and utopian purposes. The nostalgic pastoral impulse could also be associated with idealized memories of childhood, as the reliably unsentimental Samuel Johnson observed in a *Rambler* essay (21 July 1750):

[Pastoral poetry] exhibits a life, to which we have been always accustomed to associate peace, and leisure and innocence . . . In childhood we turn our thoughts to the country, as to the region of pleasure, we recur to it in old age as a port of rest, and perhaps with that secondary and adventitious gladness, which every man feels on reviewing those places, or recollecting those occurrences, that contributed to his youthful enjoyments, and bring him back to the prime of life, when the world was gay with the bloom of novelty, when mirth wantoned at his side, and hope sparkled before him.

If childhood innocence and the pastoral Golden Age of the poets were irrecoverable except in the imagination, it was still possible for the more prosperous, city-weary Augustan to enjoy a version of rural retirement which did not involve wholly forfeiting the comforts of civilisation. Just as the shepherd in the landscape stimulated associations with Virgilian pastoral, so the quiet life in a modest country residence had its venerable classical prototype; in this case, to be found in Horace's second Epode, the most frequently translated poem of the seventeenth century.[10] The Epode celebrates the contentment of the man who devotes his life to rural retirement on his small family farm. Here, to strike the keynote, is Abraham Cowley's version of the Epode's opening:

> Happy the Man whom bounteous Gods allow
> With his own Hands Paternal Grounds to plough!

> Like the first golden Mortals Happy he
> From Business and the cares of Money free![11]

The Horatian idyll has clear affinities with Golden Age longings, and endeavours to make them a practical reality. The Happy Man works his little farm, tends his vines, sheep and bees (for subsistence only, not for market gain), and is rewarded by Nature's bounty:

> With how much Joy do's he beneath some shade
> By aged trees rev'rend embraces made,
> His careless head on the fresh Green recline,
> His head uncharg'd with Fear or with Design.

For Restoration and Augustan tastes the prospect of subsistence farming proved rather too exacting (as it had for the usurer Alfius in the original Epode): but a country villa not too far from a large town became a favourite version of the Horatian ideal, and was fondly described in one of the most popular poems of the eighteenth century, John Pomfret's *The Choice* (1700). At about that date Pope's father moved from London to Binfield on the borders of Windsor Forest and there cultivated a small vegetable garden. The Binfield estate and, later, Pope's own riverside villa in what was then rural Twickenham are both versions of the Horatian ideal of country retirement. Over the artificial grotto in his garden Pope commemorated his literary inspiration with a quotation from Horace: *Secretum iter et fallentis semita vitae* ('a secluded journey along the pathway of a life unnoticed').[12]

Near the end of the century, after the improvements in roads, the country villa could afford to be rather more remote from civilisation, and indeed Picturesque tourism sometimes functions as a kind of reconnaissance for the aspiring Horatian property-owner. Many a wealthy northern industrialist enjoyed rural retirement by purchasing and developing an old cottage or building a new villa in one of the recognised beauty spots in the Lake District. Tennyson's *Edwin Morris* (1835) registers such changes:

> I was a sketcher then:
> See here, my doing: curves of mountain, bridge,
> . . . ruins of a castle . . . upon a rock
> With turrets lichen-gilded like a rock:
> And here, new-comers in an ancient hold,
> New-comers from the Mersey, millionaires . . .

Wordsworth deplored the new residents' 'craving for prospects' which meant that their houses rose from the summits of naked hills, 'in staring contrast to the snugness and privacy of the ancient houses',[13] the cottages of the dalesmen.

The country cottage has slowly developed into England's most enduring and appealing architectural expression of the Horatian ideal. In the eighteenth century this emblem of rural tranquillity, the antique 'humble cot', represented a happy blend of pastoral and Horatian aspirations:

> Remote from cities, in a rural scene,
> I lately saw the cottage of a swain;
> So neat, so private, so serene a place,
> The seat it seem'd of innocence and peace . . .
> No rich materials cou'd the building boast,
> No curious produce of a foreign coast;
> But woven hurdles, cover'd o'er with sod . . .
> A Shelter only from the winter's cold,
> As were the *Arcadian* Shepherds cots of old.[14]

So many potent associations clung to the country cottage, built of humble *native* materials as opposed to the imported Palladianism for the villas of the wealthy, that many an enterprising landowner had one built on his estate as part of the varied garden architecture catering for all moods and aspirations. In the 'Ornamented Cottage', 'chasteness and frugality should appear in every part', instructed William Marshall in his *Planting and Ornamental Gardening* (1785): if shrubs and flowers are introduced 'every thing should be native'.[15] The old, irregular, thatched cottage is, for the modern tourist as for his eighteenth-century predecessor, the *ne plus ultra* of Picturesque delight. With a *beatus ille* flourish, Payne Knight included it in his poem *The Landscape* (1794):

> Nor yet unenvy'd, to whose humbler lot
> Falls the retired and antiquated cot; –
> Its roof with weeds and mosses cover'd o'er,
> And honeysuckles climbing round the door;
> While mantling vines along its walls are spread,
> And clustering ivy decks the chimney's head.[16]

Rural retirement and the pastoral idyll favoured an Edenic, Golden Age view of life, where strenuous labour was unnecessary and where life was sustained largely by Nature's spontaneous bounty. In eighteenth-century landscape poetry the Horatian and pastoral traditions were invigorated by a classical genre which specifically celebrates rural labour, the georgic poem. The name derives from Virgil's *Georgics*, a versified treatise on farming written in 37–30 B.C. and addressed to the Roman landowners, whom Virgil exhorts to concentrate more assiduously on cultivating their estates.

Georgic writing counteracts the pastoral tendency towards passivity. Just as Genesis and Milton taught the expulsion of man from Eden and his consignment to a life of labour, Virgil declared early in his poem (here in Dryden's translation) that the mythical Golden Age of effortless abundance has been ended by Jupiter's order:

> The Sire of Gods and Men, with hard Decrees,
> Forbids our Plenty to be bought with Ease:
> And wills that Mortal Man, inur'd to toil
> Shou'd exercise, with pains, the grudging Soil.[17]

Picturesque tastes at the end of the eighteenth century, as we shall see in Chapter 3, are increasingly anti-georgic. Images of labour and cultivated countryside, so appealing to the Augustan spectator, are repudiated by Gilpin and Uvedale Price. But there is one way in which the georgic tradition encourages that nationalistic pride which is so much a part of the growth of Picturesque tourism. Virgil's celebration of labour includes three specific tributes in Book II which are echoed again and again in British Augustan poetry. He blesses the philosopher, whose knowledge and serene wisdom enable him to live free from fear. He blesses the farmer, secluded from warfare and the anxieties of public life. And he launches into a hymn of praise to Italy, to its fertility and natural resources, its benign climate, its freedom from malignant plants and animals, its beautiful cities and its heroic breed of men and women. The subjects of the first two beatitudes, the philosopher and the farmer, become in the eighteenth century quite easily conflated with the Horatian Happy Man. The Picturesque tourist's occasional impulses towards contemplative rural retirement when presented with the appropriate scenery usually carry the overtones of this Horatian-Virgilian ideal. Its extreme, reclusive, Christian exemplar is the Hermit, whose uncompromising closeness to nature intrigued Picturesque tastes. Reflecting on how crowded human society had become, Robert Heron remarked in his *Observations Made in a Journey Through the Western Islands of Scotland* (1793):

. . . I am sometimes almost tempted to fancy, that men were intended for hermits and savages . . . No wonder that living and writing, as he did, in the midst of Paris, John James Rousseau should have been led to maintain, that man was happier, more dignified, more independent in the savage state, than in a condition of polished civility.

These sentiments are endorsed again and again by the Picturesque tourists, especially by those susceptible to fashionable 'sensibility'.

Virgil's third tribute, the patriotic hymn to Italy, is ironically of the greatest importance in England for the naturalisation of imported classical versions of country life, and for quickening an awareness of Britain's own resources in natural beauty and bounty. It is ironical because, for British writers, the revered Virgil's example thus authorised defiant English panegyrics about the superiority of Britain over other, more celebrated countries, Italy included. Imitation here becomes a kind of licence for cultural emancipation.

No one took greater advantage of these opportunities than James Thomson. No single British poet contributed more to awakening and broadening the appreciation of the natural world. Joseph Warton observed:

The *Seasons* of Thomson have been very instrumental in diffusing a general taste for the beauties of *nature* and *landscape*. It is only within a few years that the picturesque scenes of our own country, our lakes, mountains, cascades, caverns and castles, have been visited and described.[18]

Thomson's masterpiece of descriptive poetry, first completed in 1730, won very great popularity. From 1750 to 1850 there were well over three hundred separate editions. *The Seasons* gained its reputation partly because of its author's omnivorous appetite for popular contemporary representations of the natural world. It consumed most of the nourishment left in those older poetic genres we have been discussing, though it could not always assimilate them.

There are set-piece passages of pastoral romance, georgic instruction and Horatian idealism scattered through the work: but these are subordinate elements. The poem's grand design and its energy spring from Thomson's contagious delight in all aspects of the natural world under the changing influence of the seasons. Up to now we have looked at poetic versions of country life in which the countryside is little more than the static, decorative setting for human activity or delicious inactivity. With Thomson that position changes: the natural world itself begins to feature as the central dramatic interest. As he wrote in his Preface to *Winter*:

In every dress nature is greatly charming . . . How gay looks the Spring! how glorious the Summer! how pleasing the Autumn! and how venerable the Winter! – But there is no thinking of these things without breaking out into poetry.[19]

Thomson's decision to break out into blank verse rather than rhymed couplets was approved as particularly appropriate for his subject. Samuel Johnson, in his *Life of Thomson*, remarked that 'Thomson's wide expansion of general views, and his enumeration of circumstantial varieties, would have been obstructed and embarrassed by the frequent intersections of the sense, which are the necessary effects of rhyme'. The step from elegantly rhymed pastoral or Horatian poetry to the more relaxed sweep of Thomson's verse is a recognition embodied in the poetic tradition itself of the scale and variety of the natural world in all its moods. The discarding of strict symmetries and neat, antithetical structures is also the prosodic equivalent of garden design over this period. William Mason in *The English Garden* (1772–81) explained his own preference for blank verse in terms which Thomson would have endorsed:

. . . numbers of the most varied kind were most proper to illustrate a subject *whose every charm springs from variety* . . . Art at the same time, in rural improvements [i.e. landscape gardening], pervading the province of Nature, unseen and unfelt, seemed to bear a striking analogy to that species of verse, the harmony of which results from measured quantity and varied cadence, without the too studied arrangement of final syllables, or regular return of consonant sounds.[20]

The enthusiasm for easing formal constraints was often related to (and justified by) the social freedoms boasted under an enlightened political constitution. Commenting on the changing tastes in gardening over the century, John Aikin wrote in the 1790s 'a taste for nature is said to be equivalent to a love of liberty and truth'.[21] Thomson, the author of *Liberty* and co-author of 'Rule Britannia', happily endorsed this kind of analogy.

Thomson the Scotsman also responded adroitly to the English nationalism of the day, which was such a force in promoting domestic tours in search of the home-grown Picturesque. Enclosing some lines of *Summer* in a letter to his compatriot David Mallet, he wryly remarked that they contained a panegyric to Britain, 'which may perhaps contribute to make my poem popular. The English people are not a little vain of themselves and their country'.[22]

### (ii) *Parnassus-upon-Thames*

> . . . the sad Nine in Greece's evil hour
> Left their Parnassus for the Latian plains . . .
> When Latium had her lofty spirit lost,
> They sought, oh Albion! next thy sea-encircled coast.[23]

The earliest tourists tended to draw on the classical writers to enhance their descriptions of scenery, especially when they travelled in countries already celebrated by those poets. In 1739 Thomas Gray, whose lines above trace the migration of the classical Muses to Britain, accompanied Horace Walpole on the Grand Tour. In crossing the Alps he was frequently reminded by the scenery of passages from Livy. Lines from Virgil and, less frequently, Homer, were piously invoked by the Grand Tourists as they made their way into Virgil's homeland. Their education had given them a fluency in the classics. But during the last half of the eighteenth century in Britain, the Roman and Greek poets were giving way to the native literature. The reading public was changing and expanding. Writers brought up under the Augustan dispensation could now no longer rely on a readership fluent in the classics. Quotations from Virgil and others had more and more often to be laboriously 'Englished'. The first two editions of William Gilpin's first Picturesque travel book *Observations on the River Wye* (1782) offer a good example of this. The second edition, of 1789, provided very loose translations of the Latin quotations which appear in the text: such translations had not featured in the first edition.

Another reason for the move away from the classical writers was the pressure of a growing impatience with the English neoclassical veneration of foreign cultures. This is expressed quite early on and with particular vigour in Thomas Tickell's *Guardian* essay (15 April 1713), where he protests against the relentless imitation of classical pastoral:

. . . our countrymen have so good an opinion of the ancients, and think so modestly of themselves, that the generality of Pastoral Writers have either stolen all from the Greeks and Romans, or so servilely imitated their manners and customs, as makes them very ridiculous.

Tickell's protest is part of that early-eighteenth-century controversy in England over the licence to naturalise the conventions of pastoral poetry.[24] Staunch neoclassicists such as Knightly Chetwood (who wrote a belligerent preface for Dryden's 1697 verse translation of Virgil's pastoral poems), John Gay and the young Alexander Pope, insisted that the classical models, Theocritus's *Idylls* and Virgil's *Eclogues*, were the only proper authorities for the pastoral poets. Against this view, writers such as Addison, Ambrose Philips and Tickell defended the poet's right to give a kind of English vernacular flavour to Pastoral; or at least to feature English shepherds in an English landscape. 'What is proper in Arcadia, or even in Italy', wrote Tickell, 'might be very absurd in a colder country'. Further absurdities arose in cases where a compromise was offered: in Pope's first Pastoral, Sicilian Muses burst into song on the banks of the Thames. By the second quarter of the eighteenth century the neoclassicists were losing ground and orthodox, quasi-Virgilian pastoral was increasingly succumbing to naturalisation.[25]

A third reason for the dwindling familiarity with the classics can be found in the growing respect for certain English poets. By the middle of the eighteenth century Shakespeare and Milton were established as rivals to Homer and Virgil, and their language was certainly more accessible for that middle-class readership from which a large proportion of the new tourists was to come. Thomas Gray is typical of those who lamented that the true native genius of poetry had been in decline in the Augustan period, and who wished to restore an older, British tradition. As we shall see during the Welsh Tour, the expression of this defiant sense of the native tradition is put into the mouth of the legendary last of the Welsh Bards. One interesting indication of the preference for the native tradition can be seen in Gray's alterations to his *Elegy in a Country Churchyard* (1751). In an early version of the *Elegy* the exemplars of the defence of the people's rights, political power, and forensic and literary eloquence were, respectively, Cato, Caesar and Cicero: in the final version they had become Hampden, Cromwell and Milton.[26]

Milton's prestige rose rapidly. Though he could hardly be called a landscape poet, he contributed to the formation of Picturesque tastes as much as did any of those poets. The descriptions of Eden in *Paradise Lost*, as we shall see later, were highly influential.* So, too, were his companion poems *L'Allegro* and *Il Penseroso* (1645). These two poems, in their invocations to Happiness and Melancholy, often celebrate landscapes which are recognisably more British than Arcadian or Italian. The most frequently quoted landscape description of all comes from this passage in *L'Allegro*:

> Som time walking not unseen
> By Hedge-row Elms on Hillocks green, . . .
> While the Plowman neer at hand,
> Whistles ore the Furrow'd Land,
> And the Milkmaid singeth blithe,
> And the Mower whets his sithe,
> And every Shepherd tells his tale,
> Under the Hawthorn in the dale.
> Streit mine eye hath caught new pleasures
> Whilst the Lantskip round it measures,
> Russet Lawns, and Fallows Gray,

*e.g. Thomas Howard's pride in his garden developments at Corby Castle in Cumberland; in 1734 he reminded one enthusiastic visitor of Milton's descriptions of Eden in Book IV, 'which very near resemble the description one wou'd give of Corby Castle' (see Peter Willis ed., *Furor Hortensis* Edinburgh, 1974, p. 32).

Where the nibling flocks do stray,
Mountains on whose barren brest
The labouring clouds do often rest:
Meadows trim with Daisies pide,
Shallow Brooks, and Rivers wide.
Towers, and Battlements it sees
Boosom'd high in tufted Trees, . . .
Hard by, a Cottage chimney smokes,
From betwixt two aged Okes . . .[27]

Milton's Happy Man 'measures' British vegetation and British architecture as he evokes landscape images expressive of joy. Many a later Picturesque tourist was to recall these descriptive phrases – especially the 'labouring clouds' resting on the mountains, and the castles 'Boosom'd high in tufted Trees' – while he gazed at Welsh or Highland landscapes where Virgilian or Homeric descriptions would have seemed incongruous.

The extraordinary popularity of these companion poems in the later eighteenth century can be judged by the number of published poems clearly influenced by them.[28] In the century following their composition about seventy-five poems demonstrate their influence. The increase in their popularity from that time on is quite remarkable: in the half-century 1750–1800 the number of such poems increases to about three hundred and twenty. No tourist who aspired to be a 'man of taste' in that later period would have been ignorant of Milton's poetic landscapes. Sixteen of those *L'Allegro* lines were quoted in William Gilpin's first discussion of landscape aesthetics, the *Dialogue upon the Gardens . . . at Stow* (1748), where they were analysed and commended as being 'quite Nature'. The 'Towers, and Battlements' couplet was mentioned in Reynolds' *Discourse XIII* (1786) as a favourite image for the painter and poet.[29] In Richard Payne Knight's poem *The Landscape* (1794), the Virgilian–Horatian Happy Man is awarded the same landscape pleasure:

Bless'd too is he, who, 'midst his tufted trees,
Some ruin'd castle's lofty Tower sees;
Imbosom'd high upon the mountain's brow.[30]

J. M. W. Turner introduced the passage into his lectures on perspective to the Royal Academy. He argued that though they were poetically beautiful in their 'Pastoral simplicity', a painter who tried to combine in the picture all the landscape components there described would soon discover harsh incongruities.[31] It was his example of the irreconcilable differences between the 'sister arts' of poetry and painting.

Two or three years before Milton composed these fairly generalised British landscapes, Mount Parnassus's traditional monopoly of the supplies of poetic inspiration had been challenged in the firm, graceful couplets of John Denham's topographical poem *Coopers Hill*.[32] A specific English location is being celebrated here, the Thames valley near Windsor. Like Michael Drayton in his *Poly-Olbion* (1622), Denham wished to enlist the 'true native Muse' for his poem on an English landscape. He argued, at the opening of the poem, that the classical haunts of the Muses, Parnassus and Helicon, were themselves created by poets, rather than being miraculously responsible for the creation of poets. This realisation consequently frees the modern poet to relocate his source of inspiration. Denham does so, and in his survey of the landscape he replaces sacred Parnassus with Cooper's Hill.

It was relatively simple but bold move to dismiss tradition in this manner, and Denham is aware of the consequences. He is now in uncharted country, a poet celebrating a landscape largely devoid of literary status. His readers would want to know what made this landscape so important that Denham was prepared to exchange more hallowed landscapes for its sake. He met their questions by offering a *paysage moralisé*, a description of a prospect in which the prominent landscape features were invested with emblematic significance. The view from Cooper's Hill included Windsor Castle, the island of Runnymede, where Magna Carta was signed, a ruined abbey (victim of the Dissolution) and the river Thames, which linked all of these in its winding course. The landscape thus offered a kind of map of English political and religious history.

Denham measures the errors and excesses of history against his view of the natural landscape itself, which he sees as a model of moderation. Two examples are particularly striking, the river Thames and the hill on which Windsor Castle stands. Unlike the fabled rivers of the ancient world, 'Whose foam is Amber, and their Gravel Gold', the unassuming Thames simply and reliably fulfils its functions as a source of irrigation and the channel for trade. The same virtues of dignity and moderation are seen in Windsor's hill:

> . . . such an easie and unforc't ascent,
> That no stupendious precipice denies
> Access, no horror turns away our eyes:
> But such a Rise, as doth at once invite
> A pleasure, and a reverence from the sight . . .
> Such seems thy gentle height, made only proud
> To be the basis of that pompous load [the Castle].[33]

To give specific, loyal point to this tribute Denham applies its emblematic significance to the King himself: 'Thy mighty Masters Embleme, in whose face / Sate meekness, heightned with Majestick Grace'.[34]

The English landscape, then, in Denham's panoramic view, exemplifies moderation, a fine combination of beauty and utility which can stand comparison with anything boasted by other countries. Pope's *Windsor-Forest* (1713) is the self-conscious successor to Denham's poem, and he acknowledges that the specific landscape he is celebrating (by and large the same, topographically, as Denham's) has already been 'By God-like Poets Venerable made'.[35] 'Let old *Arcadia* boast her ample Plain':[36] British poets could confidently turn their attentions closer to home. Once again, the same river becomes a central focus in the landscape, as 'old father Thames' announces that those fabled rivers – the gold-rich Hermus, the Tiber and the Nile – 'now no more shall be the Muse's Themes, / Lost in my Fame, as in the

1. Richard Wilson, *View on the Thames near Twickenham* (c. 1762).
Marble Hill House, Historic Buildings and Monuments Commission

Sea their Streams'.[37] Pope is now bold enough to include the Roman Tiber in his dismissal: it is clearly time for Augustan Rome to give way to Augustan England.

> No Seas so rich, so gay no Banks appear,
> No Lake so gentle, and no Spring so clear.
> Nor *Po* so swells the fabling Poet's Lays,
> While led along the Skies his Current strays,
> As thine, which visits *Windsor's* famed Abodes,
> To grace the Mansion of our earthly Gods.[38]

One final example of a celebration of the Thames valley as the successful rival to classical sites can be taken from Thomson's *Summer* (1727). The poet's view from Richmond Hill, like Denham's from Cooper's Hill, imaginatively expands to include London, Windsor's 'princely brow' and the 'silver Thames'; and then it turns to the newly developed areas of Twickenham ('where the muses haunt') and Ham:

> Enchanting vale! beyond whate'er the muse
> Has of Achaia or Hesperia sung!
> O vale of bliss! O softly-swelling hills![39]

A pictorial counterpart to the 'Enchanting vale' which competed with and has now superseded its classical counterparts, might be Richard Wilson's *View on the Thames near Twickenham* (c. 1762), a deftly classicised piece of English topography, with Claudean lighting and framing devices and the elegant pediment of Marble Hill House standing in for a Roman temple (fig. 1). The scene is thus given classical dignity without being slavishly transformed into a stretch of the Roman Campagna. For one thing, as David Solkin has noted,[40] there is some Dutch influence on the composition which subtly undercuts any idea of the pure classicism of the subject. Solkin also associates the painting with a near-contemporary topographical poem which has many an echo of Pope's *Windsor-Forest* nationalism:

> Such numerous villas along thy banks [Thames] we see,
> That royal Tiber must give place to thee.

These robust poetic declarations of independence consecrate an English landscape for subsequent celebrations. For Denham, that landscape revealed a political and moral significance: only incidentally did it suggest an appeal more purely aesthetic. Pope's *Windsor-Forest* adds a remarkable range of colour to the same view, and shows a greater sensitivity to landscape forms and chiaroscuro. Thomson, like his predecessors, respects the historical associations of the area, but responds even more fully to the beauty and grandeur of the landscape. The first version of *Summer* produces this rhapsody:

> And what a various prospect lies around!
> Of hills, and vales, and woods, and lawns, and spires[41]

'Various' is the key to the beauty of this particular view. That and the precise sequence of landscape components in the second line are designed to stimulate very specific associations, not with a pagan, classical world but with Milton's description of Eden in *Paradise Lost*. Parnassus-upon-Thames gives way to Paradise Regained.

## (iii) *The 'Picturesque Poets'*

Christopher Hussey gave the title 'Picturesque Poets' to Thomson and Dyer:

These poets look at and describe landscape in terms of pictures. Each scene is correctly composed, and filled in with sufficient vividness to enable the reader to visualise a picture after the manner of Salvator and Claude. Picturesque describes not only their mode of vision, but their method.[42]

It may seem contradictory to challenge the validity of this title as I conclude a chapter on the contribution of the poets to the development of Picturesque tastes. But I think that the acceptance of the influence of painting on these poets has been too easy and often misrepresents their descriptive writing.

The keynote struck at the end of the previous section was the 'various prospect'. The variety of the British landscape is stressed again and again in terms such as these from Gilpin: 'From whatever cause it proceeds, certain I believe it is, that this country exceeds most countries in the *variety* of its picturesque beauties'.[43] I want briefly to trace the nature and importance of this idea of variety in the tradition of descriptive poetry which culminates with Dyer and Thomson; and thereby to suggest how misapplied that title 'Picturesque Poets' can be.

Milton's Eden was a 'happy rural seat of various view'.[44] It offered a stimulating arrangement of contrasted landscape components, a 'sweet interchange /Of Hill and Vallie, Rivers, Woods and Plaines,/Now Land, now Sea'.[45] Milton amplified this 'various view':

> Flours worthy of Paradise which not nice Art
> In Beds and curious Knots, but Nature boon
> Powrd forth profuse on Hill and Dale and Plaine,
> Both where the morning Sun first warmly smote
> The open field, and where the unpierc't shade
> Imbround the noontide Bowrs . . .[46]

The young Alexander Pope paid tribute to Milton's Eden in the opening of *Windsor-Forest*. Where Denham invoked hallowed pagan landscapes, Pope associates the scenery with the 'various view' of the Christian Paradise. For him, the Forest is a microcosm of the ideal order of Nature:

> Not *Chaos*-like together crush'd and bruis'd,
> But as the World, harmoniously confus'd:
> Where Order in Variety we see,
> And where, tho' all things differ, all agree.[47]

The principle on which this exemplary landscape is founded is that of *concordia discors*, the harmonizing of discords. Denham had referred to it in *Coopers Hill*:

Such huge extreams when Nature doth unite,
Wonder from thence results, from thence delight . . .
And in the mixture of all these appears
Variety, which all the rest indears.[48]

Pope's influential contemporary, the Earl of Shaftesbury, implicitly endorsed this principle when he argued that the world's beauty was founded on contrarieties: 'from such various and disagreeing principles a universal concord is established'.[49] The ancient doctrine of *concordia discors* was, as the critic Earl Wasserman has shown,[50] central to Pope's thought, whether he was discussing the natural world, political organisation, or the ethics of the individual. It meant neither the peaceful resolution of conflict, nor its opposite extreme the reign of Chaos, but a dynamic state of controlled tensions. In man it was the active, energetic tension between reason and passion: in the political state it was the fruitful tension between anarchy and despotism. In gardening it was the 'artful wildness' commended in Pope's *Epistle to Burlington* (1731); and in the natural landscape it was the experience of controlled variety offered by Windsor Forest:

Here waving Groves a checquer'd Scene display,
And part admit and part exclude the Day
As some coy Nymph her Lover's warm Address
Nor quite indulges, nor can quite repress.
There, interspers'd in Lawns and opening Glades,
Thin Trees arise that shun each others Shades.
Here in full Light the russet Plains extend;
There wrapt in Clouds the blueish Hills ascend.[51]

The eye swings 'Here . . . There . . . Here' in its appreciation of the dynamic pattern of contrasts which distinguishes this landscape of 'various view': woodland and open country, plain and hill, clarity and obscurity.

David Solkin has argued that the principle of *concordia discors* determined the structure of one of Richard Wilson's most popular paintings *The White Monk* (early 1760s) (fig. 2), where human types and landscape forms are contrasted within, but ordered and contained by the total composition.[52] The lovers dallying under the parasol in the sunny foreground contrast with the ascetic monk on the dark, sheer cliff: plain and mountain, waterfall and placid river likewise represent the pattern of contrasts. This pictorial structure of antithesis, of 'Order in Variety', seems a plausible equivalent to Pope's lines which are organised around strong contrasts. It is far more plausible an analogy than the more obviously 'Picturesque' one suggested by Michael Rosenthal when he argues that Pope is here manipulating the Claudean principle of spatial recession by contrasting bands of light and dark. He suggests that as we move from line to line or couplet to couplet in Pope's description we are moving systematically from foreground to distance.[53] He points to the four lines of description awarded to the waving groves as evidence that they are foreground objects, more clearly distinguishable than the other, distanced features which are awarded one or two lines only. The chief objection to this is

2. Richard Wilson, *The White Monk* (early 1760s).
Toledo Museum of Art, Ohio

3. John Wootton, *Landscape with a Shepherd on a Hill* (1749).
Courtauld Institute, London

that the fanciful simile of the coy nymph which occupies the second couplet, does nothing to enhance the visual definition we expect of foreground.

The case for direct influence of landscape painting on the descriptive poetry of the first half of the century, though often asserted, can rarely be proved, except when supported by external evidence. One example where such a relationship seems proven is John Wootton's *Landscape with a Shepherd on a Hill* (1749) (fig. 3), commissioned by Lord Lyttelton. Arline Meyer[54] has pointed out how closely the painting illustrates lines in Lyttelton's own poem *The Progress of Love*:

> Begin my Muse, and Damon's woes rehearse,
> In wildest numbers and disordered verse.
> On a romantic mountain's airy head
> (While browzing goats at ease around him fed)
> Anxious he lay, with jealous cares oppress'd;
> Distrust and anger lab'ring in his breast –
> The vale beneath a pleasing prospect yields,
> Of verdant meads and cultivated fields;
> Through these a river rolls its winding flood,
> Adorn'd with various tufts of rising wood;
> Here half conceal'd in trees a cottage stands,
> A castle there the op'ning plain commands,
> Beyond, a town with glitt'ring spires is crowned,
> The distant hills the wide horizon bound.

The poet clearly directs the eye from the foreground of the mountain viewpoint through the vale beneath passing, in order, cottage, castle and town, to the horizon's bound. Wootton faithfully reproduces this structure in his painting, threading each of the principal features on his winding river.

Lyttelton's lines may be compared with a descriptive passage in Joseph Warton's poem *The Enthusiast* (1744), where the 'Lover of Nature' repudiates the great ornamental gardens such as Stowe and Versailles and then turns to the natural landscape:

> Yet let me choose some pine-topt precipice
> Abrupt and shaggy, whence a foamy stream,
> Like Anio, tumbling roars; or some bleak heath,
> Where straggling stands the mournful juniper,
> Or yew-tree scath'd; while in clear prospect round,
> From the grove's bosom spires emerge, and smoke
> In bluish wreaths ascends, ripe harvests wave,
> Low, lonely cottages, and ruin'd tops
> Of Gothic battlements appear, and streams
> Beneath the sun-beams twinkle.[55]

The images which, like Lyttelton's lines, mix *Penseroso* and *L'Allegro* moods, include cottage, castle and town, but the poet has not suggested what precise position they should occupy in his landscape. His main concern is to capture, through contrasts, the rich, relaxed variety of nature and compare it with the controlled, ornamental opulence of the great gardens. Arguments that writers like Pope and Thomson are modelling their landscape descriptions on Picturesque or Claudean principles seem to me often to be premature and reductive. They overstress the role of the visual imagination in response to a poetry which is playing on more complex associations (such as *concordia discors*) and which, implicitly or explicitly, is reviving past *literary* models (such as Milton's Eden or the mood landscapes of *L'Allegro*). An example with which I would like to finish this chapter is Thomson's celebrated description in *Spring* of a view from Lyttelton's Worcestershire estate, Hagley. Thomson called it the 'British Tempè', bringing his panegyric in line with the Parnassus-upon-Thames tradition:

> Meantime you gain the height, from whose fair brow
> The bursting prospect spreads immense around;
> And, snatched o'er hill and dale, and wood and lawn,
> And verdant field, and darkening heath between,
> And villages embosomed soft in trees,
> And spiry towns by surging columns marked
> Of household smoke, your eye excursive roams –
> Wide-stretching from the Hall in whose kind haunt
> The hospitable Genius lingers still,
> To where the broken landscape, by degrees
> Ascending, roughens into rigid hills
> O'er which the Cambrian mountains, like far clouds
> That skirt the blue horizon, dusky rise.[56]

In *The Idea of Landscape and the Sense of Place* John Barrell has argued that these lines represent a verbal equivalent of a Claude landscape in the way that the description is organised.[57] Hussey and other writers on eighteenth-century landscape poetry have also cited this passage, casually concluded that Thomson must have been influenced by Claude, and consequently acclaimed it as an early example of the Picturesque in poetry. I would not want to dispute Barrell's analysis of Thomson's manipulation of the rich view, but I am not persuaded that Claude had much to do with it. The external evidence for this claim, as the writer admits, is of little use: there is no firm proof that Thomson was particularly familiar with Claude's paintings. The case rests on the internal evidence, on the way in which the view is structured:

… the direct connection between Claude's way of looking at landscape and Thomson's was fairly generally assumed in the eighteenth century, and precisely because no other way of looking except Claude's could easily be imagined.

This is too restrictive. As Luke Herrmann points out in his *British Landscape Painting of the Eighteenth Century*, the Dutch and Flemish landscape schools were very popular in the first three decades of the eighteenth century, and it is a mistake to think that Claude had a monopoly of influence. But Thomson's landscape description seems to me to belong principally to none of these schools. One very obvious way for a poet to look at the landscape is through the eyes of his poetic predecessors. The influences on Thomson in this passage are literary rather than pictorial, and belong to the tradition we have already traced.

The lines in question come at the end of a passage of complimentary description of Hagley and its proprietor; and it is fitting that the culminating grand prospect should invoke comparison with Milton's Eden. In that first garden, nature had been made to pour forth her bounty, just as the generously 'improved' Hagley now offers this 'bursting prospect'. Eden exemplified what Milton had called the 'sweet interchange' of specific, contrasted landscape forms: 'Hill and Vallie ... Now Land, now Sea'. Pope, inspired to reproduce Eden in Stuart Windsor Forest, opens with echoed contrasts, 'Hills and Vales', and then 'the Woodland and the Plain'. Thomson follows this pattern with 'hill and dale' and then 'wood and lawn', pairings which also recall Pope's 'waving Groves' and 'Lawns', and Milton's 'unpierc't shade' and 'open field'. This controlled pattern of contrasts – the 'Order in Variety' – shapes the whole of the rest of Thomson's descriptive tribute to his patron's masterpiece. Fertile field is opposed to heath; and modest villages, which, like the *L'Allegro* towers, are 'embosomed soft in trees', are contrasted with the more assertive 'spiry towns'. In the final vivid contrast the sociable, domestic spirit is opposed to the inhospitable Sublime of the distant hills of North Wales. Thomson may have called this landscape the British Tempè, but, as he reproduces it in description, it is designed to be a Georgian Garden of Eden. The title 'Picturesque' diverts attention from this particular panegyric endeavour, and limits its appeal to the more purely formal aspects of landscape composition.

There we might leave the prospect poet, secure in his commanding position, his eye roaming beyond the parkland to that wilder country of North Wales, which, within a generation, was to become the object of one of the most popular British Picturesque tours. The aim in this chapter has been to suggest how, in British landscape poetry of the early eighteenth century, we can trace the adaptation of inherited descriptive models to new cultural and aesthetic enterprises. The gradual naturalisation of classical pastoral poetry and the imaginative re-creation of Milton's Eden in the Thames Valley or a Worcestershire landscape prepare for the Picturesque in two important ways. The first is simply to raise the status of British natural scenery and encourage tourism. The second is to prefigure Picturesque practices. In poetry, Milton's Eden is translated to a British setting both by explicit invocation and by reduplication of the internal descriptive structure. In the tourists' journals and sketch-books substantially the same practices are apparent. There are rapturous invocations to Claude or Thomson, when the tourists affect to despair of doing justice to the scenery before them; and, in their paintings, they manipulate Welsh or Lakeland views into compositional structures derived from Claude and Dughet. This pictorial process is discussed in the following chapter.

# II
# Landscape painting and the
# Picturesque formulae

'Painting has hitherto made but faint Efforts in England',[1] Horace Walpole complained in 1762 in his *Anecdotes of Painting*. National glory, which England had now secured, usually encouraged the flourishing of 'the more peacefull arts'. This had happened in Athens, Rome and Florence. England could be proud of herself in most of the peaceful arts in this period, and especially in poetry and landscape gardening. If this latter art, so closely allied to painting, had become so refined, why had the painters not taken advantage of it?

The flocks, the herds, that now are admitted into, now graze on the borders of our cultivated plains, are ready before the painter's eyes, and groupe themselves to animate his picture . . . Enough has been done to establish such a school of landscape, as cannot be found on the rest of the globe. If we have the seeds of a Claud or a Gaspar amongst us, he must come forth.[2]

Talents had appeared already in seventeenth- and eighteenth-century England, notably in portraiture and in Hogarth's genre painting. But the English School which Walpole so anxiously awaited was to be founded on landscape painting: 'In a country so profusely beautified with the amoenities of nature, it is extraordinary that we have produced so few good painters of landscapes'.[3] In painting as in poetry, the appeal to swelling nationalism was a strong pressure behind the emergence of an English school of landscape.

In the neoclassical hierarchy of genres, landscape painting held an inferior position: 'History-painting, like epic poetry, is certainly the grandest production of the art',[4] as even that dedicated landscape-student William Gilpin conceded. Gainsborough's career, which had already begun when Walpole wrote his *Anecdotes*, provides an example of the struggle of landscape painting to win respectability and (which is much the same) profitable patronage. 'I'm sick of Portraits', he complained, 'and wish very much to take my Viol da Gamba and walk off to some sweet Village where I can paint Landskips and enjoy the fag End of Life in quietness and ease'.[5] This is the painter's version of the Horatian ideal, to leave court and city life for rural retirement and obscurity. But the Horatian gesture risked forfeiture of patronage. For most of the century, those who commissioned paintings were still mainly interested in portraits and history paintings, both of which subordinated landscape to little more than a decorative backdrop. Topographical paintings, especially estate portraiture, were in some demand; and Richard Wilson's popular classicised British landscapes and country-house paintings of the 1760s and 1770s contributed significantly to the elevation of this lowly genre. As if in reply to Walpole's complaints, Lord Shelburne in the late 1760s commissioned paintings from Gainsborough, Wilson and George Barrett for his Wiltshire home, Bowood: with these he 'intended to lay the *foundation of a school of British landscapes*'.[6]

During the second half of the eighteenth century the decorative natural background to portraits, 'conversation pieces' and history paintings was brought increasingly to the fore. If Reynolds' *Discourses* exemplified the conservative, neoclassical relegation of landscape painting to a low status, the more adventurous *Monthly Review*, in a 1758 article, was concerned to elevate both the painting and poetry of landscape: 'Tho' descriptive poetry is doubtless inferior, both in dignity and utility, to ethic compositions, yet it ought to be remembered, that as in a sister-art, Landscape claims the next rank to History-painting'.[7] As the landscape artist is raised in dignity the human figures in his paintings become increasingly subordinate. They are introduced as *staffage* or merely to 'animate' a landscape. The chief use of figures in a landscape, according to Gilpin, was 'to mark a road – to break a piece of foreground – to point out the horizon in a sea-view':

If by bringing the figures forward on the foreground, you give room for *character*, and *expression*, you put them out of place as *appendages*, for which they were intended.[8]

The formal subordination of human figures restricted the practical roles they could play. For one thing, just as men were no longer to be seen commanding the landscape, so they were less often to be seen 'improving' it, agriculturally or ornamentally. The Muse of painting, as John Aikin argued in his *Essay on the Application of Natural History to Poetry* (1777), was free to 'exhibit the rural landskip, without encumbering herself with the mechanism of a plough, or the oeconomy of the husbandman'.[9] The portrayal of landscape, in other words, does not have to have a georgic justification. The figures favoured by later Picturesque tastes were the beggars, gypsies or idle shepherds, who were far from interfering with nature. As Gilpin's notorious distinction put it: 'In a moral view, the industrious mechanic is a more pleasing object than the loitering peasant. But in a picturesque light, it is otherwise'.[10] Some of the implications of this distinction are discussed in a later chapter.

Painting's sister-art had shown the way to freedom from didacticism or slavish topographical portraiture with Thomson's *Seasons*, which, according to Aikin, 'proved a refutation of those critics who deny that description can properly be the sole object of a poem, and would only admit of its occasional introduction as part of a narrative, didactic, or moral design'.[11] Such complaints about the moral obligations on the painter to make the human presence predominate over the landscape were echoed by Gainsborough:

... do you really think that a regular Composition in the Landskip way should ever be fill'd with History, or any figures but such as fill a place (I won't say stop a Gap) or create a little business for the Eye to be drawn from the Trees in order to return to them with more glee.[12]

Unfortunately for Gainsborough, the market really did think figures should be a part of the landscape, and a prominent part. Richard Wilson could more than double the price of his landscape paintings if he introduced figures. Both he and Gainsborough were dismally unsuccessful with sales of their 'regular Composition[s] in the Landskip way' in the 1770s.

Landscape painting could begin to compete with genres of a higher status in the late eighteenth century through the influence of paintings by the French and Italian landscape artists of the previous century, Claude Lorrain, Nicolas Poussin and his brother-in-law Gaspard Dughet, and Salvator Rosa. Dughet adopted his brother-in-law's surname, and it was usually he rather than Nicolas who was referred to in the numerous references to Poussin in the eighteenth century. Claude had incalculable influence on English landscape painting, an influence both liberating and constraining. His own paintings, in which the landscape predominates, were (just) classifiable as history paintings. The ineptly painted human figures from classical legend or from the Bible, were caught at historically important moments – Aeneas at Delos, St George killing the dragon, the marriage of Isaac and Rebecca, the angel's annunciation to Hagar (fig. 4). But in each case it is the landscape rather than the human drama which is most powerfully expressive of the serenity of accomplished destiny.

Claude merited several complimentary remarks in Reynolds' *Discourses*. Although Reynolds generally endorses the low status of landscape painting, he concedes that Claude's own practice conforms with the ideas on 'general nature' and the *beau idéal* he so often commends to the Royal Academy students. The 'truth' of Claude's landscapes, he argues in *Discourse IV*, is 'founded upon the same principle as that by which the Historical Painter acquires perfect form'.[13] The work of Claude and Dughet was well known not only to painters in mid-eighteenth-century England, but to the Grand Touring aristocracy and cognoscenti. In addition to the few Claudes already in England in the late seventeenth century, originals and copies were purchased in Italy and brought home to adorn the walls of the great houses. Over eighty Claudes were in English collections by the early nineteenth century, and over a hundred Rosas. Though these estimates most likely include copies, the evidence points to the considerable popularity of the Italian landscapes. Turner, in his fourth Lecture to the Royal Academy, claimed that England now possessed the choicest of Claude's works. Between 1711 and 1759, three hundred landscapes attributed to Dughet passed through the English sale rooms.[14]

The work of these painters was also popularised through engravings. Between 1741 and 1746 Arthur Pond and Charles Knapton published forty-two engravings after Old Master landscapes, amongst which were thirty Dughets and eight Claudes. Rosa's work was also known through the *Figurine* etchings and, certainly

4. Claude Lorrain, *Hagar and the Angel.*
National Gallery, London

by the 1770s, in the form of a number of engravings, according to Boydell's 1779 *Catalogue Raisonée*. Claude's *Liber Veritatis*, the collection of about two hundred drawings which he made after his oils, came into the possession of the Duke of Devonshire in the 1720s. Richard Earlom made engravings from them and they were published as sepia mezzotint prints by Boydell in 1777.

Claude's example allowed painters to concentrate much more on the disparaged landscape element in a history painting without too much violation of neoclassical canons. It was in this sense a liberating example. But the price for this freedom was a new orthodoxy. To copy Claude was, according to Gainsborough's friend William Jackson in 1798, 'the first effort of every smatterer in landscape painting'.[15] Claude became an approved model from the mid-century onwards, and departure from his practice could be regarded as heretical. Alternative landscape traditions, such as seventeenth-century Dutch paintings, were disparaged by the neoclassical critics, largely because these painters seemed less interested in idealizing the natural world than in faithfully rendering natural detail, and thus forfeited the 'intellectual dignity' prescribed by Reynolds in his third *Discourse*. Gainsborough, Constable and the Norwich School drew upon the Dutch landscape tradition, rightly recognising that their local East Anglian landscapes had more in common with Holland than with Italy. But both Gainsborough and Constable were, in this respect, at odds with the English establishment. The famous, if partly apocryphal, story of Constable's dispute with his patron Sir George Beaumont is a good example of the tenacity of these establishment prejudices. Beaumont protested that Constable should give his landscape paintings the rich brown tones associated with mellow Claude or Dughet scenes (often the result of over-varnishing), and recommended the tone and patina of an old Cremona fiddle. Constable's reply was to take the fiddle out of the studio where they were painting together and lay it down on the lawn against the fresh green of the grass.[16] Constable's subversive use of bright colour was to be invoked as a cautionary tale on several occasions. The young Holman Hunt, on showing one of his landscapes to his drawing master, received this rebuke:

Oh, dear no, certainly not . . . You haven't any idea of the key in which nature has to be treated; you must not paint foliage green like a cabbage; that'll never do . . . Constable, who is just lately dead, tried to paint landscape green, but he only proved his wrong-headedness; in fact, he had no eye for colour; there now, you see all the trees and grass, which an ignorant person would paint green, I've mellowed into soft yellows and rich browns.[17]

The search for the proper Old Master tone was a very earnest one. Gilpin recalled his own practice in the 1730s and 1740s:

I well remember . . . when a boy I used to make little drawings, I was never pleased with them till I had given them a brownish tint: And, as I knew no other method, I used to hold them over smoke till they had assumed such a tint as satisfied my eye.[18]

George Lambert, one of the earliest native-born landscape painters of any eminence, was praised in a 1782 critical essay because his sober 'master tint is firmly kept up': 'he never offends us with the gaudy glare and rawness of many modern paintings'.[19] How well that foreshadows the hostile critical reception of Turner's late work.

In addition to the obligatory, mellow master-tint, certain structural principles derived from Claude and Dughet* were adopted by the English painters. These were, particularly, the breaking down of a landscape into three distances: a background, a strongly lit middle or second distance, and a darkened foreground. Here is the versified prescription from William Mason's *The English Garden*:

> . . . three well-mark'd distances
> Spread their peculiar colouring. Vivid green,
> Warm brown and black opake the foreground bears
> Conspicuous; sober olive coldly marks
> The second distance; thence the third declines
> In softer blue, or less'ning still is lost
> In faintest purple.[20]

The tripartite structure was accompanied by the device of the *repoussoir* object, the foreground framing trees, or the tree and ruin, or mountain sides, to prevent one's eye from straying outside the canvas and to push it into the middle distance. The dark foreground frame, which might extend round at the top to an overarching bough, was known as a means of heightening visual perception in contexts other than painting. William Derham's *Physico-Theology* (1713) had explained how objects are made more striking by shading and framing the view with the hands. In the middle of the century, Joseph Spence and Philip Southcote refer to this effect in their observations on designing a garden: 'one sees a picture much stronger when the sidelights are broken all round by a proper holding up of the hand'.[21] These devices were modified by painters of the Picturesque persuasion: for example, the incisive angularity of withered trees was preferred to the more flourishing Claudean version. The devices became conventions, and the conventions in turn supplied the descriptive vocabulary of the Picturesque tourist, with his talk of 'side-screens', 'off-skips' and select distances. The artificiality of this terminology was accentuated by its association with stage design. The simplification of Claude's characteristic compositional pattern could only encourage analogy with the theatre – framing trees resembling the wings in a stage set. The antiquarian William Stukeley gives a good example of the analogy many years before Picturesque taste had formed its own jargon: 'the mountains on each side rising to a great height, one behind the other the whole length and broke off into short ones, like scenes at a playhouse'.[22] For later travellers, the flattening effect of the Claude Glass mirror-image made landscape forms, as Gilpin remarked, 'something like the scenes of a playhouse, retiring behind each other'.[23] Garden design was also now employing the kind of

---

*The early-eighteenth-century British landscape painters, particularly John Wootton and George Lambert, developed a type of composition which is often closer to Dughet than to Claude; but the typical, idealized, classicised landscapes of the period were an amalgamation of the two.

perspective tricks known to set designer and landscape painter. Joseph Spence advised a friend on the ways to create illusions of space in gardens:

To make objects that are too near seem farther off: which is done by shewing more of the intermediate ground and narrowing your view to them more and more as it recedes from you.[24]

While we are on the subject of stage design it is worth adding that several prominent landscape painters in the eighteenth century at some point in their careers, worked for the London theatres; for instance, George Lambert, Michael Angelo Rooker and Thomas Malton the younger. The best landscape painters in Scotland all worked for the theatre, and made their reputations there.[25] The best known and, in many ways, the most influential of the scene painters in London was Philip de Loutherbourg. His work at Drury Lane in the 1770s revolutionised set design, replacing architecture with landscapes, and sets of a formal, idealized kind with Picturesque and Sublime scenery.[26] For most of the century the theatres had relied on stock scenery, generalised backgrounds for the far more important action of the drama. Under de Loutherbourg, stage scenery, and especially romantic landscape scenery, became in itself one of Drury Lane's greatest attractions. His triumph came with his sets for *The Wonders of Derbyshire* (1779) for which he designed twelve scenic views, from sketches taken during a tour to the Peak District.

A good example of the Picturesque vocabulary, with its 'screens' and 'distances', is found in James Clarke's *Survey of the Lakes* (1787), as he directs the Picturesque artist to various prime viewpoints on Ullswater:

Next proceed to a little bay in *Hallin-Hagg*, where the painter will meet with employment for his pencil in two most beautiful landscapes. The best of these, in my opinion, faces Glencoyn, and contains many good objects not crouded too close together. The side-screens will be Ewe-Cragg, the rising ground in Gowbarrow Park, and some other less striking objects on the right hand: on the left, a small coppice, Sandwich-Dod, Sandwich-Cascade, and Birk-Fell: the front screen will take in Glencoyn-House, Lyulph's Tower, and the picturesque ground on which they stand; whilst Glencoyn Pike, Common-Fell, Catesby Pike, and Helveylin, succeeding each other in just degrees of distinctness, close the distances.[27]

Such scrupulous directions to an exact viewpoint were often combined, incongruously, with encouragement to take liberties in rearranging the components of the scene. R. H. Newell did for Welsh scenery what Clarke and Thomas West had done for the Lakes: he established very specific 'Stations' for the artists. Here are his instructions for getting the right angle on Llaugharne Castle after mounting the first hill on the Tenby road out of Llaugharne:

Bring the Castle exactly *within the angle* made by the sloping hill and woody steep *before* it. Then ascend or descend, till the *water* and *three* of the promontories appear above the castle. In this station the sea bounds the distance, Nature's compositions are seldom complete or correct; but here nothing seems in the wrong place, and little which one

5. William Payne, 'Laugharne Castle', from R. H. Newell, *Letters on the Scenery of Wales* (1821). National Library of Wales, Aberystwyth

would wish away. The only liberties necessary to be taken are, a tree or stump, planted at the *left* corner, and the uniformity of the long hedge on the right of the foreground somewhat broken.[28]

Fig. 5 shows how loyally Gilpinesque Newell's principles are. One may compare it with Gilpin's two 'Mountain Landscapes' (fig. 6) designed to illustrate Picturesque principles.[29] In the non-Picturesque version (6a) the smooth converging lines of the mountains cradle an equally smooth middle-distance. In the Picturesque version (6b) these lines are roughened and irregularized, and produce a model landscape upon which Newell bases his view of Llaugharne Castle.

Gilpin, it should be noted, was not a whole-hearted admirer of Claude. But then we should remember that he had reservations about Nature's own competence in designing her landscapes. He praised Claude's colouring, and his 'aerial' distances, but remarked that 'we rarely find an instance of good composition in any of his pictures, and still more rarely an exhibition of any grand scene or appearance of Nature'.[30] He felt Claude's landscapes were too cluttered and lacked simplicity. Even so, Gilpin's structural conventions in landscape painting more often than not seem dependent on Claude's example: 'the more redundant designs of Claude are simplified' he wrote in introduction to some of his own drawings which he offered for sale.[31] Gilpin's version of this simplified Claudean design can be seen in fig. 7, an archetypal Picturesque composition.

6a & b. William Gilpin, 'Non-Picturesque and Picturesque Mountain Landscapes',
from *Three Essays* (1792: plates from 1808 ed.)
Victoria and Albert Museum, London

7. William Gilpin, *Landscape Composition.*
British Museum, London

By the turn of the century the Picturesque vocabulary, both verbal and pictorial, had hardened into a jargon, and impatience with it became more marked:

The old mode of composing pictures by certain formulae, like apothecaries' prescriptions, or receipts in cookery, seems (at least in landscape) to have given way to the study of nature.[32]

This is the point at which the search for the Picturesque gives way to innovations which we associate with Constable's naturalism, and, later, Ruskin's call to artists to observe Truth in their paintings of the natural world. But the old formulary mode was tenacious. William Craig, in his *Essay on the Study of Nature in Drawing Landscape* (1793), lamented its noxious influence: 'amongst many practitioners in drawing, a certain set of signs has been employed, as by agreement, to represent, or signify, certain objects in nature, to which they have intrinsically little or no resemblance.'[33] These highly stylized modes of both execution and design survived long into the nineteenth century, in spite of Ruskin's polemics. Elizabeth Fry's sister, Richenda Gurney, was tutored by the Norwich painter John Crome, and her landscape compositions evidently exhibited the characteristics of ossified Claudean conventions. They were:

resolutely picturesque, as though the drawing-master had stood looking over the shoulder of the artist, pointing out the bough of a tree should always chance to arch over the foreground, and a figure in a red cloak pass across the middle distance . . . The facts of the landscape gave way if they conflicted with the rules of the game.[34]

Richard Jefferies was more impatient with the old conventions. In *The Open Air* (1885) he tells of his encounter with an artist who seems to favour a generalised Dutch School manner:

He had pitched his easel where two hedges formed an angle, and one of them was full of oak trees. The hedge was singularly full of 'bits' – bryony, tangles of grasses, berries, boughs half-tinted and boughs green, hung as it were with pictures like the wall of a room. Standing as near as I could without disturbing him, I found that the subject of his canvas was none of these. It was that old stale device of a rustic bridge spanning a shallow stream crossing a lane. Some figure stood on the bridge – the old, old trick. He was filling up the hedge of the lane with trees from the hedge, and they were cleverly executed. But why drag them into this fusty scheme, which has appeared in every child's textbook for fifty years? Why not have painted the beautiful hedge at hand, purely and simply, a hedge hung with pictures for any one to copy?

Indeed, why bother at all to paint on location if the scene on the canvas is to bear so little relation to the scenery viewed?

Close attention to nature was of little importance to the artist who was painting to a formula. It could be argued that the neoclassical principle of the *beau idéal*, the 'central form', positively discouraged literal representation in painting of individual and particular objects in the landscape. 'There is an absolute necessity for the Painter to generalize his notions', insisted Reynolds; 'to paint particulars is not to paint nature, it is only to paint Circumstances'.[35] Under this dispensation, the landscape painter might as well make do with miniature facsimiles of trees, hills and cattle:

> . . . in some paintings we have all beheld
> Green baize hath surely sat for a green field:
> Bolsters for mountains, hills, and wheaten mows;
> Cats for ram-goats, and curs for bulls and cows[36]

Uvedale Price remembered early excursions into the country with Gainsborough, when the artist would collect roots, stones and mosses to compose rural foregrounds in his studio.[37] Rough tree-bark could be simulated by wrapping wet grey paper around a stick and squeezing it tight. Paul Sandby even had a fire-proof model cottage so that he could study the effects of smoke rising from the chimney.[38]

The limitations of the Claudean orthodoxies had important consequences for the Picturesque tourist, whether or not he was himself a painter. It limited the kinds of landscape eligible for praise and study. As the agricultural writer William Marshall observed in 1785, 'Nature scarcely knows the thing mankind call a *landscape*'.[39] Most landscapes therefore needed to be 'improved' if they were to qualify for Claudean treatment. Gainsborough complained that he had never seen any place in England that 'affords a Subject equal to the poorest imitations of Gaspar or Claude'.[40] We have already seen how some of the poets dealt with such disparagements of British scenery. The painters took considerably longer to do justice to the subject, and were indeed encouraged by the example of the great success of Thomson's *Seasons*. It is an irony often noted that the rapid growth of interest in views of British scenery was largely prompted by a foreign initiative. The Empress of Russia in 1773 commissioned a vast table-service from the Stafford-shire firm of Wedgewood and Bentley. The service was to be decorated with views of British scenery. It was put on exhibition in London the following year and greatly acclaimed. Together with views of ruins, country houses, and gardens, the 'picturesque landscapes of Great Britain' were depicted, in such a way as to 'merit the attention of all travellers'.[41]

As a consequence of the popular reception of the exhibition, *The Copper Plate Magazine* came into being, and between 1774 and 1778 issued 24 engravings, mostly country-house views drawn by Paul Sandby. This was followed by *The Virtuosi's Museum* (1778–1781), which specifically referred to the Empress's initia-tive in order to spur the British themselves not to neglect their own country. Again, the enterprise was substantially the work of Paul Sandby. George Barrett and Francis Wheatley were called upon to supply paintings for Middiman's *Select Views*: some 15 of the 30-odd engravings featured Lake District scenery. In 1782 Joseph Pott in his *Essay on Landscape Painting* was urging that 'if the painter should pant for sublime scenes, stupendous mountains, precipices, waterfalls, he will find ample scope to improve his imagination in the Welch counties, or in Derbyshire, and the west of England'.[42] By the 1790s, when the Continent was closed to British tourists, the print-shop windows were crowded with Picturesque views of various parts of Britain. The tourist setting out for specific regions equipped him-self with a selection of the relevant prints as a guide to the beauty spots. But idealiza-tion or various Picturesque adjustments to the topography made the prints un-reliable as guides. 'I last year took drawings of waterfalls with me into the North,' grumbled John Byng; 'and return'd to London – without being able to discover them; tho' I have since learned that I was within a mile, or two, of some of them'.[43]

By the end of the century these landscapes had won their own Picturesque reputations. In an 1801 verse epistle to Sir George Beaumont, *On the Encouragement of the British School of Painting*, William Sotheby lists the locations which we will be exploring with the tourists later in the book:

> What lovelier views than Albion's scenes display,
> Lure the charm'd wanderer on his varied way?
> Whether he gaze from Snowdon's summit hoar,
> Or scale the rugged heights of bold Lodore,
> Down Wye's green meads, white cliffs, and woodlands sail,
> Catch inspiration from Langollen's vale,
> In Dove's still dell the world's far din forsake,
> Or hermit visions feed on Lomond's lake.

Sometimes these home landscapes, in painting, would be strangely lit, especially if the artist was an afficionado of Italian landscapes: a mellow Mediterranean light would suffuse a Welsh valley. Richard Wilson was the master of this kind of trans-figured native landscape, and he represents an important transitional stage in the development of the English School. Italian light on a British landscape was one form of adaptation. Another was to give an Italian foreground to a British background. One of Turner's 1799 watercolours shows Caernarvon Castle in a hazy distance with a Claudean foreground, and a middle-distance graced with a Claudean bridge (see fig. 39). Such hybrid landscapes were extremely popular in painting; and, of course, could be brought to life in the 'improved' gardens of the great houses such as Stowe and Stourhead.

Many of the difficulties in translating and then naturalising the Claudean idiom were simply overcome by an enterprising nationalism, which we have already seen as a shaping force in the development of descriptive poetry in the eighteenth century. Take for instance the matter of ruins in a landscape. Those trim or crumbling classical temples which grace many a Claudean Italian landscape were simply not available in the British countryside, and consequently had to be manufactured for the gardens of the wealthy. But eventually even this practice came to be censured. In *The English Garden* William Mason allows 'classic rules' to be applied to the houses occupied by the wealthy, but not to their garden ruins. The building of fragments of Greek or Roman architecture in Britain is 'but a splendid lie which mocks historic credence':

> Hence the cause
> Why Saxon piles or Norman here prevail:
> Form they a rude, 'tis yet an English whole[44]

Mason's caution was reinforced by Richard Payne Knight: 'No decoration should we introduce, / That has not first been nat'raliz'd by use'.[45] There were, of course, medieval ruins in abundance, abbeys and castles as evocative to Britons of their own history as were the ruined Roman temples to the seventeenth-century Italians. The English Gothic revival, a distinctly nationalistic phenomenon, performed a great service in promoting the aesthetic appeal of the ruins of native antiquities, and thereby consecrating them for inclusion in quasi-Claudean British landscape painting:

Although the refined in taste may prefer the chaste and noble proportions of Grecian art, to the more irregular and wild ideas of northern climes . . . yet, in the venerable state of ruin, there is an awful romantic wildness in the Gothic remains, that moves the mind very powerfully.[46]

The improbable Italian light was fading from British landscapes as the century neared its close. This was to a great extent due to developments in watercolour painting, and its more faithful, subtle rendering of damper atmospheres and changeful skies in soft washes. This medium, peculiarly suited to the conditions of the British landscape and climate, saw its most spectacular development in England in the last two decades of the eighteenth century. It was, in many respects, original to England, and, consequently, was freer from the influences of convention and tradition than oil painting. Considerable claims have been made for watercolour painting in this respect: 'It gave the final blow to the persistence in landscape art of those classical accessories which may be thought of as the graphic equivalents of the Latinized metaphors and similes of Pope and Dryden'.[47] The 'final blow' is an apt phrase: we have already noted a succession of challenges to neoclassicism in painting and poetry through the century.

In its earliest form watercolour painting was simply 'tinted drawing', usually for the purposes of topographical record. The first stage in such compositions was the careful delineation of forms in pen or pencil. Rudimentary light and shade were then introduced with Indian ink, and the whole was coloured with simple washes. At a later period in the medium's development, the rigid outlines were subdued, a greater variety of colour was introduced, and the picture was built up principally through the series of washes. In Paul Sandby's practice, this 'improved style' involved the deepening repetitions of tinting as the objects approached the foreground.[48] The transitional phases from tinted drawing to watercolour painting gave to these pictures a puzzling, anomalous status – half drawing, half painting – as the 1782 reviewer of John Robert Cozens' work observed:

[His drawings] are, for composition, keeping, and effect, superior to any thing of the kind. They have a peculiar excellence, in which they resemble painting; for the effect is not, as is usually the case, produced from outlines filled up, but is worked into light, shade, and keeping, by a more artful process, the masses being determined in the first making out.[49]

The novel subtleties of watercolour began to attract attention from 1760 onwards. That was the year of the first open exhibition of works on sale by living British artists, which offered the watercolourist a new kind of independence, 'a double market for his produce', as the historian of the Old Watercolour Society explains:

Hitherto the worker on copper had furnished the sole medium through which the designer's art could be presented to the public eye . . . It had now become his [the painter's] interest to make his drawing attractive for its own sake, and desirable to possess as an original and unique work of art, besides being suited to the publisher's purpose of multiplying it by the agency of the press.[50]

One consequence of this greater independence was the way in which delineation (making the engraver's task easier) gave way to subtler compositions of washes, which the printer found hard to compete with and difficult to reproduce.*

The change from line-and-wash drawing to painting in watercolours may be compared with some of those changing attitudes towards landscape which we have observed elsewhere. What began as a means of topographical and documentary record developed into a medium for expressing certain emotional responses to natural scenery, and raised the status of landscape painting. If the landscape

---

*The delay in publishing Gilpin's various manuscript *Observations* was largely due to these circumstances: see below Part II, pp. 86.

painter can create images *'analogous to the various feelings, and sensations of the mind'*, wrote Gilpin near the end of his life, then 'where would be the harm of saying, that landscape, like history-paintings hath its ethics!'[51] At the turn of the century John Stoddart's *Remarks on Local Scenery* reflected that even Reynolds 'seems to have had little feeling of those delicious and powerful emotions, which, in an uninitiated mind, the forms of nature are capable of producing'. Cozens' controversial, melancholy mountain landscapes offer some of the earliest examples of this expressive watercolour painting: 'Cozens is all poetry', Constable said. In the work of Turner and Girtin in the later 1790s this power is brought to early maturity. In 1799 Turner was reported as saying how much he disliked the 'mechanically systematic' methods of watercolour painting, as practised, for instance by John 'Warwick' Smith: 'Turner has no settled process but drives the colours about till he has expressed the idea in his mind'.[52] Turner and Girtin supplied what was felt to be missing in both the topographical tradition and the formulary Picturesque mode – the poetry of landscape.

# III

# The evolution of Picturesque taste, 1750-1800

Mr. Pitt . . . ordered a tent to be pitched, tea to be prepared, and his French horn to breath Music like the unseen Genius of the woods . . . After tea we rambled about for an hour, seeing several views, some wild as Salvator Rosa, others placid, and with the setting sun, worthy of Claude Lorrain.[1]

This is from a letter written in 1753 by Mrs Elizabeth Montagu, the distinguished 'bluestocking'. The glamorous picnic took place not on the Roman Campagna but near Tunbridge Wells in Kent. It is an early instance of what was, later in the century, to become a descriptive commonplace, and it suggests that the vogue for invoking Rosa and Claude in this manner may well have started during those fashionable 'conversaziones' in mid-century London society.

Five years before Mrs Montagu's letter, James Thomson had published his *Castle of Indolence*. The stanza in Canto I which describes the landscape paintings adorning the Castle concludes with this couplet:

> Whate'er Lorrain light-touched with softening hue,
> Or savage Rosa dashed, or learned Poussin drew.

The three distinct characters of seventeenth-century idealized landscape paintings are fixed for the next three generations in those lines.

As we have seen, one of the chief excitements for the Picturesque tourist was the recognition and tracing of resemblances between art and nature. That particular pleasure of comparison and association is, of course, much older than the late eighteenth century. It is clearly formulated, for instance, in Addison's 1712 *Spectator* papers on 'The Pleasures of the Imagination'. Addison categorizes the primary sources of the imagination's pleasures, chiefly those objects or prospects which are distinguished by Greatness, Uncommonness or Beauty. He then turns his attention to what he calls the secondary pleasures of the imagination. Amongst these is our love of comparing objects and tracing resemblances. We are particularly pleased when we compare 'the Ideas arising from the Original Objects, with the Ideas we receive from the Statue, Picture, Description, or Sound that represents them'.[2] On this principle, 'we find the Works of Nature still more pleasant, the more they resemble those of Art'.[3] This secondary pleasure was of crucial importance for the Picturesque tourists. One might even say that, in many cases, Addison's secondary pleasure becomes their primary pleasure; when, to revive an earlier example, the glimpse of a scene in North Wales beguiles the spectator because it seems a nearly perfect native facsimile of a Dughet landscape, or when a pastoral poem suddenly comes to life on the banks of Ullswater. How profoundly satisfying for the poet Samuel Rogers was this moment's vision during a tour in Wales:

I have seen a ragged shepherd boy . . . throw himself down in an attitude that Raphael would not have disdained to copy.[4]

This is life accidentally imitating art – the purest of Picturesque pleasures.

It is the opportunity for just this kind of secondary pleasure which enhances Mrs Montagu's appreciation of her 'picturesque picnic'. I have already mentioned Richard Payne Knight's associationist argument about natural scenery's having greater appeal for the person familiar with classical pastoral poetry (see above, p. 4). He goes on from there to assert that, 'The spectator, having his mind enriched with the embellishments of the painter and the poet, applies them, by the spontaneous association of ideas, to the natural objects presented to his eye, which thus acquire ideal and imaginary beauties'.[5] The association is seldom as spontaneous as Knight suggests, but his is a very clear formulation of the Picturesque habit of mind.

His mention of 'ideal beauties' born of the interaction between natural objects and associated ideas may remind one not only of Pope's rendering of Windsor Forest in terms of Milton's Eden, but also of certain strategies in neoclassical portraiture. Idealization through literary or pictorial allusion had been a professional practice in many a fashionable portrait, where a particular subject could be given an enhanced dignity by being deliberately posed in attitudes reminiscent of Renaissance paintings. Ronald Paulson has shown how, for example, Reynolds' celebrated *Mrs. Siddons as the Tragic Muse* (1784) adopts the pose of a Michelangelo prophet from the Sistine ceiling, and thus adds a religious dimension to the idea of tragedy.[6] So when Mrs Montagu describes the views of the countryside around Tunbridge Wells as 'worthy of Claude', she is both expressing her pleased recognition of the resembles and enhancing the prestige of a particular landscape.

But if these pleasures are to be shared, it is clear that all parties must understand the aesthetic premises. Mrs Montagu's circle was composed of a cultivated élite whose familiarity with the work of Claude, Dughet and Rosa – as with that of Thomson and Milton or Virgil and Homer – guaranteed the life of this kind of associationist code. The later Picturesque tourists, who came, by and large, from the same class of society, had certainly equal and perhaps greater familiarity with this *painterly* code, though perhaps rather less familiarity with the classical *literary* code.

Most of the story so far has shown how British tastes in natural beauty were derived initially from foreign models, from images of Italian scenery rendered by the Latin poets and the seventeenth-century landscape painters. The Picturesque comes into play in this context as a kind of intellectual recreation favoured by a self-confident élite, whose education in the classics might have been completed by the Grand Tour and the opportunity to see the works of Claude, Dughet and Rosa in Italy and in the English collections. But in this third quarter of the century there are clear signs of a disturbance to the cultural supremacy of this élite. There is an erosion of confidence in the Augustan culture which expresses itself in a variety of ways. Milton and Thomson are beginning to seem rivals to Homer and Virgil. Thomas Gray experiments with Celtic mythology as a new source for poetic ideas and images. A sense of the decline of literature and the fine arts is being voiced by a number of distinguished critics.[7] The idea of an absolute standard of taste, governed by rational rules and supported by reference to the example of the ancients, collapses in a succession of essays by the leading writers on aesthetics, who prove, sometimes unintentionally, that the recognition of beauty is subjective and individual.[8] Graveyard musings and Sublime aesthetics encourage exploration into the darker recesses of the psyche. The taste for Gothick and Chinoiserie in domestic design sorts oddly with the Palladian ideal. Ancient Rome herself had by now been visited by many an Englishman shocked to see at first hand the citadel of the classical world reduced to a rubble of masonry and a few cadaverous, crumbling structures. As David Solkin has argued,[9] the moral lessons to be drawn from Rome's decline in the later Empire were very important for mid-century English culture. Even the veneration of Augustan Rome was waning, with Augustus himself being seen as the enemy to republican liberty and to the arts.

Melancholic, introverted, eclectic and hesitantly nationalistic, many writers and artists of the period seem often in a state of paralysis, bewildered about the present, impatient with the immediate past, fascinated by the remote past. From all this there emerges a sense of the Picturesque which becomes far more complex than Mrs Montagu's accolade to Kentish scenery. I want to focus this mid-century retreat from certain Augustan values, and its contribution to later Picturesque tastes, in two topics, ruins and gardening. The two chief theorists of the Picturesque, William Gilpin and Uvedale Price, both began their writing careers with discussions of garden design; and both, in developing their Picturesque theories, are haunted by that appropriate emblem of a period of decaying confidence, the ruin. This approach might help to explain why 'like a picture' becomes inadequate as a definition of late-eighteenth-century Picturesque, and indeed of our modern, casual 'picturesque'.

## (i) *The Interpretation of Ruins*

'Pleasing melancholy' and 'agreeable horror' were two types of emotional experience induced by the contemplation of ruins. Both feature prominently in mid-century taste. At the end of the century Charles Heath, the author of one of the best-known tour guidebooks, asserted that 'no two pieces of Poetry, in the English language, have been more universally read, or admired, than Dr. Blair's "Grave", and Mr. Gray's "Elegy in a Country Churchyard" '.[10] Both these pieces belong in composition to the 1740s, and, along with Edward Young's *Night Thoughts* (1742–45) and Thomas Parnell's *Night Piece on Death* (1722), constitute what, in a later age, came to be known as the Graveyard School of poetry.

One critic, C. A. Moore, who has made a particular study of this mid-century phenomenon has claimed that, statistically, the period deserves to be called the Age of Melancholy. Melancholy was a notoriously English affliction, and even earned the name the 'English Malady'. That was the title of an authoritative book on the subject in 1733 by Dr George Cheyne, who, in his Preface, attributed these *'nervous Distempers'* and *'Lowness of Spirits'* to several factors such as the dampness of the English climate, the richness of diet and sedentary occupations of the 'better sort (among whom the *Evil* mostly rages)', and the crowded conditions of the big towns. He also noted the recent rise in the suicide rate and judged that it was caused largely by this Malady. In the 1750s and especially in 1755, suicide seems to have reached epidemic proportions. Moore suggests that the Graveyard poets and their successors who felt the impulse to indulge the melancholy mood were forced by the prevailing ethos to resort to methods of indirection. Thus the 'meditatio mortis' in ruined abbeys and country churchyards became much favoured as a kind of religious screen for morbid emotionalism.[11] In the later decades of the century the religious pretext is dropped. Robert Aubin, in his authoritative study of topographical poetry, notes that by the 1780s most English poets had substituted unabashed sentiment for charnel-house horror.[12] The uninhibited indulgence of 'pleasing melancholy' becomes one of the most compelling motives for the Picturesque tourist to visit ruined abbeys and castles.

One reason for this later freedom to discard the religious pretext for such intense emotional indulgence could be found in Edmund Burke's influential formulation of the Sublime in the late 1750s. In his *Philosophical Enquiry into the Origin of Our Ideas of the Sublime and Beautiful* (1757: revised and expanded in 1759) he argued that the two strongest instincts known to man are self-preservation and the social impulse. All that directly threatens self-preservation causes terror; and terrifying experiences are the source of the Sublime. Our experience of the Sublime is far greater in intensity than our experience of Beauty. Beauty attracts and reassures: the Sublime intimidates. Beauty draws out one's social instincts. The intensification of social intimacy is the source of the sexual impulse, which in turn assures the continued propagation of the race (a kind of macrocosmic self-preservation). Burke's linking of Beauty and sexuality leads him to characterise Beauty according to the age's general sense of what constitutes feminine attractiveness: weakness, softness, gentle curves, delicate colouring, and so on. For the later Picturesque connoisseur it was an easy matter to find these feminine qualities in the soft, hospitable, mellow landscapes of Claude: accordingly, Beauty in landscape could be analysed in Burkean, psychological terms. The characteristics of the Sublime, on the other hand, include terrifying power, obscurity, and sharp contrasts; and the corresponding painter was Salvator Rosa. The thrill of the Sublime, this 'agreeable horror', depends on one's being able to enjoy danger at a safe distance. The relationship between the spectator, the recoiling figures and the catastrophe in de Loutherbourg's *An Avalanche in the Alps* (fig. 8) is very much an experiment in the Sublime. David Hartley had described this particular kind of pleasure in landscape terms in 1749:

8. P. de Loutherbourg, *An Avalanche in the Alps* (1803).
Tate Gallery, London

If there be a precipice, a cataract, a mountain of snow, etc in one part of the scene, the nascent ideas of fear and horror magnify and enliven all the other ideas, and by degrees pass into pleasures, by suggesting the security from pain.[13]

The important stress in the *Enquiry* is on the sensationist interpretation of both the Sublime and the Beautiful. Beauty is not determined by such hallowed Renaissance criteria as proportion, utility or 'fitness', for these are intellectual judgements. Beauty and Sublimity seize the mind before it can collect its thoughts. We shall see later, on the Tours, many such responses recorded in Burkean terminology. Even Gilpin acknowledged that the chief pleasure in Picturesque travel was not the 'scientifical' analysis of scenery (though that afforded great amusement) but the irrational response:

We are most delighted, when some grand scene, tho perhaps of incorrect composition, rising before the eye, strikes us beyond the power of thought . . . every mental operation is suspended . . . We rather *feel*, than *survey* it.[14]

Burke's *Enquiry* classified and gave a dignity to primary emotional drives, and correspondingly had some effect in further discrediting rationalism. It endorsed a number of contemporary challenges to rationalism among the moral philosophers – e.g. Hume's *Enquiry Concerning the Principles of Morals* (1752), Adam Smith's *Theory of Moral Sentiments* (1759) – and was instrumental in promoting 'sentiment' or 'sensibility', a vogue which grew as the century advanced, especially in the response to the natural world. 'Till Rousseau's time, there had been no "sentimental" love of nature',[15] wrote Ruskin. In this climate a genteel melancholy became a psychologically interesting condition: 'Melancholy itself is a source of pleasure to a cultivated mind', according to John Aikin in the 1790s.[16] Thus the religious pretext for Gothic horrors and morbid emotionalism could be discarded.

As Hartley indicated, the Sublime in landscape terms required dangerous, awe-inspiring scenery, particularly wild mountain country. Marjorie Hope Nicolson's classic study of Sublime aesthetics, *Mountain Gloom and Mountain Glory* (1959), has demonstrated how, at least in the first third of the century, wilderness and mountain scenery were a minority taste. Nonetheless, there were several remarkable expressions of it, such as Addison's discussions in his 1712 *Spectator* papers 'The Pleasures of the Imagination', and Bishop Berkeley's challenge to the reader not to feel a 'pleasing horror' at the sight of gloomy forests, huge mountains and other manifestations of an 'agreeable horror'.[17] More eloquent was the famous rhapsody to uncultivated country in the Earl of Shaftesbury's *The Moralists* (1709):

I shall no longer resist the passion growing in me for things of a natural kind, where neither art nor the conceit or caprice of man has spoiled their genuine order by breaking in upon that primitive state. Even the rude rocks, the mossy caverns, the irregular un-wrought grottos and broken falls of waters, with all the horrid graces of the wilderness itself, as representing Nature more, will be the more engaging, and appear with a magnificence beyond the formal mockery of princely gardens.[18]

Notice the phrase 'genuine order'. It is a skilful anticipation of Augustan objections to misshapen, unruly wilderness with its threat to the sense of order imposed on nature by enlightened, civilised man. Shaftesbury's rhapsodist, fortified by confidence in the well-regulated Newtonian universe, now insists that raw nature – rude, irregular, unwrought, broken – is the source of genuine order, compared with which the human equivalent is just 'formal mockery'. Those 'princely gardens', of course, soon caught up with changing tastes: if nature herself proved niggardly, the proprietor could commission 'Capability' Brown or others to instal broken falls of water and exquisitely irregular and apparently unwrought grottos.

'Agreeable horror' and 'pleasing melancholy' are nourished by images of decay, by monstrous, broken and irregular forms, in both natural scenery and the works of man. There is a fascinating essay by Barbara Maria Stafford on these new tastes in landscape at the end of the eighteenth century, particularly the taste for Chaos.[19] Recognising Burke's classifications, she argues that Chaos 'hints at masculine, virile sublimities in opposition to the feminine charms of the ordered'. Travellers now relish 'those parts of nature which are vast, misproportioned or "torn and mangled" by Palladian standards. Chaos has form, form of a special kind which existed before the overlay of sophisticated cultures'. Ruined architecture represents a return to the state of nature, and thus acquires a positive value. In order to clarify the complexity of attitudes towards ruins, as we trace the evolution of later Picturesque tastes, I shall, at the risk of seeming over-schematic, isolate four or five main types of response. The first is that indulgence of melancholy and horror associated with Graveyard poetry and Sublime aesthetics. This can be termed the *sentimental* response to ruins. The second might be called the *antiquarian* response, which seeks to reconstruct the ruin in the imagination and draws upon some architectural expertise. The third is the *aesthetic*: that is the pleasures of form and colouring, the decorative nature of the ruin. John Aikin, writing in the 1790s, believed this response was a very recent development in taste:

The newest and most fashionable mode of considering them [ruins] is with respect to the place they hold in the *picturesque*; and it is chiefly under this head that they have become such favourites with landscape painters and landscape writers.[20]

Aikin is, in fact, inaccurate about the novelty of this response, which was exemplified at the beginning of the eighteenth century in the story of the intended design for Blenheim Park. Sir John Vanbrugh, Blenheim's architect, was invited to assist Henry Wise in laying out the grounds. He wanted to retain as a feature in his landscape design the ruined medieval manor of Woodstock. One of the reasons he gives is claimed by some to be the germ of the whole Picturesque movement. Vanbrugh insisted that were the old building to be glimpsed rising from trees and thickets (with perhaps a recollection of *L'Allegro*'s towers 'Boosom'd high in tufted Trees'), 'it wou'd make One of the most Agreable objects that the best of Landskip Painters can invent'.[21] Another early example of the aesthetic appreciation of ruins, tinged with sentimentality, occurs in the painter-poet John Dyer's letters from Rome (c. 1724):

There is a certain charm that follows the sweep of time, and I can't help thinking the triumphal arches more beautiful now than ever they were ... a certain greenness ... a certain disjointedness and moulder among the stones, something so pleasing in their weeds and tufts of myrtle, and something in the altogether so greatly wild, that mingling with art, and blotting out the traces of disagreeable squares and angles, adds certain beauties that could not be before imagined.[22]

A fourth type of response is the *moral*, neatly expressed in an analogy by Robert Ginsberg: 'A ruin on one's estate once served like a skull on one's desk'.[23] In the moral view the ruin becomes a *memento mori* and an emblem of that favourite eighteenth-century theme, the Vanity of Human Wishes. This is elegantly exemplified in Dyer's *Grongar Hill*, when the poet contemplates one of the ruined castles in the landscape:

> Yet Time has seen, that lifts the low,
> And level lays the lofty Brow,
> Has seen this broken Pile compleat,
> Big with the Vanity of State;
> But transient is the Smile of Fate!
> A little Rule, a little Sway,
> A sun-beam in a Winter's Day
> Is all the Proud and Mighty have,
> Between the Cradle and the Grave.[24]

The moral appeal is here closely related to an historical awareness which cherishes the ruin as an image of Nature's levelling of haughty tyranny: in other words, a fifth kind of response, which we might call the *political*. For the eighteenth century the ruined castle is a potent emblem of liberation from Gothic feudalism. 'Believe me', exclaims Addison, in Hurd's imaginary *Moral and Political Dialogues*, 'I never see the remains of that greatness which arose in the past ages on the ruins of public freedom and private property, but I congratulate with myself on living at a time, when the meanest subject is as free and independent as those royal minions; and when his property, whatever it be, is as secure as that of the first minister'.[25] The religious counterpart to the castle, the ruined abbey, represents the triumphant banishment from England of Popish 'superstition'. 'The ruins of these once magnificent edifices', writes Uvedale Price, combining the political and aesthetic criteria, 'are the pride and boast of this island: we may well be proud of them; not merely in a picturesque point of view: we may glory that the abodes of tyranny and superstition are in ruin'.[26] Viewed in this light, the Reformation's destruction of the abbeys of Britain could be commended, and frequently was. William Shenstone called Henry VIII's action 'righteous havoc':

> Then from its towering height with horrid sound
> Rush'd the proud abbey: then the vaulted roofs,
> Torn from their walls, disclosed the wanton scene
> Of monkish chastity! Each angry friar

9. Batty Langley, 'An Avenue in Perspective, terminated with the ruins of an ancient Building
after the Roman manner', from *New Principles of Gardening* (1728). British Library, London

> Crawl'd from his bedded strumpet, muttering low
> An ineffectual curse. The pervious nooks . . .
> Imbide the novel daylight, and expose,
> Obvious, the fraudful enginery of Rome.[27]

Gilpin referred to Henry VIII's vandalistic successor, Oliver Cromwell, as 'that
picturesque genius', who 'omitted no opportunity of adorning the countries,
through which he passed, with noble ruins'. Such mixed attitudes, incidentally,
were not exclusive to the eighteenth century: even during the two or three generations following the dissolution of the monasteries in the 1530s, nostalgia and
antiquarian enthusiasms intensified at the same time as the release from Popery
was being celebrated.[28]

For Shenstone these ruins left in the landscape have now become of use only

> . . . to grace a rural scene,
> To bound our vistas, and to glad the sons
> Of George's reign, reserved for fairer times!

Fig. 9, a plate in Batty Langley's *New Principles of Gardening* (1728), shows the way
of deploying a ruin – here to terminate an avenue perspective. Shenstone, like
Price, acknowledges two types of ruin interest, the political appraisal (conquest of
arrogant feudalism and 'superstition') and the aesthetic ('grace a rural scene', 'bound

47

our vistas'). To these he adds a few more when he discusses ruins in his essay on gardening,[29] an important text to which we shall return later:

> RUINATED structures appear to derive their power of pleasing, from the irregularity of surface, which is VARIETY; and the latitude they afford the imagination, to conceive an enlargement of their dimensions, or to recollect any events or circumstances appertaining to their pristine grandeur, so far as concerns grandeur and solemnity.

Three sources of pleasure are identified here: formal variety, fanciful architectural reconstruction, and romantic, historical association. The later, more complex developments in Picturesque taste grow out of all these varied attitudes towards ruins in the middle decades of the eighteenth century – varied and often incompatible. Nowhere are the tensions between the characteristically Augustan response to ruins (predominantly as moral and political emblems) and the Picturesque, predominantly aesthetic response (delight in formal variety) more sharply marked than in Gilpin's earliest discussion of landscape aesthetics, *Dialogue upon the Gardens . . . at Stow* (1748).[30]

The *Dialogue* features a debate between two gentlemen visitors to Stowe. As they enter the gardens from the south, one of the first sights they encounter is the artificial Rock-Work which separates the Octagon Pond from the lake, on the borders of which is an artificially ruined Hermitage. The scene is judged by both to be 'vastly picturesque'. This is, incidentally, the first recorded published use of the term by Gilpin. However, one of the visitors is puzzled by the strong appeal of these ruins, and wonders 'why we are more taken with Prospects of this ruinous kind, than with Views of Plenty and Prosperity in their greatest Perfection'. To this his friend gives a reply that is to be crucial in the development of Picturesque theory later in the century:

> Yes: but cannot you make a distinction between natural and moral Beauties? Our social Affections undoubtedly find their Enjoyment the most compleat when they contemplate, a Country smiling in the midst of Plenty, where Houses are well-built, Plantations regular, and everything the most commodious and useful. But such Regularity and Exactness excites no manner of Pleasure in the Imagination, unless they are made use of to contrast with something of an opposite kind.

That distinction between natural and moral beauty would have made most Augustans very uneasy, so clearly does it fly in the face of cherished neoclassical values, where physical beauty is seen as the expression of moral beauty. But Gilpin insists on the separation of the two. Although he can interpret, iconographically, Stowe's garden architecture, he is not concerned here with the kind of moral or political pleasure in ruins enjoyed by Shenstone and Dyer. The implication of Gilpin's remarks is that the imagination is amoral. It has very little to do with social considerations, with utility or convenience:

> The Fancy is struck by *Nature* alone . . . Thus a regular Building perhaps gives us very little pleasure; and yet a fine Rock, beautifully set off in Claro-obscuro, and garnished with flourishing Bushes, Ivy, and dead Branches, may afford us a great deal.

The appeal has become almost exclusively visual. We may find it more comfortable to live in a regular building, but the *imagination* can only be fully pleased with 'a ragged Ruin, with venerable old Oaks, and Pines nodding over it', such as Stowe's 'old' Hermitage. The division is complete. The imagination or 'Fancy' craves satisfactions which seem wholly contrary to those required by morality, the 'social Affections'. Since it is above all the painter who is concerned chiefly with what gives *imaginative* pleasure, the adjective 'picturesque' is duly applied to this type of aggressively anti-utilitarian scenery.

The setting for Gilpin's *Dialogue* raises a problem in itself. Garden ruins could not legitimately inspire historical reflections. In spite of the Hermitage's being described several times by the two visitors as impressively old, it was no more ancient than Gilpin himself. The sentimental confusion caused by skilfully executed artificial ruins is amusingly illustrated in the story of the naïve gentleman visitor to a famous landscape garden. He observed to the gardener who was his guide that the splendid ruin before him must be very old indeed. 'Oh sir', said the gardener, 'the next my Master builds will be much older'.[31] The real age of these ruins did not seem to matter very much, nor did the fact that they had never existed in a pre-ruined state as intelligible architecture. Garden theorists such as Thomas Whateley might well advise strict architectural accuracy in contriving these dilapidated fragments, and insist that the supposed original design should be clear; but not many ruin builders were so scrupulous. Antiquarian curiosity can seem ludicrously inappropriate in the case of artificial ruins. They were designed either for didactic, emblematic purposes, such as the telling satirical relationship between Stowe's beautifully intact Temple of Ancient Virtue and its ruined Temple of Modern Virtue, or simply in order to stimulate vague, sentimental associations.

But what of those cases when authentic medieval ruins were annexed by the landscape gardener (as, for example, Vanbrugh had wanted at Blenheim) and viewed alongside contemporary architectural follies? A good example is Fountains Abbey which John Aislabie incorporated into his Studley Royal garden in the late 1760s. The problem here was how to harmonize the true antique with modern imitations and modern garden design. Aislabie failed, according to Gilpin, because he showed insufficient respect in his garden design for the venerable antiquity of the Abbey. The lawns around the crumbling remains had been neatly shaved, and the proprietor was trying to restore the ruin. 'The very idea of giving a finished splendour to a ruin, is absurd', thought Gilpin: 'the *recent* marks of human industry' were wholly unnatural in a place evidently forlorn and deserted by man. A true ruin has ceased to be wholly the work of man:

Rooted for ages in the soil; assimilated to it; and become, as it were, a part of it; we consider it as a work of nature, rather than of art.[32]

Ruins fascinated the Picturesque tourist partly because, in spite of Gilpin's recommendations to separate moral and aesthetic responses, they raised so many questions about the relationship between man and nature, as well as presenting interestingly broken lines and varied tints. According to Aikin, for those who travel in search of the Picturesque, 'the regular lines of art but ill harmonize with the free strokes of nature', but ruins represent that surrender of art to nature:

> The ivy creeping along gothic arches, and forming a verdant lattice across the dismantled casements; bushes starting through the chasms of the rifted tower . . . are the fantastic strokes of nature working upon the patterns of art, which all the refinement of magnificence cannot imitate.[33]

However, ruins caused considerable problems for some of the Picturesque theorists. As we shall see, it becomes necessary for Uvedale Price to leave aside discussion of ruins, because ruins, especially on a monumental scale, stimulate too complex a response for the theorist concerned to isolate specifically formal, Picturesque qualities. Gilpin however, although his concern is principally with matters of form and colour, allows the rich complexity of associations a free role in determining his response to ruins. There is the very occasional stock moral reflection, but usually his response is a blend of vague, sentimental associations and the painter's relish of broken lines, abrupt chiaroscuro and the subdued variety of colours and textures. In this emphasis he is typical of the Picturesque tourists in the last third of the century. Familiar with Sublime aesthetics, tinged with fashionable 'sensibility', and equipped with the connoisseur's vocabulary in landscape analysis, these later ruin enthusiasts are primarily interested in mood, colour and composition. Their Augustan predecessors, by and large, were excited by allegorical interpretation of garden architecture and sculpture and by the moral and political connotations of ruined castles and abbeys. 'All these devices', wrote Thomas Whateley of garden statuary, 'are rather *emblematical* than expressive . . . they make no immediate impression, for they must be examined, compared, perhaps explained, before the whole design of them is well understood'.[34] These are intellectual exertions which the later tourists usually find too strenuous and too prosaic. David Solkin has dated these changing attitudes to the 1760s, during which 'a number of British artists had begun to produce ruin-pieces that emphasised particular details at the expense of general ideas or ideals of order, and which offered vague emotional pleasure as opposed to specific intellectual instruction'.[35]

### (ii) *Moral, Sentimental and Picturesque Gardening*

The history of the English garden to the end of the eighteenth century is a paradigm of these changing tastes, as Ronald Paulson, John Dixon Hunt and others have demonstrated. In the early stage the garden and its architectural ornaments were to be read like an emblem book or *paysage moralisé*, much as Denham had interpreted the view from Cooper's Hill: many features in that view were indeed later manufactured and miniaturised for the gardens – gentle hills and valleys, glades for contemplation, and fragments of ancient architecture. Aaron Hill's planned Moral Rock Garden takes this version to its extreme.[36] His garden was to have been a kind of moral test, inviting the visitor to choose from a number of paths at the perimeter, with titles like Honour, Riches and Industry, only one of which led to the Temple of Happiness and Cave of Content at the centre. Elsewhere emblematic architecture (Stowe's Temple of Virtue) and emblematic statuary elaborated various moral precepts. Jonathan Tyer's estate near Dorking included a Valley of the Shadow of Death where the effigy of an unbeliever dying in agony was positioned opposite to a Christian dying serenely.[37]

At a later stage, the garden is toured like a gallery of three-dimensional seventeenth-century landscape paintings (which themselves deployed modified iconographic systems): 'every journey is made through a succession of pictures'[38] observed Horace Walpole of this kind of garden. Pope and William Kent were reckoned to have been the first who 'practised painting in gardening'. Pope, according to Spence, maintained that 'all gardening is landscape painting'.[39] The landscape painter becomes the model for the management of distances. Philip Southcote at Woburn contrived a view which, with a few native variations, might almost fit a description of a Claude painting. The hill and ruined church refer to St Anne's, the very ruin which Denham, a century before, had included as emblematic of religious excesses, but which now serves only to 'bound a vista' in decorative fashion:

From the line that leads to the house, the foreground is the meadow, the mid-ground a winding stream with clumps and trees scattered about it, and the background is the rising of the hill and the line of trees to the ruined church.[40]

The painter also influences the distribution of colour, as Henry Hoare observed: 'The greens should be ranged together in large masses as the shades are in painting'. On similar principles 'the lights and shades in gardening are managed by disposing the thick grove-work, the thin, and the openings in a proper manner, of which the eye generally is the properest judge'.[41] The chief beauty of Shenstone's Shropshire estate, The Leasowes, according to Robert Dodsley's 1764 'Description', was its range of 'distinguishable scenes'.[42] The tour of the gardens was a circuit punctuated by seats affording a great variety of views. Each view was captioned, like a painting, with an appropriate inscription on or near the viewing seat. Such a garden still catered for cultivated, patrician tastes, as Shenstone suggested in his 'Thoughts' on gardening: 'Objects should be less calculated to strike the immediate eye, than the judgement or well-formed imagination, as in painting'. With its interplay between selected viewpoint and Latin verse inscription this is landscape evidently designed for the connoisseur. But The Leasowes was also attuned to the age of Sensibility. The mood, or 'peculiar character' of the landscape – the 'savage', the sprightly, the melancholy, the horrid – could each be enhanced by 'suitable appendages' such as funerary urns, and lovers' benches.

The picture-gallery phase of gardening blends with or gives way to this third, sentimental phase in which the garden, now largely shorn of significant statuary and classical monuments, becomes a landscape of variety, to be *felt* as a medley of moods. The Picturesque begins to flourish in the second phase, runs confusedly into the third, and eventually becomes impatient with gardens altogether. 'The more refined our taste grows from the *study of nature*', wrote Gilpin, 'the more insipid are the *works of art*'.[43]

In this rather oversimplified tabulation of phases, we need to identify more precisely that crucial change, signalled in Gilpin's *Dialogue*, from the predominantly moral to the predominantly aesthetic response to landscape. It may be useful at this point to recall the Horatian principle (endorsed by the Augustans) that a work of art should instruct or delight, or combine the two functions. 'The End and Design of a good Garden, is to be both profitable and delightful', remarked Batty Langley in his *New Principles of Gardening* (1728).[44] If we apply this to the appreciation of landscape then we expect a balanced combination of the emblematic and aesthetic satisfactions: Pope's *Windsor-Forest* offers such a combination, as we have seen. John Dyer also discovered it in his view from Grongar Hill. As befits the Augustan painter-poet, he enjoys the beauty of the expansive, sunlit landscape, but he also enjoys the perception of analogies between the river's course and the flow of human life, and the ruined castle as an emblem of retribution for the Vanity of State. The twin satisfactions – moral profit and aesthetic delight – are then neatly formulated:

> Thus is Nature's Vesture wrought,
> To instruct our wand'ring Thought,
> Thus she dresses green and gay,
> To disperse our cares away.[45]

This landscape both instructs and delights, balancing moral and aesthetic values. The tilting of the balance away from the moral and towards the aesthetic becomes most evident, as I have already suggested, in the middle decades of the century. But there were clear anticipations of the shift in taste in those 1712 *Spectator* papers on the 'Pleasures of the Imagination'. The pleasures with which Addison was chiefly concerned are those which arise from visible objects, since sight is 'the most perfect and most delightful of all our Senses'. Once sight, and the pleasures dependent on sight, are isolated and elevated like this, it is not too bold a step to allow the visual sense that degree of aesthetic autonomy which so distinguishes Gilpin's account of the Picturesque – 'the tyranny of the eye' in Wordsworth's later disparaging phrase.[46]

Pope's landscapes, as we saw in *Windsor-Forest*, preserve a careful blend of the moral and aesthetic. His famous advice on gardening in the *Epistle to Burlington* (1731) emphasises Good Sense, respect for Nature, and Use, in order to counteract the abuse of riches when lavished indiscriminately on an estate. Good taste here is always a moral quality, and the garden should express that quality in its design and economic function. His ideal, he declares, can be found in the gardens at Stowe, 'a work to wonder at'. The Stowe gardens, seventeen years later, become the setting for Gilpin's *Dialogue*, which adapts the *concordia discors* couplet from *Windsor-Forest* as its epigraph: 'Here Order in Variety we see, / Where all Things differ, yet where all agree'. There his spokesman finds it necessary to advocate the dissociation of moral and aesthetic criteria in order to explain the peculiar appeal of the ruins and artful Rock-Work. The other speaker in the *Dialogue* has doubts about this explanation and later challenges the dissociation by quoting a line from Pope's *Epistle*: ' 'Tis Use alone that sanctifies Expence'. How, he asks, can Stowe's proprietor justify the sacrificing of such a wide expanse of fertile land to visual pleasures only? How can an expensively ornamented garden be of any public 'Use'? For all his emphasis on imaginative pleasure and its sources in the 'natural' garden, Addison was aware (*Spectator* 414) of the economic consequences of promoting ornamental gardening and disturbing the profit/pleasure equilibrium:

> It might, indeed, be of ill Consequence to the Publick, as well as unprofitable to private Persons, to alienate so much Ground from Pasturage, and the Plow . . . But why may not a whole Estate be thrown into a kind of Garden by frequent Plantations, that they may turn as much to the Profit, as the Pleasure of others.

In the *Dialogue* various justifications for ornamental gardening are offered. There is, first of all, the economic argument (another borrowing from the *Epistle*) that work on this estate provides employment for many poor families and invigorates local trade. Then comes this defence of refined aesthetic pleasure:

> I must own there appears a very visible Connection between an *improved* Taste for Pleasure, and a Taste for Virtue: when I sit ravished at an Oratorio, or stand astonished before the Cartoons, or enjoy myself in these happy Walks, I can feel my Mind expand itself, my Notions enlarge, and my Heart better disposed either for a religious Thought, or a benevolent Action: In a Word, I cannot help imagining a Taste for these exalted Pleasures contributes towards making me a better Man.

This is, of course, a very convenient moral vindication of ornamental gardening on a grand scale. Stowe's version of 'improved' nature has become a valuable work of art, like a grand musical composition or a High Renaissance painting. Logically then, it must be appraised by the sort of criteria and indeed vocabulary which are normally reserved for art criticism. On these terms, consideration of the economic contributions of the great estate has no place, for they afford no aesthetic pleasure. Consequently those manifestly functional parts of an estate where efficiency is enhanced by regularity and uniformity of design – e.g. kitchen garden, estate offices, large-scale timber-plantations – have to be separated off, concealed or disguised (Gothic façades to modern dairy-buildings). It is but a step from here to the belief that beauty in landscape is chiefly to be associated not with cultivated fields and neat estate-architecture but with wild country and ruined buildings. 'The painter gains from what the merchant has lost',[47] muses Gilpin as he surveys the Picturesque remains of formerly prosperous Winchelsea.

If Pope's moral and economic criteria for garden design are scarcely more than a passing gesture in Gilpin's predominantly formalist debate on landscape aesthetics, they are virtually abandoned in Shenstone's 'Unconnected Thoughts on Gardening' written in the early 1760s. The title itself emphasises the unsystematic nature of the essay, appropriately Picturesque in its irregularity of design. Shenstone divides gardening into three 'species': kitchen gardening, *parterre* gardening, and 'landskip, or picturesque-gardening'. It is the last species with which he is concerned, and he holds that it 'consists in pleasing the imagination, by scenes of grandeur, beauty, or variety' – again, Addison's prescription almost word for word. Utility or 'convenience' is excluded from consideration in this sort of garden, as Gilpin had wanted to do in his appreciation of Stowe. Shenstone clearly knows his predecessors in the discussion of aesthetics – Addison, Gerard, Burke – and just as he endorses Addison's three sources of imaginative pleasure, so he agrees with Burke that the Sublime has generally a more profound effect than the merely beautiful. His principal concern is to suggest ways of managing garden design so as to afford the maximum pleasure to the eye. For this specific purpose he thinks the landscape painter is the gardener's best designer. The painter knows best how to arrange a view and introduce a stimulating variety of form and colour. *Variety* is again presented as a key concern in the appreciation of landscape: 'Are there not broken rocks and rugged grounds, to which we can hardly attribute either beauty or grandeur, and yet when introduced near an extent of lawn, impart a pleasure equal to more shapely scenes?' Variety must occupy an aesthetic position not catered for by either the Sublime or the Beautiful, and yet it must be recognised as equal to each in the pleasure it affords. Variety applies both to the broken lines and rugged textures of the rocks and to the pleasant visual transitions made from neat lawns to rough pasture, or from *parterre* to mountain scenery:

Variety appears to me to derive a good part of it's effect from novelty [cf. Addison's 'Uncommonness' or 'Novelty']; as the eye, passing from one form or colour, to a form or colour of a different kind, finds a degree of novelty in it's present object which affords immediate satisfaction.

This variety must of course remain a controlled effect, just as the painter who forms such pictures on canvas is principally interested, according to James Clarke's *Survey of the Lakes* (1787), in views characterised by 'a sort of irregular symmetry'. The eye passes from one form or colour to a form or colour of a different kind, as we had been invited to experience in the 'Here . . . There . . . Here' structure of Pope's description of Windsor Forest (see above, p. 18). Shenstone's 'variety', adapted from Addison's 'novelty', is derived from the principle on which those descriptive passages from Milton, Pope, Dyer and Thomson are based. It springs from *concordia discors* and organises the descriptions of views such as the 'Ever Charming, ever New' landscape seen from Grongar Hill. But how does Shenstone's 'variety' come to be associated with the *Picturesque*? Why not simply refer to it as Variety? The reason is that the ultimate authority on the management of this controlled variety is no longer an intellectual theory (the *concordia discors*), but the art of the landscape painter. 'Landskip should contain variety enough to form a picture upon canvas'.

The gardener therefore must be well acquainted with the work of the landscape painters, as Shenstone advised. He should also know the celebrated passages of landscape description in poetry. Stephen Switzer's popular book on garden design,

*Ichnographia Rustica* frequently commends Milton's description of Eden and Pope's opening lines to *Windsor-Forest* as models for the natural garden. The other authority for the gardener is Nature herself. 'First follow Nature', Pope advised the poet and critic in his *Essay on Criticism*, 'and your judgement frame / By her just standard'. This is Nature in the more abstract sense, the principle of order, stability and permanence in the universe. But this Nature was, through imperceptible shifts, increasingly identified with the natural world in its physical manifestations, with all that stood separate from Art or Artifice, and beyond the reach of meddling man. 'The Fancy is struck by *Nature* alone; and if *Art* does anything more than improve her, we think she grows impertinent', wrote Gilpin in his *Dialogue*. Therefore the connoisseur of landscape gardening must not only be familiar with the appropriate poets and painters, but he must become qualified as a connoisseur of Nature – Nature as she exhibits herself in fine natural landscapes. He must combine these two types of connoisseurship. In other words, he must become the Picturesque tourist.

This prerequisite is already hinted at in Gilpin's *Dialogue*. One of the friends mentions a visit he made three years earlier to east Cumberland (near Gilpin's birthplace). From many a fine natural landscape there he was particularly struck by one, and he could not help wishing that Stowe's proprietor had had such materials to work with: for then, 'it could not be but he would make a most noble Picture':

There is the greatest Variety of garnished Rocks, shattered Precipices, rising Hills, ornamented with the finest Woods, thro' which are opened the most elegant Vales that I have ever met with: Not to mention the most enchanting Views up and down the River, which winds itself in such a manner as to shew its Banks to the Best Advantage, which, together with very charming Prospects into the Country, terminated by the blue Hills at a distance, make as fine a Piece of Nature, as perhaps can any where be met with.

Here then is a fine 'Piece of Nature', distinguished chiefly by the variety of its components and by its charming prospects. A landscaping genius, claims the speaker, could here so exert himself as to convert this 'Piece' into 'a most noble Picture'. This, with little modification, is exactly the activity of the Picturesque tourist as he travels through the spectacular regions of Britain. John Stoddart, who wrote a record of his Scottish tours in 1799 and 1800, defined the Picturesque traveller as one who 'reviews the scenes of nature and the rules of art, with which he is already acquainted, and in imagination adapts to this standard the scenery which he expects to behold'.[48] To place Nature under the direction of Art for the purposes of improvement is the professional role of the landscape gardener. The Picturesque tourist is simply carrying on this function, but in the imagination only as he fills his tour journal and sketch-book with appraisals and modifications of the landscapes through which he travels.

Gilpin's *Dialogue* and Shenstone's 'Thoughts' bring into rough focus ideas and arguments which lead us into the heart of Picturesque theory as it developed in the last three decades of the century. Burke's *Enquiry* had delivered a powerful blow to neoclassical aesthetic criteria by arguing that the perception of beauty was dependent not on the intellectual recognition of utility or good proportion in the object viewed, but on the immediate response to formal qualities such as gradual variation, smoothness and smallness: 'The influence of reason in producing our passions is nothing near so extensive as it is commonly believed'.[49] Shenstone, Gilpin and Uvedale Price in their later development of Picturesque aesthetics endorse this challenge to neoclassicism. They go further: Picturesque taste by the 1790s has not only dismissed utility and proportion but positively recommends obsolescence and rugged disproportion as having the most exquisite aesthetic appeal. Variety has become of paramount importance. A vigorous variety of texture and contour contributes to the cherished ruggedness and irregularity of the ruin and, more generally, of garden design in the later decades of the century, to the exclusion of symmetry and utility. The sharpening taste for variety is the beginning of that later Picturesque obsession with roughness and dishevelment, just as the anti-utilitarian bias is to issue in that notorious Picturesque fondness for ruins, hovels, gypsies and beggars.

(iii) *Humble Stations: Picturesque Theory in the 1790s*

Gilpin's first tour-book *Observations on the River Wye* (1782) announced a 'new object of pursuit' for the tourist. Instead of inquiring into the culture of soils or the manners of men in various parts of Britain, the tourist is recommended 'to examine the face of a country *by the rules of picturesque beauty*'. For this purpose the Wye Valley was finely suited. Soon after his return from that tour in the summer of 1770, Gilpin wrote enthusiastically of 'such a display of picturesque scenery, that it is beyond any commendation'. Judged by Gilpin's 'rules', many of the river scenes appeared to him to be remarkably 'correct': 'Indeed very little more is necessary than to transfer them upon canvas, and they are pictures'.[50] This last sentence explains what Gilpin means by 'picturesque' at this stage. It conforms with his 1768 definition in the *Essay upon Prints*: 'a term expressive of that peculiar kind of beauty, which is agreeable in a picture'.[51]

As has often been noted, Gilpin uses the phrase 'picturesque beauty' quite freely, seeing no particular incompatibility between Picturesque and Beautiful. But the distinction is already latent. What he calls that 'peculiar' kind of beauty so agreeable in a picture is not quite the same beauty we see in the world around us. This latter beauty therefore usually needs some correction if it is to become agreeable in a picture. Such issues were at the heart of the debates over the Picturesque in the 1790s.

William Gilpin, schoolmaster and country clergyman, was a reluctant theorist. He wrote to his publishers in 1802: 'I am far more anxious to have you push my religious works ... I have figured so much lately as a picturesque man, that I should be glad to redeem my character as a clergyman'.[52] But he had created a fashion for which the public had developed an insatiable hunger; and as he was, in the words of the *Monthly Review*, 'the venerable founder and master of the Picturesque School', his hundreds of tourist pupils would not easily let him return to his primary vocation. Apart from brief, incidental remarks on the term 'Picturesque' in his various travel books, nearly a quarter of a century passes between his *Essay upon Prints* definition and the publication of his more extended theoretical discussion 'On Picturesque Beauty' in *Three Essays* (1792).[53] All his tours took place during that period, including the Wye Valley tour in 1770, the tour to the Lakes in 1772 and the tour into the Scottish Highlands in 1776.

The essay 'On Picturesque Beauty' sets out to clarify that distinction between Beautiful and Picturesque objects or scenes: 'between those, which please the eye in their *natural state*; and those, which please from some quality, capable of being *illustrated in painting*'. Gilpin argues that whereas beauty in '*real objects*' is distinguished, as Burke rightly observed, by smoothness and neatness (elegant architecture and improved pleasure-grounds are his examples), beauty in '*picturesque representation*' is distinguished by roughness and ruggedness, as in the outline and bark of a tree or the craggy sides of a mountain:

Picturesque composition consists in uniting in one whole a variety of parts; and these parts can only be obtained from rough objects.

Why? Because rough objects allow the artist a 'free, bold touch' in execution, and enable him to lavish the 'graces of his art' upon his subject. Once Gilpin has established the painter's preference for rough objects, he broadens the issue to consider why roughness should make an '*essential difference*' between the objects of nature and the objects of artificial representation. This he candidly admits he cannot ultimately answer. As he finds himself pursuing his enquiries into the first principles of aesthetics he realises the futility: 'we go on, without end, and without satisfaction'. The tentative nature of the essay is confirmed in Gilpin's concluding remark to the reader that he sent the piece to Sir Joshua Reynolds, hoping for his '*imprimatur*'. Reynolds wrote a kind reply, venturing the opinion that the adjective 'picturesque' was more properly applied to 'the excellences of the inferior schools', Rubens and the Venetian painters for example, and not to Raphael or Michelangelo. It is, in his opinion, inimical to the Grand Style: 'variety of tints and forms is picturesque; but ... the reverse of this – (uniformity of colour, and a long continuation of lines) produces grandeur'. By and large, Gilpin agrees with this distinction, and hints that he had not really given it much attention:

With regard to the term *picturesque*, I have always myself used it merely to denote *such objects, as are proper subjects for painting*: so that according to *my definition*, one of the cartoons, and a flower piece are equally picturesque.

So we are back to where we started.

The reader of Gilpin's essay is likely to gain more from the application and exemplification of the ideas in play, and will be particularly struck by Gilpin's first example of how a Beautiful 'real object' can be made Picturesque:

A piece of Palladian architecture may be elegant in the last degree. The proportion of it's parts – the propriety of it's ornaments – and the symmetry of the whole, may be highly pleasing. But if we introduce it in a picture, it immediately becomes a formal object, and ceases to please. Should we wish to give it picturesque beauty, we must beat down one half of it, deface the other, and throw the mutilated members around in heaps. In short, from a *smooth* building we must turn it into a *rough* ruin.

Such drastic measures taken in order to render an elegant building suitable for the painter carry implications of which neither Gilpin nor Uvedale Price (who takes a similar example) seems aware. They are ostensibly preoccupied only with formal matters. But for us the sense of iconoclasm is inescapable. Palladian elegance, the neoclassical ideal of beauty, is being dismantled before our eyes. The agency for this in Gilpin is the mallet smashing the work of the patient chisel, ostensibly in the interests of art. In Price's example there are subtler changes, which we shall come to shortly.

Sir Uvedale Price was the doyen of Picturesque theorists. His own estate at Foxley in Herefordshire exemplified the aesthetic principles for which he argued at length in his *Essay on the Picturesque* (1794).[54] He found both William Kent and 'Capability' Brown too meanly formal in their garden designs – shaven lawns, and trees in careful 'clumps' – and urged a greater freedom and relaxation. In this he was supported by his friend and neighbour Richard Payne Knight, who dedicated his didactic poem *The Landscape* to Price in 1794.

Price is dissatisfied with Gilpin's essay. He wishes to give to the Picturesque a status quite distinct from the Beautiful or the Sublime, and to identify objects that are inherently and peculiarly Picturesque. 'The picturesque', he argues near the start of his *Essay*,[55] 'by being discriminated from the beautiful and the sublime, has a separate character, and not a mere reference to the art of painting'. It is at this point, when the reference to painting is swept to the margin, that another term might well have been introduced to replace 'Picturesque'; but it was too late. The debate centring on the term 'Picturesque' had already generated too much momentum.[56]

Like Gilpin, Price early in his discussion focuses attention on the classical ruin, and his description compares interestingly with Gilpin's:

A temple or palace of Grecian architecture in its perfect entire state, and with its surface and colour smooth and even, either in painting or reality is beautiful; in ruin it is picturesque. Observe the process by which time, the great author of such changes, converts a beautiful object into a picturesque one. First, by means of weather stains, partial incrustations, mosses, etc., it at the same time takes off from the uniformity of the surface, and of the colour; that is, gives a degree of roughness and variety of tint. Next, the various accidents of weather loosen the stones themselves; they tumble in irregular masses, upon what was perhaps smooth turf or pavement, or nicely trimmed walks and shrubberies; now mixed and overgrown with wild plants and creepers, that crawl over and shoot among the fallen ruins. Sedums, wall-flowers, and other vegetables that bear drought, find nourishment in the decayed cement from which the stones have been detached: birds convey their food into the chinks, and yew, elder, and other berried plants project from the sides; while the ivy mantles over other parts and crowns the top.

As with Gilpin's description, the reader must be registering more than simply the formal changes, 'roughness and variety' replacing 'uniformity'. Nature's reclamation of her raw materials is observed in detail with great relish. Organic life is spontaneously resumed, during time's slow, relentless destruction of symmetry.

Shortly after his examination of the ruined Grecian temple, Price decides that the spectator's Picturesque pleasure in contemplating such ruins may be confused with other responses, for instance with that to the Beautiful or the Sublime ('the elegance or grandeur of their forms') or with the sentimental or moral responses ('the veneration of high antiquity – or the solemnity of religious awe'). In other words, the ruin, so long a prominent feature in the *paysage moralisé* and now so encrusted with emblematic significance, provokes a response too complex for him to discuss in purely Picturesque terms. So he resorts to humbler subjects which certainly cannot be thought of as having elegance or grandeur or religious solemnity, and which, he seems to imply, have a more restricted range of connotations and are thus unlikely to interfere with the purely Picturesque appreciation of forms and colours. He chooses as prime Picturesque material hovels, cottages, dilapidated mills, the interiors of old barns, 'old mossy, rough-hewn park pales of unequal heights', disturbed surfaces of water, certain kinds of tree (oak, elm) – particularly when shattered by storm – shaggy goats, and sheep with ragged fleeces. His depressing list of the derelict and obsolescent is finished off with a few human subjects eligible for Picturesque treatment, the gypsies and beggars, 'who in all the qualities which give them that character, bear a close analogy to the wild forester and the worn-out cart-horse, and again to old mills, hovels, and other inanimate objects of the same kind'. In effect, only ruined human beings are Picturesque. All these rugged, angular forms are a continual stimulus to the eye, and they are cherished specifically for that reason. Price's criterion of 'visual irritation' indicates his relation to Burke's sensationist aesthetic. Thus the long tradition of the *paysage moralisé*, the landscape designed for interpretation and instruction as well as for visual enjoyment, gives way to what might almost be called a *paysage amoralisé*, if not *démoralisé*.

The shift from the Grecian temple or Palladian building in its entire state to a dismembered ruin, and from there to the old hovel, in a sense exemplifies those more gradual shifts of interest over the last part of the eighteenth century: public taste increasingly draws away from a sophisticated metropolitan, classical culture towards an interest in the humbler, more remote, native ways of life. Gainsborough's cottage subjects and Goldsmith's *Deserted Village* (1770) typify these new tastes in the representation of the rural poor. 'Sensibility', 'soft' primitivism, the rise of evangelicalism – these and other pressures manipulated the images of the rural poor and their environment, and endowed them with complex moral and political associations. The trouble is that the Picturesque enterprise in its later stages, with its almost exclusive emphasis on visual appreciation, entailed a suppression of the spectator's moral response to those very subjects which it could least hope to divest of moral significance – the ruin, the hovel and rural poverty.

10. Thomas Bewick, woodcut illustration to Goldsmith's works.

Consider these lines from Goldsmith's *The Traveller*, elegantly illustrated in Bewick's woodcut (fig. 10):

> . . . in those domes where Caesars once bore sway,
> Defaced by time, and tottering in decay,
> There in the ruin, heedless of the dead,
> The shelter-seeking peasant builds his shed;
> And, wondering man could want the larger pile,
> Exults, and owns his cottage with a smile.[57]

We can hardly dissociate these images (and Goldsmith certainly does not) from familiar themes in eighteenth-century literature – the vanity of human wishes, the Horatian retreat from court and city, and the simplicities of pastoral. At the same time such a scene is prime Picturesque material. Michael Angelo Rooker made a speciality of this kind of subject.[58] The peasant's humble shelter built into the ruins of imperial Rome is a close parallel to Price's description of animal and vegetable life starting up again in the ruins of the Grecian palace, in which his emphasis is purely on the conversion of beautiful form into Picturesque form. In spite of all his formalist emphasis, those images of ruin and hovel, beggar and gypsy, remain charged with values beyond mere ruggedness and irregularity. Under the terms of Price's discussion a Picturesque iconography, in the sense of a value-laden system of imagery, ought almost to be a solecism, but clearly it is not; and in the remainder of this chapter I want to indicate how this pure formalism could not be sustained, even by Price himself.

The social descent – palace to ruin to hovel – has an interesting analogy with the painter's changing viewpoint in the eighteenth century. The neoclassical position is put by Joshua Reynolds in his third *Discourse*, as he urges the apprentice painter to concentrate on general nature, 'the eternal invariable idea of nature':

... the whole beauty and grandeur of the art consists, in my opinion, in being able to get above all singular forms, local customs, particularities, and details of every kind.[59]

We can see this principle in practice if we literalize Reynolds' phrase 'get above'; for that is the right description of the characteristic position adopted by the neo-classical landscape painter and poet. The painter favours a high viewpoint as does the prospect poet; in each case he has *physically* 'got above' the particularities and details spread before him, and can hardly help but generalize what he can see only at a considerable distance.

Reynolds' advice was issued in 1770, the year after Thomas Gray had set out to tour the Lake District. While exploring Derwentwater, Gray decided that 'all [view]points that are much elevated, spoil the beauty of the valley, and make its parts, which are not large, look poor and diminutive'. This observation caught the attention of William Mason when he edited Gray's descriptions of the Lakes for publication in 1775, and he added a significant footnote:

The *Picturesque Point* is always ... low in all prospects: A truth, which though the Land-scape Painter knows, he cannot always observe; since the Patron who employs him to take a view of his place, usually carries him to some elevation for that purpose, in order, I suppose, that he may have more of him for his money.[60]

The releasing of the artist from private patronage alters the viewpoint, and, as we shall see on the Tours, the Picturesque painter often goes to absurd depths to find the lowest possible angle on his subject. The preference for the low angle is demonstrated in a pair of drawings by Gilpin, which feature the conventional side-screen trees, middle-distance bridge and castle tower, and mountain background. Fig. 11a, though hardly a 'prospect', is still, for Gilpin, relatively un-Picturesque. The horizon line is about half-way up the composition and the spectator is nearly on a level with the bridge. In fig. 11b the viewpoint is much lower, down in the gorge. The spread of the arch is more impressive and the multiplied mountain peaks now nearly reach the top of the picture. A few other touches soften or break up the rectilinear architecture. The spectator has much more the sense of being enveloped by the landscape.

The distinction between these two viewing positions and the sense of envelop-ment by the scenery have counterparts in the development of the English garden and its relationship to the house. The geometrical garden was meant to be seen from the drawing room on the *piano nobile* or from a raised terrace. Its organisation

11a. William Gilpin, *Landscape Composition*.
Fry Gallery, London

could be appreciated from one elevated vantage point (to which the commissioned painter would be directed). But in the landscape garden, as Ronald Paulson has described, the general feeling is of '*going down into*, of *being in* and *moving through*'.[61] There is a closer involvement, a willingness to submerge oneself in the landscape once one is moving through rather than surveying it. This later preference is seen in Benjamin Malkin's assessment of Hafod, the Sublime landscaped estate in Cardiganshire, which was one of the attractions on the tour of North Wales:

The inducement to explore should never be withdrawn, by a sweeping survey from a balcony or a portico: however wide the range, the idea of magnitude is impaired, by the very possibility of comprehending it all at once.[62]

Mark Girouard, in *Life in the English Country House*, has discussed the late-eighteenth-century preference for having the main rooms of the house more in touch with the garden, 'not just by views through the windows . . . but also by means of having the rooms at ground level . . . The rooms thus flowed out into the garden'.[63]

The idea of wandering through and perhaps even losing oneself in the natural garden is reflected in the vogue for artificial 'wildernesses' in gardens, select areas where one could enjoy the *frisson* of being lost, 'a-mazed', 'be-wildered'. It is reflected also in the lowered viewpoint prescribed by Mason. One of the consequences for the artist is the increasing prominence of the natural foreground, which

11b. William Gilpin, *Landscape Composition.*
Fry Gallery, London

now replaces the rectilinear drawing-room window frame or the terrace balustrade. The natural details and particularities which were, in every sense, beneath the neoclassical painter's notice, now surround the Picturesque artist. He can hardly avoid, even if he wishes to, the delicious varieties of tints and textures so relished by Price. 'When the whole plan of a garden is visible at one cast of the eye, it takes away even the *hopes* of variety',[64] remarked Philip Southcote. The new stress on the foreground is clearly made by Gilpin: 'we consider the foreground as the *basis, and foundation of the whole picture*';[65] and again, '*Foregrounds* are essential to landscape: *distances* are not'.[66] The accentuation of foreground was also an incidental effect of the convex Claude Glass so favoured by the tourists.

The 'prospect' had been a commanding view, favoured in an age of confidence and optimism. 'Prospect' means literally a 'looking forward'. In the seventeenth century, as James Turner has shown, 'the prospect from a high place was well-established as an image of political foresight and inquiry'.[67] The repudiation of the high viewpoint in late-eighteenth-century Picturesque theory suggests a failure of confidence. The long view now needs to be screened off: better not to see too far ahead. Towering mountains may afford panoramic viewpoints, but, like ruined architecture, they must also remind arrogant man of his insignificance. Human figures can be introduced only to accentuate this, never to disturb it. They may be seen in postures of awe at the sight of mountains and cataracts, or as Nature's gallery attendants obsequiously pointing out her beauties from the sideline, or as vagrants traipsing along the old worn paths, remote from civilisation's new highways. Like the painter's viewpoint, they occupy humble stations.

The various challenges to neoclassical orthodoxy implicit in the lowered viewpoint, in the more particularised rendering of detail, and in the demolition of the Grecian or Palladian ideal, were partly a revolt against the constraints imposed by the commissioned topographical portraits of elegant country seats, where, as Mason's footnote suggests, the patron required something like a pictorial map of his estate from a viewpoint which would display all its tasteful organisation. It was a revolt that extended beyond the treatment of objects to the painter's choice of objects themselves. On the good estate everything is in neat working-order, so the liberated Picturesque painter will prefer old barns and decrepit watermills; for, as we noticed in the earlier discussion on ruins, utility in a Picturesque view becomes antagonistic to beauty. Instead of the neat post-and-rail boundary to fields, he will prefer Price's 'old, mossy, rough-hewn park pales of unequal heights': he will, that is, unless the neat hedgerows, palings and other property boundaries are thrown into the remote distance, in which case they can become 'one rich blended surface'.[68] Even the most intractably non-Picturesque scenery could be accommodated in this way, as Wordsworth implies in his telling phrase 'by distance ruralized'[69] as he casts a backward glance on the smoky city of Bristol near the beginning of *The Prelude*. Instead of smooth parkland the Picturesque artist will prefer rough pasture; instead of well-shorn sheep, the shaggy goat; and instead of the commissioned Stubbsian portrait of the 'sleek, pampered steed', grooms and jockeys, he will prefer the 'wild forester, and the worn-out cart-horse'.

The list of new preferences could extend indefinitely. The Picturesque eye is habitually drawn to the humble, uncultivated parts of nature and human society; and that becomes the tourist's goal. As we noted in his *Dialogue* at Stowe, Gilpin is always anxious to distinguish what is simply pleasing to the spectator as he views the countryside from what is Picturesque:

In general indeed, when we meet with a description of a pleasing country, we hear of hay-cocks, or waving cornfields, or labourers at their plough, or other circumstances and objects, which the picturesque eye always wishes to exclude.[70]

The Picturesque eye, in other words, is anti-georgic. Man's presumptuous 'improvements' are repudiated by the Picturesque eye, which 'ranges after nature, untamed by art, and bursting wildly into all it's irregular forms'.[71] Man is humbled before the untamed grandeur of Nature. Price's choice of human subjects exemplifies these Picturesque preferences. True Picturesque taste chooses not the busy field-labourer and estate manager but the gypsy and beggar, who are both quite beyond the parkland pale. Humans of a higher social scale must also be humbled, just like the painter's viewpoint and the razed temple:

. . . a Belisarius, or a Marius in age and exile, have the same mixture of picturesqueness and of decayed grandeur as the venerable remains of past ages.

Price's main target in his *Essay* is 'Capability' Brown, whom he accuses of creating very dull landscapes with his 'smoothing and levelling'. 'Levelling' is an activity which Price deplores, in both its horticultural and political senses, and his Picturesque preference for the forms of humble life should not be mistaken for egalitarianism. He is fully conscious of this double sense of 'levelling' as he pursues his argument.[72] 'Despotism is the most complete leveller', he reminds his reader. But he is also wary of any move in the opposite direction: the Revolution and Reign of Terror in France had scared any liberal principles he had. He was frightened by what he called the dreadful 'anarchy' resulting from the French people's bid for liberty. As a property owner he was very conscious of his own vulnerability, as his earnest *Thoughts on the Defence of Property* (1797) addressed to other Herefordshire landowners illustrates.

Price had in mind almost the reverse of egalitarianism. He wished to restore the old hierarchy with its clear social distinctions, because that was Nature's original design. The same principle, accordingly, should be applied to gardening:

A good landscape is that in which all the parts are free and unconstrained, but in which, though some are prominent and highly illuminated, and others in shade and retirement; some rough, and others more smooth and polished, yet they are all necessary to the beauty, energy, effect, and harmony of the whole. I do not see how a good government can be more exactly defined.[73]

We have almost returned to the *paysage moralisé*. Here again is 'Order in Variety'. Man's meddling 'improvements' to Nature threaten to dissolve these interesting distinctions into a dreary uniformity, a dead level. Thus Variety, Nature's spontaneous variety, enriched over the centuries, becomes the guiding principle. The moment that smoothing and levelling begin:

. . . adieu to all that the painter admires – to all intricacies – to all the beautiful varieties of form, tint, and light and shade; every deep recess – every bold projection – the fantastic roots of trees – the winding paths of sheep – all must go; in a few hours, the rash hand of false taste completely demolishes what time only, and a thousand lucky accidents, can mature, so as to become the admiration and study of a Ruysdael or a Gainsborough.[74]

For the Picturesque connoisseur, nothing attracts the attention like neglect. The Picturesque eye, maintains Gilpin, 'must find its own beauties; and often fixes . . . on some accidental rough object, which the common eye would pass unnoticed';[75] and which agricultural or horticultural improvement had not disturbed. As John Clare put it, the man of true taste 'loves each desolate neglected spot / That seems in labours hurry left forgot'.[76] Neglect is, after all, the best cosmetic for the ruin, that most poignant emblem of desuetude.

The reactionary, anti-utilitarian element in Picturesque taste has here reached its apogee. It is hostile to the engineering of social change and prizes the human anachronisms left in the wake of such change. Wordsworth, who was no lover of the Picturesque, caught the sentimental charms of obsolescence, in both landscape and economic terms, when he gave to his Wanderer, the anachronistic pedlar, these elegiac lines in *The Excursion*:

> With fruitless pains
> Might one like me *now* visit many a tract
> Which, in his youth, he trod, and trod again,
> A lone pedestrian with a scanty freight . . .
> Among the tenantry of thorpe and vill;
> Or straggling burgh, of ancient charter proud,
> And dignified by battlements and towers
> Of some stern castle, mouldering on the brow
> Of a green hill or bank of rugged stream.
> The foot-path faintly marked, the horse-track wild,
> And formidable length of plashy lane, . . .
> Have vanished – swallowed up by stately roads
> Easy and bold, that penetrate the gloom
> Of Britain's farthest glens.[77]

Price and his followers in the 1790s want to turn the clock back, to rediscover landscapes where there are not only no traces of contemporary industrialization, land enclosure and estate improvement, but where the georgic idyll in all its forms is lost and where the terrifying 'levelling' influences from across the Channel can never come. In flight from Brownian landscapes, the Picturesque tourist is now willing to trek hundreds of miles to find a world 'That seems in labours hurry left forgot'. The painter is very willing to satisfy the same needs:

. . . at all times, and everywhere, one great end of Landscape painting is to bring distant scenery, – and such more particularly as it is wild and not easily accessible, – under the eye, in a cultivated country . . . and not to expose itself, by a faint imitation of the views which are seen from the windows of the room, for which the representations are intended as furniture.[78]

The search for the Picturesque begins with exactly this 'one great end' in mind.

# IV

# Travelling 'knick-knacks'

James Plumptre, a Cambridge clergyman and Fellow of Clare Hall, made a tour through northern England, the Scottish Highlands and parts of Wales in the summer of 1799. He calculated that of the total distance travelled (well over 2000 miles), 1774¼ miles were on foot.[1] He felt able to claim such precision because he carried a pedometer in his breeches' pocket. The pedometer was one item in a very full list of travelling 'knick-knacks', as he called them. These included pieces of tinted glass through which to view the landscape, drawing pads, memorandum books, a small watercolour set, pens and pencils, a telescope, a barometer, maps, the pocket edition of William Cowper's poems, and abridged versions of various tour books by Dr Johnson, Thomas Pennant and others. Before embarking on the Tours themselves I would like to consider some of these 'knick-knacks', in particular the Claude Glass, the memorandum book or tour journal, and the sketch-book.

## (i) *The Claude Glass*

The Picturesque tourist is typically a gentleman or gentlewoman engaged in an experiment in controlled aesthetic response to a range of new and often intimidating visual experiences. The new vocabulary, the methodical classification of different kinds of scenery, the development of technical skills in drawing and painting to enable the viewer to 'fix' a landscape, the establishment of Stations affording composed prospects – these all formed a subtle psychological protection to the tourist freshly exposed to daunting and often disorienting landscapes. Those terms 'fix', 'Station', and 'composed' indicate precisely the nature of this protection, the stability given to these new experiences, by the selection and isolation of landscape components. Untamed landscapes can thus be controlled.

The search for the Picturesque is analogous to the sport of hunting. 'The draughtsman was driven into the recesses of the mountains, for the subject of his pencil',[2] William Marshall had noted in his brief, 1795 history of landscape painting. There is something of the big-game hunter in these tourists, boasting of their encounters with savage landscapes, 'capturing' wild scenes, and 'fixing' them as pictorial trophies in order to sell them or hang them up in frames on their drawing-room walls. Gilpin himself tests the hunting analogy, perhaps to entice the Squire

12. Claude Glasses.
Science Museum, London

Westerns of his day to forsake their licentious pleasures in favour of the Picturesque tour:

Shall we suppose it a greater pleasure to the sportsman to pursue a trivial animal, than it is to the man of taste to pursue the beauties of nature? to follow her through all her recesses? to obtain a sudden glance, as she flits past him in some airy shape? to trace her through the mazes of the cover . . .[3]

The Picturesque tourist pursued his prey with a Claude Glass rather than a gun (fig. 12). He could fix and compose elusive landscape features in a matter of seconds. 'My Convex Mirror brought every scene within the compass of a picture'[4] recalled one tourist with delight, as he reduced the extensive views at Lake Windermere into manageable proportions. The Claude Glass was an optical device which took various forms, of which perhaps Thomas Gray's was the most typical: 'a Plano-convex Mirror of about four inches diameter on a black foil, and bound up like a pocket-book'.[5] The convexity miniaturised the reflected landscape. Except in the foreground, details were largely lost, and something like a *beau idéal* emerged, freed from particularities and deformities. Gilpin felt that the mirror was particularly advantageous where the painter was interested in foregrounds, since the convexity sometimes shrank distances out of sight.

The Claude Glass could trace its ancestry back to the studio mirrors used by

Renaissance painters, and to instruments such as the *camera obscura*.* William Mason thought the Claude Glass 'perhaps the best and most convenient substitute for a Camera Obscura, of anything that has hitherto been invented'. The term 'Claude Glass', or sometimes 'Gray Glasses', could also apply to transparent coloured glasses through which one viewed a landscape, tinted but not necessarily modified in shape. Gilpin, perhaps surprisingly, makes little mention of these devices on his many tours, even though, as Norman Nicholson has suggested, his own drawings, 'both in their oval shape and the carroty colours of the aquatints, were in great part an imitation of the image in the mirror'.[6] Gilpin is actually disparaging about the Glasses (as distinct from the mirror):

How far the painter should follow his eye, or his glass in working from nature, I am not master enough of the theory of colouring to ascertain. In general, I am apt to believe, that the merit of this kind of modified vision consists chiefly in it's novelty; and that nature has given us a better apparatus, for viewing objects in a picturesque light; than any, the optician can furnish . . .[7]

The term 'Gray Glasses', as an alternative to 'Claude Glass', was a tribute to the poet whose own devotion to their use is exemplified in his account of trying to capture a Lake District sunset in his mirror:

[I] fell down on my back across a dirty lane with my glass open in one hand, but broke only my knuckles: stay'd nevertheless, & saw the sun set in all its glory.[8]

This contrivance with its special ability to afford the tourist a 'kind of modified vision', raises some teasing aesthetic problems. The mirror, as Jean Hagstrum has argued,[9] paradoxically provides both faithful realism and stylized idealism: it reflects whatever landscape is presented to it, and yet it also modifies that landscape. To this extent it was invaluable for painters who were still loyal to neoclassical prescriptions – *generalised* Nature and the *beau idéal* – but who nonetheless toured in search of very specific landscapes. With the Claude Glass all sorts of compromise between generalisation and particularisation were possible. One such caught Gilpin's interest. He remarked that the human eye cannot concentrate on *'general effect'* and *'particular objects'* at the same time, nor can it hold simultaneous focus on foreground and distance. But the mirror can manage both:

. . . in the minute exhibitions of the convex-mirror, *composition*, *forms*, and *colours* are brought closer together; and the eye examines the *general effect*, the *forms of the objects*, and the *beauty of the tints*, in one complex view.[10]

The Glass thus performed a very important aesthetic function, even if it was a tourist toy. Its 'complex view' helped the apprentice painter; and, for the non-painting tourist, its darker tinting and distortion helped to superimpose something like a Claudean idiom on British landscape. It was a portable means of realising the efforts of the idealizing imagination, as Gilpin discovered when he used it from the window of his travelling chaise:

*The two ladies in Sandby's *Roslin Castle* (see below, fig. 68) are using a *camera obscura*.

A succession of high-coloured pictures is continually gliding before the eye. They are like the visions of the imagination; or the brilliant landscapes of a dream. Forms, and colours, in brightest array, fleet before us; and if the transient glance of a good composition happen to unite with them, we should give any price to fix, and appropriate the scene.[11]

The manipulative potential of the Glass was often exploited by the tourists. In a matter of seconds the time of day or the season could be altered. The darkened glass, tinted blue and grey, could suffuse a varied afternoon scene with moonlight. The yellow, or 'sunrise' glass, when used at noon, conveniently afforded a glowing dawn view, 'without the obscuration of the morning mist'.[12] Through the hoar-frost tinted lens, distant corn stooks became snow drifts. The tourists could rationalise these fancies by claiming that such artifice was, after all, only a means of anticipating what Nature herself would be doing in a few hours' or a few months' time with the same landscape. Since the tourist was essentially a visitor, with little time to spare, he could reasonably try to condense twenty-four hours of changing light effects into a couple of hours' play with his Glasses. It was a kind of artistic licence.

The coloured Glasses were also useful for introducing a tonal harmony into the scene, and this was important for the painter brought up to respect the 'master tint'. Of course, tonal harmony could always be conferred by fortunate accidents of light and weather, in which case the Glasses could be laid aside. Mist could soften and give tonal unity to a sharply angular landscape, and pleasantly dissolve horizon lines, *à la* Claude. A rich sunset could harmonize an assemblage of hetero-geneous forms and colours. Smoke or the hot air from a fire could create some fine blending, idealizing effects, as Coleridge noticed while having tea on Grasmere island:

I lay & saw the woods, & mountains, & lake all trembling, & as it were idealized thro' the subtle smoke which rose up from the clear red embers of the fir-apples which we had collected.[13]

As anyone who has witnessed such effects will testify, images like this are indelible, though very simply achieved. The Glasses were popular because they could con-veniently offer a near facsimile of such idealizing effects. Coleridge briefly developed the analogy of the Claude Glass to explain the way in which the mind habitually receives the impressions of the natural world:

In the country, all around us smile Good and Beauty – and the Images of this divine καλοκἀγαθόν are miniatured on the mind of the beholder, as a Landscape on a Convex Mirror.[14]

The implications of the Glass as an idealizing medium can be helpful when we think of the terms in which the increasing importance of the imagination was discussed by these early Romantics. The naked eye sees the landscape as a collection of disparate elements: but the imagination can reconstitute and transfigure that landscape into an image of harmony. We shall see shortly how Wordsworth does

13. Thomas Rowlandson, *An Artist Travelling in Wales*.
National Museum of Wales, Cardiff

this with the Wye Valley. His nephew's *Memoirs of William Wordsworth* (1851) explains this mediating power of the Romantic imagination very well, and introduces a suggestive analogy:

Imagination is a subjective term: it deals with objects not as they are, but as they appear to the mind of the poet. The imagination is that intellectual lens through the medium of which the poetical observer sees the objects of his observation, modified both in form and colour.[15]

The imagination as an 'intellectual lens' approximates it to the Claude Glass, which can modify and enhance a particular landscape. All the special properties of the Glass are present in Coleridge's well-known account of the origins of his poetic collaboration with Wordsworth,[16] and their agreement about the two cardinal points of poetry: 'the power of exciting the sympathy of the reader by a faithful adherence to the truth of nature, and the power of giving the interest of novelty by the modifying colours of the imagination'.* Truth to nature and the modifying imagination seem incompatible principles. But Coleridge offers an illustration of how the two might be combined; and he does so in terms which might equally well be a tribute to the powers of the Claude Glass:

*Cf. Constable's enthusiastic endorsement of a remark made by one of his friends: 'The whole object and difficulty of the art (indeed of all the fine arts) is to *unite imagination with nature*' (quoted in C. R. Leslie, *Memoirs of the Life of John Constable* [ed. J. Mayne, 1951], p. 179).

14. Thomas Hearne, *Sir George Beaumont and Joseph Farington Sketching a Waterfall* (? 1778).
Coll. Sir Francis Beaumont

The sudden charm, which accidents of light and shade, which moon-light or sun-set diffused over a known and familiar landscape, appeared to represent the practicability of combining both. These are the poetry of nature.

### (ii) *Sketch-books and Journals*

In Rowlandson's picture of *An Artist Travelling in Wales* (fig. 13) the wretched, determined artist is setting out encumbered by the tools of his trade. A large sketch-book or perhaps portfolio is slung over his back, a cumbersome tripod easel lies across his lap, and tied to it are his palette, water-flask and palette knife. Such is his dedication to the Picturesque that the rest of his luggage for sustaining himself on the tour is proportionately insignificant. This is a touring artist of rather slender means. The wealthier breed travelled by coach and could take a small retinue of servants with them. To judge by the drawing of Sir George Beaumont painting a waterfall, these servants must have had to clamber up precipitous slopes with their arms full of easels, sketch-pads, paints and brushes, and umbrellas to keep the spray off the artists and their painting surfaces (fig. 14). *Plein air* oil painting, which Beaumont and his friends seem to be engaged in, was rarely practised in this period, and the artists usually relied on pencil, pen and watercolour. Sketch-pads came in all sizes, the size used presumably depending on carriage circumstances in the tour. The same applied to the notebooks. For the pedestrian, or solitary traveller, a pocket memorandum was the most convenient, but afforded space for little more than a topographical record. At the other extreme is *A Travelling Journal* (fig. 15), a more lavish, purpose-built volume, published with that title printed on its cover in London in 1789 and used that year for a tour in Scotland. The tourist was meant to use a whole two-page opening at one time. Two narrow columns were provided for recording dates and place-names, and two broad ones for 'Observations, etc' and 'Omissions'. The status of the Omissions column is a little enigmatic. It seems it could be filled in with anything from documentary enlargements on well-known places and paintings missed during a country house visit to afterthoughts on the atmosphere of a particular site. The methodical layout would have pleased the first Duchess of Northumberland, who, on her travels in 1760, carried with her a questionnaire of 150 items, including the query 'Is the place chearful melancholy romantic wild or dreary?'[17]

Another important item for the tour was the guidebook. As these began to proliferate over the last two decades of the eighteenth century, the choice became increasingly difficult, especially for the pedestrian or equestrian traveller:

... a traveller of all others can least carry a library about with him. He therefore who judiciously combines together in a portable volume from such laborious authorities the facts by which the places in any beaten route are distinguished, and adds them to his own observations on their present state, is doing a service both to the traveller, and to him who sits at home.[18]

Several such compendia appeared eventually. Charles Heath's *Excursion down*

We arrived at our Inn with not a dry Thread about us, & situated on the Forth.

+ The Galic Interpretation of the word Linlithgow is Lin — a loch, Lith — a withy, and gow or cow — a large Dog; the Town Arms are — a Dog tied to a Tree in the middle of a lake.

# This Lake has a small Island in the eastern extremity, and abounds with fish.

The Great Room of the Palace is well proportioned being 90 ft long — 30 wide and 30 high: in the fourth one stood a very elegant fountain but now entirely destroyed; as are likewise 2 beautiful figures of the Pope and 2 Cardinals.

+ whose office is over the Police

15. *A Travelling Journal* (1789).
National Library of Scotland, Edinburgh

of a Sublime Heathen

*Suave mari magno turbantibus æquora Ventis &c.*

The Ride from hence to Queensferry, a small Town on the coast about 9 miles distant, may perhaps be extremely pleasant, but I am sure that we had no reason to think so, being overtaken by a violent storm which raged with increasing fury for the space of 3 hours. — In the morn? ride to Hopeton House the seat of the Earl of Hopeton a most superb structure distant about 3 miles from Queensferry. — As the House was painting we were not permitted to see it, but if the inside corresponds with the out, there must be very few in Scotland equal to it. — The Pleasure Grounds around the House are extremely pleasant and the View from them, which extends above 30 miles East and West, beggars all description. Hence thro' a well-cultivated country to Linlithgow the ruins of whose Palace are still sufficient to shew it's ancient grandeur. the shew the Room where Queen Mary was born: The Town is pleasantly situated on the Borders of a small lake. In the Church which is contiguous to the Palace is preserved an antique stone beautifully sculptured — on one half Genius is betrayed and seized while with his right hand he is healing the servant of the high Priest, whose ear Peter had cut off on the other half — is Genius with 8 Disciples praying. — Linlithgow is governed by a Provost (to whose civility & willingness acknowledge myself highly indebted) a Dean of Guild and 4 Bailies. — About 2 miles from Linlithgow cross the

Queensferry

June 25.
Hopeton House

Linlithgowshire
Linlithgow

Palace

antique Stone

the *Wye* (1799) was a judicious anthology of extracts from Gilpin and other published Picturesque tours, to which he added copious historical and topographical information. William Mavor in 1798–1800 brought out a small-format, six-volume edition of *The British Tourists*, which could have been quite easily accommodated even by those who travelled light.

'Tour writing is the very rage of the times', remarked John Byng in 1782, surprised to find himself very much *à la mode* as he indulged the 'description-passion' in his 'Ride into the West' that summer.[19] What was the tour journal designed to achieve? Was it to be a purely topographical record, or a highly personal, impressionistic account? The decision over what kind of journal was appropriate was often debated in prefatory remarks in the journals themselves, as the tourists presented their credentials and apologised for being tempted yet again 'to stain paper, & attempt description'.[20] As more and more journals appeared, whether printed and published or circulated in manuscript, the need to distinguish one's own tour record from others became increasingly important:

Tours have become a very fashionable sort both of writing and reading . . . the generality of them are deficient in all the points which make new tours necessary, since they are nauseous repetitions of each other.[21]

The jaded tour-reader needed to find the customary woods, lakes and mountains 'mingled with historical, fabulous, and romantic associations' if he was not to turn from the descriptions with indifference or disgust. This staleness was infecting much of the descriptive poetry of the late eighteenth century, which, like the formulaic modes of landscape painting, 'degenerated into a kind of phraseology, consisting of combinations of words which have been so long coupled together, that, like the hero and his epithet in Homer, they are become inseparable companions'.[22] The mechanical quality of descriptive essays struck Thomas Bernard, a young barrister, as he examined his own attempts at a tour journal. He had the impression that these writers calculate in advance their vocabulary, phrases and expressions and then distribute them quite indiscriminately among the objects visited: 'The consequence is that the Lake of Geneva & the Duck-pond at Deptford are depictured in the same Colours, & produce the same Idea'.[23] There is an amusing example of a tourist struggling with his repertoire of epithets in the manuscript of Bishop Percy's 'Observanda' for his 1773 Scottish tour:

. . . the immense Group of stupendous Mountains beyond it to the North, rising up in gigantic scenery beyond one another, form a succession of Picturesque wonderfully great, astonishing & ~~picturesque~~ fine ~~Picturesque~~ beyond all description, & to which no Language can do justice.[24]

– *quod erat demonstrandum*. Descriptive staleness was inevitable, given the peculiar nature of Picturesque tourism, in which the object was not so much to find something new to describe and then experiment with a new vocabulary, as to find scenery which resembled familiar paintings or poetic descriptions. If you found the right scenery, then your tour journal would logically proclaim the discovery in the appropriate current vocabulary.

Along with 'beautiful', 'sublime' and 'picturesque', the adjective 'romantic' was becoming indiscriminately applied to any attractive aspect of the natural landscape. Robert Heron, the Scottish historian and topographer, complained of the way the term had become debased in current usage, and paused during his Highland tour to trace its degeneration:

The time was, when *romances*, filled with a peculiarly refined, lofty, and notwithstanding these qualities, in some instances simple system of morals, manners, scenery, and incidents, held that place in the estimation of the gay and the idle, – which is now occupied by novels. The scenery particularly, which was described in those works of fiction, was of a character of wild sublimity or fanciful beauty, such as bore little or no resemblance to either the beauty or the sublimity marking the scenery of cultivated regions . . . Beside that particular species of scenery, any scenes which have a tendency to withdraw the mind from the associations of real life, and to carry the imagination to rove through *Fairy-land*, and to call up her own wild creations, were, with little impropriety, ranked in the same class of romantic scenery.[25]

Heron seems to be suggesting that the increasing realism of contemporary fiction was frustrating more extravagant imaginative needs: 'romances' have become novels, so we must look elsewhere, in the wilder scenery of the world about us, to realise 'romantic' fictions. This was certainly one motive for the Picturesque adventure, as is demonstrated by William Maton's response to the gothicised Lyulph's Tower on the banks of Ullswater:

This building reminded us, in every particular, of the airy castles described in romances, as being situated in the midst of impenetrable forests for the custody of some unyielding damsel hurried away from her relatives by a cruel baron.[26]

The Tower is romantic because it looks as if it had come straight out of a romance, and thus affords the same kind of associative pleasure as the recognition of resemblances between a British landscape and a Claude painting. Indeed, Maton goes on to say of the Tower that if it had been met with only in description – 'from the pen of a Radcliffe for example' – he would have doubted its existence anywhere except in the novelist's imagination.

Those whose journals strained to avoid perpetual repetition of the same images accompanied by their stock epithets were forced into descriptive extravaganzas; and these generated the reactionary taste for cool, accurate representation, as Dr Thomas Herring indicates:

I am a little afraid, if I should be particular in my description, you would think, I am playing the traveller upon you; but, indeed, I will stick religiously to truth.[27]

In this same letter of 1739, he recalls his previous year's 'picture of North Wales' on which his friend had complimented him for his 'poetical fancy'. William Bingley castigated two of his predecessors on the Welsh Tour, who had 'introduced the novelist too often in their works'.[28] The phrase 'playing the traveller' upon some-one implies a kind of descriptive coquetry: but fidelity in landscape description proved far from simple. Samuel Ireland determined to concentrate on such fidelity when he set out to record in words and drawings the Wye Valley scenery. It was his aim 'that his drawings should, like the transparent mirror of his stream, truly reflect the landscape that exists around, as well as the objects that decorate its banks'.[29] Charles Dibdin thought such faithful reflections rather like literal translations: 'they are correct and vapid, I therefore shall call what I have done effects . . . these are free and liberal, and not slavish, but spirited'.[30] Gilpin would have been sympathetic with this, since his own practice was to give the *character* of the scenery and not a literal transcript. What was the point of a faithful view anyway, asked Dibdin. It could be very misleading for subsequent tourists: 'I have continually recommended effect, which will for ever remind you of a place instead of views which time and innovations will alter and confound'.

The writer or painter can never anyway truly reflect his subject:

. . . picturesque Descriptions of any kind give a very indistinct idea to others visiting the same spot. Tourists vary in their Descriptions, as the prominent Objects strike them at the Moment, & what may appear to one as deserving particular Attention, may appear to another of very little consequence.[31]

Short of giving an exhaustive, indiscriminate inventory of the objects in view, the tour writer must select and therefore discriminate. Warren Hastings lucidly expresses the difficulty in the journal of his 1787 tour:

Nor do I suppose that any Description could convey the Imagery of a perspective View to the Mind of another as it appears to the Eye of a Spectator; it being impossible to enumerate in the Order of their relative Positions all the minute parts of the general Composition, or by a successive Arrangement, to which the greatest Powers of Language are restricted, to impress on the steadiest Attention that Combination of objects which the Eye takes in at a single Glance.[32]

One tourist, acutely aware of the need to establish some consistent descriptive principle for his journal, resolved on the following:

About to enter on the most beautiful scenery, I shall, hereafter, in describing, fix one spot in a landscape, whence the best bird's eye view of the whole is to be had, and beginning in front, shall go round to the right hand, and returning by the left, make a complete sweep.[33]

One might well prefer a little 'playing the traveller' to this daunting promise of an eye on a mechanical swivel. This methodical tourist was probably following an old tradition in the composition of a landscape painting. William Sanderson's *Graphice* (1658) issued the following advice to the painter interested in 'Landskip':

*Take* your *Station* upon the rize of ground, or top of an *Hill*, where you shall have a large *Horizon*; And skore your *Tablet into three divisions* downwards, from the top to the bottoms, set your face directly opposite to the midst of your *Horizon*, and keeping your body fixed, observe what is comprehended directly before your eyes, and draw that into forme upon your *Tablet* in the middle-*Division*. Then turning your *Head* only, (not your body) to the right hand, draw likewise what is presented to your *sight* . . .[34]

Anyone who tries to describe at length a grand view is faced with these problems of organisation. As the Picturesque tourists make clear, compositional problems occupy much of their attention. Let us take an example which features two well-known participants, John Dyer and William Gilpin. In 1770 Gilpin visited the Towy Valley in South Wales, the scene described in Dyer's *Grongar Hill* (1726). Gilpin quotes a part of that description:

> Below me Trees unnumber'd rise,
> Beautiful in various Dies;
> The gloomy Pine, the Poplar blue,
> The yellow Beech, the Sable Yew . . .
> And beyond the purple Grove . . .
> Lies a long and level Lawn,
> On which a dark Hill, steep and high,
> Holds and charms the wand'ring Eye!
> Deep are his Feet in Towy's Flood,
> His Sides are cloath'd with waving Wood,
> And antient Towers crown his Brow,
> That cast an awful Look below;
> Whose ragged Walls the Ivy creeps,
> And with his Arms from falling keeps.[35]

Gilpin's main criticism here is that Dyer's distances cannot easily be distinguished from his foregrounds.[36] The trees below the poet compose the foreground, and they can be identified and given separate foliage colours. That is as it should be, thinks Gilpin. The eye moves beyond these to the 'purple Grove'. Gilpin, who perhaps misinterprets the adjective, feels that purple is more properly the colour of the most distant objects and that it is prematurely introduced at this stage by Dyer. But his principal objection is to the description of the castle. Dryslwyn Castle viewed from Grongar is a distant object; but 'instead of being marked with still fainter colours, than the *purple-grove*, is touched with all the strength of a fore-ground. You see the very ivy creeping upon the walls'. Gilpin then introduces the familiar couplet from Milton's *L'Allegro*:

> Towers, and battlements he sees
> Bosomed high in tufted trees.

This he says is 'picturesquely' accurate:

Here we have all the indistinct colouring, which obscures a distant object. We do not see the iron-grated window, the portcullis, the ditch or the rampart. We can just distinguish a Castle from a tree; and a tower from a battlement . . .

However controversial the matter of organising the description, there was broad agreement on Thomas Gray's advice, which was much quoted: 'Half a word fixed upon or near the spot, is worth a cart-load of recollection'.[37] Such guarantees of authenticity became a familiar boast of the journals, and, for many, constituted their greatest value:

It was merely with a view to that species of amusement which arises from the recollection of interesting scenes, and the emotions which they excited at the time when they passed under observation, that the Writer of the following memorandums ever thought of committing them to paper.[38]

The emphasis is on 'at the time when they passed under observation'. Gilpin's own 'observations' were, he asserted, more likely to be founded on truth, 'as they are not the offspring of theory; but are taken warm from the scenes of nature, as they arise'.[39] The first impression was especially important in a period keen to cultivate 'sensibility', the spontaneous response, warm from the heart. 'First impressions' became a kind of cliché, as Jane Austen recognised when she used the phrase for her original title to what became *Pride and Prejudice*. Authenticity and originality were equally stressed by the tourists:

I follow no written guide, lest I should enter too much into other people's ideas, and not give nature scope to my own: I shall do the best I can, frequently writing upon the spot from whence the object strikes me.[40]

Many a watercolour drawing was similarly executed: the painter Francis Towne made a practice of noting on the back of his pictures the fact that they were taken 'on the spot'. On-the-spot sketching was best done, according to Gilpin, with a soft black-lead pencil: 'Nothing glides so volubly over paper, and executes an idea so quickly'.[41] Distances in a complicated landscape could be marked in with a few written references. Then, at a later stage, pen strokes and ink washes could be added for *chiaroscuro*. Both sketch and written memorandum could be worked up at a later stage.

Many journals underwent textual alteration as they evolved from on-the-spot jottings to neat fair copy or printed book form. The working-up process sometimes involved the insertion of reflective passages made to seem as if they arose naturally out of the particular experiences recorded, and designed to give more weight and dignity to the journal. The question of authenticity then becomes more complicated. Although, like the finished painting, the 'worked-up' text may sometimes contribute in its elaboration to the development of the 'poetical fancy' in description, it need not jeopardize the integrity of that first experience 'taken warm from the scenes of nature'. It is ironic that the Oxford English Dictionary gives one definition of the word 'Picturesque' which makes it nearly synonymous with 'poetical fancy': 'Of language, narrative etc . . . Strikingly graphic or vivid; sometimes implying disregard of fact in the effort for effect'. The sober Gilpin felt constrained to apologise for the 'too luxuriant' language used in his *Lakes* tour: 'I can only say, I endeavoured, as I could, to adapt my language to my subject; and as *picturesque description* was rather a novel mode of writing, I thought I had some little right to adopt my own'.[42]

As far as Gilpin was concerned, Picturesque practice always involved some 'improvement'. In this, as in other respects (e.g. his stress on *decorum*) he remains loyal to neoclassical criteria. The *'faithful portrait'*, though justified as the artist's first impression of his subject, should never characterise the final picture. Nature is the 'great archetype', but Nature needs a little adjustment by reference to her 'best forms':

> Then deem not Art defective, which divides,
> Rejects, or recombines: but rather say,
> 'Tis her chief excellence.[43]

This is the source of all those later parodies of Picturesque manipulation of scenery. James Plumptre, the author of *The Lakers* (1798), one of the earliest and best of the satires, wrote a letter of apology to Gilpin in 1801, hoping that feelings had not been hurt. In his reply Gilpin took up the point about the Picturesque artist's high-handed attitude towards Nature and tried to explain his position:

... we consider nature as y$^e$ grand storehouse of all our picturesque ideas. At y$^e$ same time, we do not suppose her magnificence stoops to all those little requisites of composition, light, balance of foreground, & distance, w$^h$. we expect in a picture – a term, w$^h$. we have surely a right to define. Nor do we depreciate nature, but exalt her. With an open hand she gives us corn; but she does not condescend to make a loaf.[44]

That last adroit analogy is revealing, perhaps in more ways than Gilpin realised. The Picturesque artist 'appropriates'* natural scenery and processes it into a commodity. With the aid of his 'knick-knacks' he converts Nature's unmanageable bounty into a frameable possession.

Journal and sketch-book enjoy a close partnership over this period. Both are subject to the same Picturesque imperatives. Both function, rather like the Claude Glass, as the means of mediating and modifying natural scenery. Both become valued trophies of a new kind of adventure. Gainsborough's challenge to his *literary* predecessors, just before he sets out for the Lakes in 1783, indicates a vigorous competitiveness which quite ignores the conventional boundaries of the two media:

[I] purpose when I come back to show you that your Grays and Dr. Brownes were tawdry fan-Painters. I purpose to mount all the Lakes at the next Exhibition, in the great stile.[45]

*    *    *

A list, from an anonymous 1789 journal, of antiquities, romantic scenery and picturesque views, is a good index of contemporary tastes in travel:

Tho' it is an easy Thing to sit by your Fire-side and read the Adventures of others, and glut your Imagination with various Descriptions of Ancient Towns and Castles, Romantic Scenery, picturesque Views, and Churches once dedicated to the Almighty falling to

---

*The term is used by Gilpin: see above p. 70.

Decay . . . yet the knowledge makes but little Impression on the Mind; it comes and goes like a Shadow; From ocular Demonstration alone are we to expect any lasting Impression, or hope for any thorough Improvement; It is from this alone that we become in after Times a source of Pleasure to Ourselves, an Ornament to our Friends, and a desirable companion to all.[46]

The modern Georgian city is left behind in the search for wild landscapes and the remains of ancient buildings. A hundred years earlier, Samuel Brewer had set out from his Cumberland home to visit London:

I was resolved with my self to goe & see Their Fashions, methods & waies in their Philosophy & natural Learning (where to my Inclinations most led me). I am not ignorant how that many of my Country-men will laugh at me, & ask what it hath got me – Such sordid People as these do not deserve a reply . . .[47]

But the tourists from the mid-eighteenth century onwards reversed Brewer's route: they headed away from London and up to Cumberland, and they went in search not of new 'Fashions' and 'Philosophy' but of primitive, obsolescent ways of life, tinged with paganism. Cultivated minds, like cultivated country, were out of fashion. Mary Anne Hanway gave specific instructions to her coachman 'to go *sentimentally*' through the country, not at his usual brisk, professional pace; and she rode 'pencil in *hand*' to catch the great forms of Nature.[48] Another sentimental traveller, Joseph Budworth, prefaced his journal with a warning to sophisticated readers: 'I have no fine houses, no fine paintings, no compliments to great people, to swell out my book with – *my portraits* are cottagers, my *pictures* what Nature has lavished around them'.[49] These are sentiments deeply-rooted in the late-eighteenth-century sensibility. We recall Gainsborough's growing 'sick of Portraits', and longing to 'walk off to some sweet Village'.

# PART II

# The Picturesque Tours

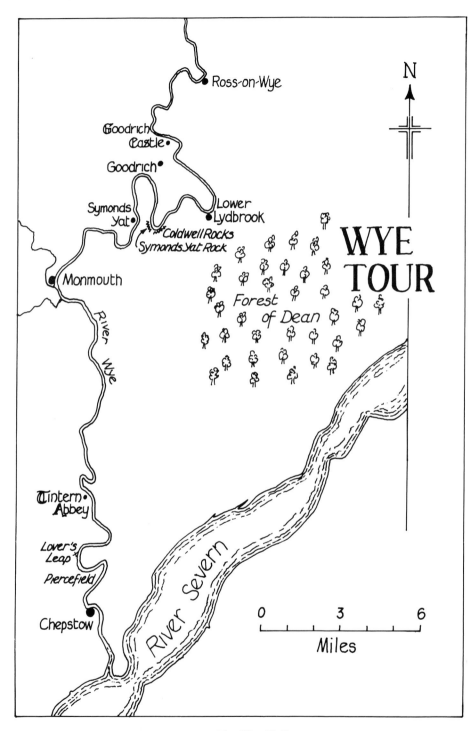

Map 1. The Wye Valley

# V

# The Wye Valley tour:
# river scenery and ruins

‑‑‑‑‑‑

                                              – Once again
Do I behold these steep and lofty cliffs,
Which on a wild secluded scene impress
Thoughts of more deep seclusion; and connect
The landscape with the quiet of the sky.
The day is come when I again repose
Here, under this dark sycamore, and view
These plots of cottage-ground, these orchard-tufts,
Which, at this season, with their unripe fruits,
Among the woods and copses lose themselves,
Nor, with their green and simple hue, disturb
The wild green landscape. Once again I see
These hedge-rows, hardly hedge-rows, little lines
Of sportive wood run wild; these pastoral farms
Green to the very door . . .

                              [William Wordsworth]


When all these regular forms are softened by distance – when hedge-row trees begin to unite, and lengthen into streaks along the horizon – when farm-houses, and ordinary buildings lose all their vulgarity of shape, and are scattered about, in formless spots, through the several parts of a distance – it is inconceivable what richness, and beauty, this mass of deformity, when melted together, adds to a landscape.[1]

                              [William Gilpin]


The opening paragraph of Wordsworth's 'Lines Written a Few Miles above Tintern Abbey' is a very carefully constructed, highly selective description of the scenery of the Wye Valley in the 1790s. The poet seems to have taken Gilpin's advice on the softening effects of distance: his selection and organisation of landscape features ensure that the finished composition will emerge as an image of profound harmony. Pastoral beauty and mountain Sublimity, man and nature – these potential antagonists are all reconciled. The cottage-ground plots and the orchard-tufts do not disturb the wild, green landscape. In the description of 'These hedge-rows, hardly hedge-rows, little lines / Of sportive wood run wild', the succession of qualifying phrases enacts the scarcely perceptible merging of the cultivated with the wild. Wordsworth is celebrating his return to the Wye Valley in 1798 after an absence of five years. Consequently memory and association are even stronger influences on his feelings now than is the impact of the physical scenery itself, which accordingly occupies in description only about an eighth of the whole poem. In the main body of the poem Wordsworth turns inwards to examine those memories and associations, to come to terms with gains and losses in his changing relationship with the natural world, and eventually to declare himself a 'worshipper of nature'. It is the *locus classicus* of Romantic nature worship, and for Wordsworth it involves his acknowledging the immaturity of the purely visual, unreflective delight in Nature's forms and colours: what is implied is the repudiation of Picturesque values. 'Tintern Abbey' launches a new phase in man's relationship with the natural world, on the spot where, a generation earlier, Picturesque tourism itself was launched.

Two days before Wordsworth and his sister set off on their walking tour of the Wye Valley, in the summer of 1798, they dined with the Revd. Richard Warner, whose *Walk through Wales, in August 1797* had appeared earlier in the year and who, no doubt, spoke very highly of the Wye scenery. They probably also took with them the earliest and most famous of the Picturesque tour guide-books, Gilpin's *Observations on the River Wye, and Several Parts of South Wales, etc. relative chiefly to Picturesque Beauty; Made in the Summer of the Year 1770*.[2] The publication of this book, in 1782, is traditionally credited with having initiated the vogue for Picturesque tourism in Britain, and by the end of the century it had reached its fifth edition. Although the general public discovered Gilpin in 1783, his 'Observations' had been circulating in manuscript, accompanied with its author's pen and wash sketches, for at least a decade earlier. As the book's Dedication makes plain, Thomas Gray had requested the loan of the manuscript in 1771, the year after he had made his own visit to the Wye Valley. Both Gray and his friend William Mason urged Gilpin to publish his tour, but it was delayed for twelve years, largely because Gilpin could find no adequate way of reproducing the line and wash illustrations he thought so necessary to his purpose.* In the mid-1770s Paul Sandby published sets of aquatints which proved much more faithful to the medium of watercolour than the old-style engravings. Gilpin's nephew, the artist William Sawrey Gilpin, reproduced the sketches for that first edition through a rather crude process which combined etching and aquatint. For the second edition, of 1789, only aquatinting was used, and Gilpin was better pleased with the result:

It . . . certainly comes the nearest of any mode we know, to the softness of the pencil [i.e. brush]. It may indeed literally be called *drawing*; as it washes in the shades.[3]

*Mason's later reactions to these highly generalising illustrations of Wye scenery suggest that his earlier enthusiasm had cooled a little. As he wrote to Gilpin in 1784: 'If a voyager down the river Wye takes out your Book, his very Boatman crys out, "nay Sir you may look in vain there no body can find one Picture in it the least like".' (quoted in C. P. Barbier, *William Gilpin* [Oxford, 1963], p. 71). In spite of the 1782 publication date on the title page, the book did not appear until the following year.

*the front-skreen, & also one of the side-skreens complex.*

*the front-skreen complex; and both ye side-skreens simple.*

16. William Gilpin, 'Sketches of River Scenery'.
National Library of Wales, Aberystwyth

17. William Gilpin, 'View of the Wye from Ross churchyard', and adjacent page, from the
MS Wye tour notebook (1770). Bodleian Library, Oxford

Thomas Gray had made the river voyage from Ross to Chepstow only a few weeks before Gilpin. He thought the journey 'a succession of nameless wonders'.[4] Gilpin agreed. 'If you have never navigated the Wye', he wrote to a friend soon after his return, 'you have seen nothing. Besides three or four capital views upon it, the whole is such a display of picturesque scenery that it is beyond any commendation'.[5] The boat journey down the Wye specifically for the purpose of admiring the scenery and antiquities pre-dates Gilpin's tour by at least a quarter of a century. John Egerton, the Bishop of Durham, was the 'Father of the Voyage down the Wye', according to the local topographer Charles Heath. Egerton's father, the Bishop of Hereford, appointed him Rector of Ross in 1745, and soon afterwards he had a pleasure-boat built so that he could take his friends on summer excursions down the Wye. A quarter of a century later, the tour had become commercialised and impersonalised. Gilpin paid his fare and took a covered boat, navigated by three men. By the end of the century at least eight pleasure-boats, equipped with coverings against the sun and rain, and tables for drawing or writing, were carrying tourists back and forth from Ross to Chepstow throughout the summer months.[6]

River scenery, which was the particular attraction of the Wye tour, offered the connoisseur Picturesque pleasures of a very specific kind. Unlike travel in a jolting carriage, the smooth passage of the boat relaxed the tourist and encouraged concentration on the very steady unfolding of views. Each of these views had, according to Gilpin, 'four grand parts': 'the *area*, which is the river itself; the *two side-screens*, which are the opposite banks, and mark the perspective; and the *front-screen*, which points out the winding of the river' (see fig. 16). The chief delight of the Wye Valley was that the views, 'though composed only of these *simple parts*, are yet *infinitely varied*'. Side-screens converge or recede, rise or sink, sometimes obscuring and sometimes abruptly revealing a background. The boat glides along, allowing the tourist to feel that a series of stage-sets is being slid into position for his pleasure. The theatrical analogy is frequently implied in the tourists' descriptions. William Coxe, for example, praised 'the beauties of the ever shifting scenery . . . appearing, vanishing, and re-appearing, in different shapes, and with different combinations of wood and water'.

The popularity of the Wye tour reached its peak by the turn of the century. In the Introduction to his thorough and very well-known guide-book *The Excursion down the Wye from Ross to Monmouth* (1799), Charles Heath speculated on the recent growth of interest in the area:

Whether it be owing to the unsettled state of affairs on the Continent, which renders travelling, if not unsafe, at least disagreeable, – or to that well-founded curiosity, which excites the Man of Observation to survey its attractions, – certain it is that *Monmouth-shire* has, in the course of the last four or five years, been honoured with a very large share of Public Notice.

Ross itself was a good starting point. It was famous as the home town of the legendary philanthropist John Kyrle, the exemplary 'Man of Ross' featured in Pope's *Epistle to Bathurst* (1733). Kyrle's home in the later eighteenth century had become one of the inns frequented by the tourists. Another advantage in starting from Ross was the panoramic view from its churchyard. This commanded a broad, horse-shoe sweep of the river and was much admired as a prospect. As we see from his Wye tour notebook (fig. 17), Gilpin took some time to decide on the proper classification of this view. He changed 'very beautiful' to 'amusing', and declared it was not Picturesque for a number of reasons: the viewpoint was too high; the extensive scene was broken up into too many parts; and there were no objects of sufficient distinction. His pen-and-ink sketch of the scene shows also the lack of a good foreground and side-screens.

After paying their one and a half guineas for the first stage of the journey, travellers embarked, frequently at dawn, just below the seven-arch bridge. One conscientious tourist, whose journal survives in the National Library of Wales, made good use of a short delay in loading the boat by producing a watercolour of the scene, which he later worked up for his fair-copy journal[7] (fig. 18). Ross bridge is silhouetted against the early morning sun, with an imaginary tower-capped hill rising steeply behind it. The little canopied pleasure-boat waits in the foreground. The local oarsmen were not always as sensitive to the delicacy of their passengers as might be wished. But Charles Heath reassured tourists that the proprietors of the boats would accompany them from the inn down to the river, 'so the ear is not pained with a coarseness of language, too frequently heard from the navigators of public rivers'. After this initial hurdle, and as long as the weather remained fine, there was nothing but pleasure awaiting the tourists.

The first great spectacle was about three miles below Ross, the ruins of Goodrich Castle, acclaimed by Gilpin as one of the grandest views which can be imagined:

... we rested on our oars to examine it. A reach of the river, forming a noble bay, is spread before the eye. The bank, on the right, is steep, and covered with wood; beyond which a bold promontory shoots out, crowned with a castle, rising among the trees.

The four grand parts of river scenery are here magnificently deployed. The 'area' is a noble formation; the side-screen banks are distinct but finely contrasted; and the bold front-screen features a ruined castle which could well be described as 'Boosom'd high in tufted Trees' (fig. 19). The castle adds that touch of perfection prescribed by Gilpin in his earlier general remarks on river scenery:

When we introduce a scene on canvas ... we want the castle, or the abbey, to give consequence to the scene. And indeed the landscape-painter seldom thinks his view perfect, without characterizing it by some object of this kind.

Consequently, this particular view 'I should not scruple to call *correctly picturesque*'. This was very high praise from the fastidious Gilpin, whose observations at this point continue with strictures on Nature's general incompetence in the matter of scenic compositions.

18. 'Mr M.', 'View of Ross Bridge', from a MS 'Tour to South Wales, etc' (1801).
National Library of Wales, Aberystwyth

19. Thomas Hearne, *Goodrich Castle on the Wye*.
Yale Center for British Art, Paul Mellon Collection

The river scenery became increasingly impressive after Goodrich as the gorge of the Wye deepened. The young Samuel Rogers in his 1791 expedition records a number of features at this stage of the journey which Wordsworth selects for his poem seven years later: 'cottages perched one above another, half sheltered with wood, and often discovered only by the blue wreaths of smoke that ascended from them . . . a chain of orchards, the apple-trees twisting into a thousand forms'.[8] The Revd. Stebbing Shaw delighted in these perched cottages, so 'richly recluse' he thought, and no doubt free from poverty and anxiety: 'a more primaeval scene cannot well be conceived to exist'. But Rogers and others remarked on another, and far from primaeval aspect of the Wye Valley which, though it was hard for the eye or ear to miss, was significantly excluded from Wordsworth's image of natural harmony. At Lydbrook, about three miles below the castle, there was a coal wharf: 'a busy scene', thought Rogers, 'but properly softened down by the woods that nearly envelop it'.[9] Rogers' description reassures the reader that the signs of vigorous commerce and industry do not seriously disturb the tranquillity of the natural setting. This could not be said of the second grand scene on the tour, the ironworks at New Weir. Tourists who arrived at this point on their voyage would very likely have borne in mind Thomas Whateley's striking description, originally published in *Observations on Modern Gardening* (1770)[10] and reprinted in Heath's guide-book. This stretch of the river, thought Whateley, 'so far from being disturbed, becomes more interesting and important, by the business to which it is destined'. He describes the landscape at this point as a chasm between two ranges of hills which rise almost perpendicularly from the water. Dark tree-covered crags protrude here and there:

In the midst of all this gloom is an iron forge, covered with a black cloud of smoak, and surrounded with half burned ore, with coal, and with cinders; the fuel for it is brought down a path, worn into steps narrow and steep, and winding among precipices; and near it is an open space of barren moor, about which are scattered the huts of the workmen. It stands close to the cascade of the Weir, where the agitation of the current is encreased by large fragments of rocks which have been swept down by floods from the banks, or shivered by tempests from the brow; and the sullen sound, at stated intervals from the strokes of the great hammers in the forge, deadens the roar of the water-fall.

The natural scene itself is awesome, and therefore positively enhanced by the presence of industry: 'machinery, especially when its powers are stupendous, or its effects formidable, is an effort of art, which may be accommodated to the extravagancies of nature'. Together with this mighty din, the turbulent current at New Weir made the ferry, the little fishing coracles and the pleasure-boat itself seem peculiarly frail to Gilpin:

[Here] all the employments of the people seem to require either exertion or caution; and the idea of force or of danger which attend them, gives to the scene an animation . . . perfectly compatible with the wildest romantic situations.

Strenuous, purposeful activity such as centres of industry offered generally displeased Gilpin and his tourist successors; but he did concede that there could be accidental Picturesque advantages from such scenes: the smoke from the charcoal burners 'is frequently seen issuing from the sides of the hills; and spreading its thin veil over a part of them, beautifully breaks their lines, and unites them with the sky'. Little plumes of smoke can be seen in Thomas Hearne's picture of Goodrich Castle.

Partly because the banks of the Wye were so sublimely steep and wild, most tourists welcomed the energies released by industry as 'harmonious appendages' to the landscape. The spectacle of New Weir amid the amphitheatre of romantic beauties presented by Coldwell Rocks and the very abrupt rise to 470 feet of Symonds Yat Rock gave the tourist a thrilling taste of the Picturesque modulating swiftly into the Sublime (fig. 20). Fosbroke's 1818 guide-book recommended the views from the top of Symonds Yat: the long prospect, which 'may be called from Claude's Pictures, the painter's map style' complemented the view of the immediate, craggy scenery which evoked the spirit of Rosa.

In another six or seven miles the passengers reached the end of this first stage of the tour, Monmouth, where Gilpin arrived a little after sunset. Fosbroke classified the scenery of that first part of the tour 'Grand and Beautiful'. The remaining twenty miles or so to Chepstow were 'Sublime and Awful' – well worth another guinea and a half.

The first stretches of the river below Monmouth ran through meadows which Gilpin was pleased to note were devoted to pasture rather than to crops: 'Furrowed-lands, and waving corn, however charming in pastoral poetry, are ill-accommodated to painting'. There are two reasons for this: the painter never likes to see signs of the division of property in landscapes which should belong to Nature; and cornfields are simply monotonous in colour and texture. Pasture on the other hand, gives Nature her freedom, and the grazing cattle add variety and animation to the scene.

Tintern village, eight miles below Monmouth, was largely ignored by tourists anxious to catch sight of the Abbey just round the bend in the river. But George Cumberland thought such neglect quite unmerited: 'an artist, possessed of the rare talent of knowing how to chuse, might soon fill his portfolio' with studies of this charming village.

By common consent the chief architectural glory of the Wye Valley was the ruined Tintern Abbey (fig. 21). Its gaunt, melancholy splendour in this natural setting generated countless descriptions in verse, prose, watercolour and oil. There were transparencies too, such as Fanny Price enjoyed at Mansfield Park, where, on the three lower panes of one of the windows, 'Tintern Abbey held its station between a cave in Italy, and a moonlight lake in Cumberland'. The ruins had drawn tourists long before Gilpin and Gray arrived in the summer of 1770. The Revd. Sneyd Davies's topographical poem of 1742 set the tone for many later responses to the scene:

20.  William Day, *View on the River Wye* (1788).
Victoria and Albert Museum, London

21. Michael Angelo Rooker, *Tintern Abbey*.
Private collection

At length our pilgrimage's home appears,
Her venerable fabric *Tintern* rears;
While the sun, glancing in its calm decline,
With his last gilding beautifies her shrine; . . .
Here, my lov'd friend, along the mossy dome,
In pleasurable sadness let me roam,
Look back upon the world, in haven safe;
Weep o'er its ruins, at its follies laugh.[11]

In the middle of the eighteenth century, the period particularly susceptible to 'pleasurable sadness', Tintern Abbey was frequently the object of secular pilgrimages. Jeremiah Milles paused here, also in 1742, on his way from London to Holyhead, to admire, in its 'romantik' situation, 'One of ye lightest and most beautifull Gothick buildings I have seen in England'.[12] Most of the various attitudes towards ruins which I discussed earlier were stimulated by the sight of the Abbey. Samuel Ireland seems to have had a checklist to hand:

Approaching this sublime and sequestered spot, the enthusiastic lover of simplicity in art and nature, the admirer of the picturesque and beautiful, the antiquary and the moralist will feel the effect, as it were, of enchantment, and become lost almost in a pleasing melancholy.

Few were immune to its enchantment, though some thought it fell short of the Sublime. 'Here, at one cast of the eye, the whole is comprehended, nothing being left for the spectator to guess or explore', thought the antiquarian Francis Grose: the Abbey lacked 'that gloomy solemnity so essential to religious ruins; those yawning vaults and dreary recesses which strike the Beholder with a religious awe, and make him almost shudder at entering them, calling into his mind all the Tales of the Nursery'.[13] What exactly was 'religious awe'? It seems to have been less devotional enthusiasm (it was after all a Roman Catholic site) than a sharp spasm of pleasing melancholy. But Lucy Wright's experience suggests that occasionally the adjective 'religious' is wholly appropriate to one's response to Tintern Abbey: 'even the Atheist, and free thinker could not divest themselves, in these ruins, of sentiments of religion, which they would be ashamed to own as being a degradation of their reasons'.[14] 'Sentiments of religion' keeps the response safely this side of idolatry and enthusiasm, and attunes it to anti-rationalist 'sensibility'. The stylistic flourishes of a number of descriptions suggest that even if the tourists' immediate sight of the Abbey was not spiritually overwhelming, they knew, nonetheless, what were the appropriate attitudes to strike. Two good lines of blank verse are audible in this piece:

In treading these spacious aisles where once the pealing anthem swelled the gale and choral voices joined in song to heaven, we felt an impressive sense that led to meditation . . . The light laugh was stifled, sedateness ruled the hour.[15]

The tourists covered reams of paper trying to evoke a scene which they usually insisted was beyond description, as John Skinner demonstrates:

22. John 'Warwick' Smith, *Tintern. Approach from Village of Tintern.* 'Few views of this ruin are more picturesque than this, but it is interrupted by a mean modern house, which has been built close to it.' National Library of Wales, Aberystwyth

A magnificent colonade of gothic arches and pillars, extending nearly 100 yards, terminated by green foliage, through the gigantic window to the East, a velvet green, stretching beneath the feet; the lofty roof open to the blue canopy of Heaven; luxuriant Ivy, and various tinted shrubs, hanging from the walls; these were the objects which collectively burst upon the sight in all their charms, far beyond the powers of my pen to describe, or my pencil to delineate.[16]

Hyperbole aside, there was, in fact, a peculiar difficulty for the painter at this site, because his perspective on the Abbey's exterior was baffled by a cluster of distinctly un-Picturesque huts and cottages. 'The outside did not entirely answer my expectations', continued John Skinner; 'and this I attribute to the miserable approach through a dirty lane bounded by ruinous huts'. Richard Colt Hoare visiting it in 1797 and 1798 complained that the magnificent west front 'would be a most beautiful object, could it be seen in its proper point of view, which now it cannot, owing to the obstruction of the cottages and orchards'.[17] His wish that the Abbey's owner, the Duke of Beaufort, had included the removal of these obstacles in his other local 'improvements' echoed John Byng's impatient remarks in 1781:

At some trifling expense, the surrounding cottages and orchards might be removed; and then the abbey could stand nobly back'd by woods, and open to the water: at present it is shamefully block'd up.

23. P. de Loutherbourg, *The River Wye at Tintern Abbey* (1805).
Fitzwilliam Museum, Cambridge

24. J. M. W. Turner, *Interior of Tintern Abbey* (1794).
Victoria and Albert Museum, London

But there were also good Picturesque reasons for retaining the cottages, as Samuel Ireland argued: 'so far from diminishing the grandeur of the general effect, [they serve] rather on the contrary as a scale, and give magnitude to the principal object'. It was perhaps this kind of effective contrast which John 'Warwick' Smith was aiming at in placing his blockish cottage in front of the abbey ruins (fig. 22).

While Colt Hoare was sketching the interior, his companion William Coxe, in search of a better Picturesque viewpoint, crossed to the opposite bank and walked about half a mile downstream:

From this point the ruins assuming a new character, seem to occupy a gentle eminence and impend over the river, without the intervention of a single cottage to obstruct the view. The grand east window, wholly covered with shrubs and half mantled with ivy, rises like the portal of a majestic edifice embowered in wood. Through this opening and along the vista of the church, the clusters of ivy, which twine round the pillars or hang suspended from the arches, resemble tufts of trees, while the thick mantle of foliage, seen through the tracery of the west window, forms a continuation of the perspective, and appears like an interminable forest.

From this angle the Abbey's harder lines are softened, and when ivy-clad pillars can resemble trees, it becomes possible to see the architecture as a whole assimilated into the surrounding landscape, offering (as did Wordsworth's lines of description) a 'pleasing intermixture of wildness and culture'. This may well be near the point from which de Loutherbourg's 1805 oil, *The River Wye at Tintern Abbey*, is taken (fig. 23). The Abbey is barely visible on the left, but Loutherbourg has reorientated it so that one of the windows with richer tracery than the east window is presented to the view.[18] The ruin is thus discreetly 'Boosom'd high in tufted Trees'.

The search for the right viewpoint was also necessary in order to blur the Abbey's hard, straight lines. Both Colt Hoare and Coxe echoed Gilpin's great regret that:

. . . a number of gabel-ends hurt the eye with their regularity; and disgust it by the vulgarity of their shape. A mallet judiciously used (but who durst use it?) might be of service in fracturing some of them; particularly those of the cross isles, which are not only disagreeable in themselves, but confound the perspective.

Picturesque artists had to find other ways of modifying these shapes. Moss and the heavy festoons of ivy could be useful in this respect, and many a watercolourist broke up or blurred these austere lines by introducing or exaggerating such vegetation. Turner's 1794 watercolour delicately illustrates the principle (fig. 24). There were other considerations than those of the purely Picturesque in retaining the ivy inside Tintern Abbey. Its presence in such abundance stimulated that pleasing melancholy at the thought of how vulnerable to time are man's works: 'an intermixture of a vigorous vegetation, intimates a settled despair of their restoration', observed Whateley, who had recommended the Abbey as a model for fictitious ruins in landscaped gardens. The sensation of 'settled despair', which tourists had come a long way to enjoy, was a delicate creature, and needed constant nourishment: John Byng wished the owner had adorned the interior '(instead of the well-mowed floor) with evergreens, cypresses &c. and [made] the doors in gothic character'. Clearance of the interior had begun as long ago as 1756, under the orders of the Duke of Beaufort, and before Picturesque tastes had fully evolved. Francis Grose regretted the conscientious tidying up undertaken by the poor folk who lived in the vicinity of the Abbey:

. . . by [their] absurd labour the ground is covered over with a turf as even and trim as that of a Bowling-green, which gives the building more the air of an artificial Ruin in a Garden, than that of an ancient decayed Abbey.[19]

'Ruinated' garden architecture should emulate Tintern Abbey, but authentic ruins should not aspire to the condition of art. The poor folk, ignorant of such connoisseurship, thought they were doing the tourists a favour by grooming the ruins; whereas the only grooming required by the ungrateful tourists should have been concentrated on the shabby condition of the poor themselves. On the whole, they were an embarrassment, an irritation that added to the obstructed approach to the Abbey. Crowds of them importuned the tourist soon after he had stepped out of the boat, 'as if a place, once devoted to indolence, could never again become the seat of industry,' Gilpin reflected. Many of them occupied ramshackle huts set up amongst the monastery ruins, and the tourist could only avoid them by exercising a little charity. Some of the beggars could legitimately offer themselves as guides. The Duke kept the Abbey under lock and key, 'the showing of it being given to an Old Woman, who picks up a tollerable Livelyhood by the Parties which constantly come hither from Bath & Bristol'.[20] This was probably the old woman who showed Gilpin the monks' library in the ruins:

She could scarce crawl; shuffling along her palsied limbs, and meagre, contracted body, by the help of two sticks. She led us, through an old gate, into a place overspread with nettles, and briars; and pointing to the remnant of a shattered cloister, told us, that was the place. It was her own mansion . . . I never saw so loathsome a human dwelling. It was a cavity, loftily vaulted, between two ruined walls; which streamed with various-coloured stains of unwholsome dews.

The old woman died in the workhouse, as Samuel Rogers learned on his visit twenty years later.[21] The tourist to Tintern Abbey must have found such experiences most discomforting. It was all very well to indulge pleasing melancholy at the prospect of this monumental, ivy-clad emblem of Mutability: but to do so involved avoiding any disturbance from Mutability's human victims. The Picturesque imagination was endlessly resourceful in such circumstances, as John Byng demonstrates:

I enter'd the abbey accompanied by a boy who knew nothing, and by a very old man who had forgotten every thing; but I kept him with me, as his venerable grey beard, and locks, added dignity to my thoughts; and I fancied him the hermit of the place.

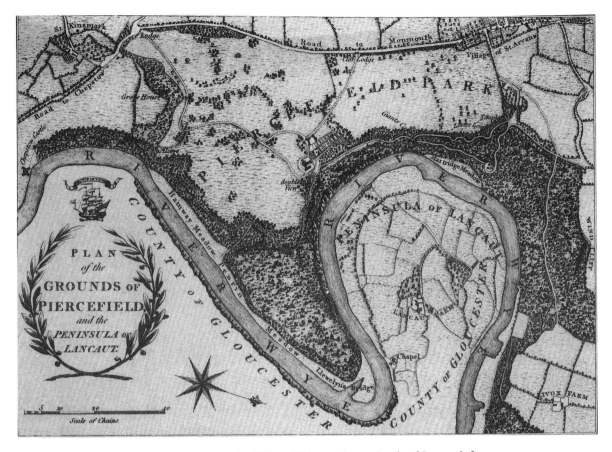

25. 'Plan of the grounds of Piercefield, and the peninsula of Lancaut', from
William Coxe's *An Historical Tour in Monmouthshire* (1801).
British Library, London

26. George Cumberland, 'Scene at Piercefield', in his MS 'Tour in North Wales' (1784).
National Library of Wales, Aberystwyth

Seventeen years later, in 1798, yet another dotard (unless, improbably, it was the same) was acting as a hopelessly incompetent cicerone:

. . . the task of being the historian of the abbey had for several years devolved on the veteran, a few abstract and unconnected ideas floated in his vacant mind, which had been so long stationary there, that he imagined his brain the sole repository of information and himself the only genuine chronicler.[22]

When the exploring, sketching and scribbling had been completed, and the melancholy mood properly indulged, the site offered other attractions:

The way to enjoy Tintern Abbey properly, and at leisure, is to bring wines, cold meat, with corn for the horses; (bread, beer, cyder, and commonly salmon, may be had at the Beaufort Arms); spread your table in the ruins; and possibly a Welsh harper may be procured from Chepstow.

This is one of John Byng's many inspirations for Picturesque picnic sites. Quite fortuitously, the Beaufort Arms provided alternative forms of Picturesque or Sublime entertainment. Francis Grose, on his 1775 tour, happened to look out of the inn window, and 'saw a kind of Fireworks occasion'd by the Sparks which ascended from the Forges, which having a high Dark Mountain for a Back Ground and the Night being rather cloudy exhibited a pleasing Appearance'.[23] The proximity of these ironworks to the Abbey must often have stimulated contradictory responses (fig. 25). Edward Davies, in his 'Poetical Description of Tintern Abbey', is thrilled both by the desolate ruins and by the tremendous energy of the forges:

> These fruits of industry enrich the place,
> Where plenty smiles in every busy face:
> The lazy drones [i.e. the monks] are driven from the hive,
> For here the active only live and thrive.
> Such is the state of ABBEY at this day,
> For sloth, affrighted, fled with monks away.[24]

That curious economic partnership of modern ironworks and antiquarian tourism at least brought some prosperity to the area for a while. But by the end of the century, improvements in agriculture had cleared much of the neighbouring forest and thereby reduced charcoal supplies to the local industries.[25]

Back in the boat, and continuing the voyage downstream, Gilpin soon noticed a regrettable difference in one aspect of the Wye scenery: the influence of the tide. The clear mirror of the river became muddied and the banks appeared sludgy. But there were compensations. The cliffs on either side began to rise much more steeply as the boat approached Piercefield (fig. 25). This awesome natural setting where the river makes a tight loop around the peninsula of Lancaut had been fully exploited by the prodigal Valentine Morris, one-time Governor of St Vincent.[26] He inherited and improved this 300-acre estate on the right bank of the river with the assistance of his wife, Mary Mordaunt, sister-in-law to Sir William Milner, the owner of another famous garden, Nun Appleton in Yorkshire. Visitors were admitted to Morris's 'Walks' in these cliff-top gardens every Tuesday and Friday. Gilpin disembarked here and after a zig-zag ascent of the cliff surveyed and commended Morris's improvements, but added:

We cannot however call these views picturesque. They are either presented from too high a point; or they have little to mark them as characteristic; or they do not fall into such composition, as would appear to advantage on canvas. But they are extremely romantic; and give a loose to the most pleasing riot of imagination.

This is almost exactly the same catalogue of failings as Gilpin had recorded at Ross churchyard in appraising that famous view. But if the scenes were awkward as pictorial compositions they were, by general agreement, highly romantic. There was one view, confessed Arthur Young, who visited Piercefield in 1768, 'at the very idea of describing which, my pen drops from my hand ... the eyes of your imagination are not keen enough to take in this point, which the united talents of a *Claud*, a *Poussin*, a *Vernet*, and a *Smith*, would scarcely be able to sketch'.[27] Charles Heath echoed Gilpin's remarks and complained of the lack of variety: 'the general criticisms which arise on viewing the rocks, hanging woods, and deep precipices of PERSFIELD, are all those of the *sublime*'. William Coxe, on the other hand, discovered an invigorating *concordia discors* in 'the majestic transition from the impervious gloom of the forests to open groves; from

27. Samuel Ireland, 'Chepstow &c from Persfield', from *Picturesque Views on the River Wye* (1797).
British Library, London

meadows and lawns, to rocks and precipices, and from the mild beauties of English landscape to the wildness of Alpine scenery'.

Piercefield was a formidable challenge to the amateur watercolourists, and it is no wonder that many felt disappointed with their own work and helplessly invoked Claude and Dughet. The gardener was the only artist to triumph in a work of this scale. Morris was nearly a casualty to his own enthusiasm: while exploring the 'capabilities' of his garden he fell off Lover's Leap, the viewpoint 180 feet above the Wye, but was saved by some sturdy shrubbery a little way below. He called in William Knowles, the Chepstow builder who had cleared the ruins of Tintern Abbey for the Duke of Beaufort, and created ten principal Views, including Lover's Leap, Windcliff, Grotto (recommended as another good dining site by the ever-alert John Byng) and Giant's Cave. The Cave had a bizarre embellishment, as Charles Heath describes:

... in a cavity on the top of the rock is placed an Herculean figure, who held in his hands an enormous stone, which with full force he was about to hurl on the head of the passing visitor ... but his *gigantic majesty* being assailed by a powerful enemy, called *frost*, he soon became divested of his terrific influence, his arms falling off from their joints at the elbows, – in which decrepid and mutilated state he now remains.

Each of these Views, approached by serpentine paths, was evidently chosen with scrupulous attention to Picturesque prescriptions for organised prospects. Consequently, the most appropriate tributes paid by the tourists were that the Views resembled works of art, a painting by Claude, or a stage-set, as Stebbing Shaw describes:

... opposite the cave are bow railings with a seat, which if we may compare the works of nature with those of art, may be called a front box of one of the compleatest theatres in the universe ... Here wants no painted canvas to express its scenery, nature's sweet landscape is quite enough. [Fig. 26]

Although he despaired of doing justice to one of the views towards Chepstow – 'adapted only to the talent and pencil of a Claude', yet again – Samuel Ireland did produce a characteristic Claudean composition, *Chepstow &c from Persfield* (fig. 27). It conforms with another enthusiastic description by Arthur Young:

The town and castle of Chepstow appear from one part of the bench, rising from the romantic steps of wood, in a manner too beautiful to express: a small remove discovers the steeple, so dropt in the precise point of taste, that one can scarcely believe it a real steeple, and not an eye-trap.[28]

A carefully organised view can thus seem to 'landscape' the country beyond the garden boundaries and give it an artificial status. This is a triumph of Picturesque management. The spectator is treated to 'all the picturesque beauties of a natural *camera obscura*'.[29]

In 1784 George Smith bought the estate from the bankrupt Morris and continued to develop it over the next ten years. In order to save the tourists from undue fatigue, he straightened the winding approach paths, and made other alterations bitterly regretted by Samuel Ireland:

With his roller and shears, insipid uniformity has identified the ever changeful scene; and the slime of this snail has scarce less deformed its dells, its craggy hills and its groves, than has the mud of the Severn that polluted its waters.

The intrusion of the mud from the Severn reminded the tourists that they had nearly reached the end of the Wye voyage. For Gilpin it was indeed the end of his exploration of river scenery. The tide was out when he left Piercefield. The boat drew too much water to complete the journey downstream, so he and his companions were obliged to walk the rest of the way into Chepstow.

The river scenery from Ross to Piercefield received what was perhaps its highest accolade when Fosbroke published his *Wye Tour* in 1818. In the opening pages he claimed that the Wye Valley was, in character rather than in details, 'a portrait of the celebrated Grecian Tempe enlarged'. To prove this is not idle flattery, he proceeds to quote passages from a recent travel account of a visit to the supposed original Vale of Tempe in northern Greece. Each quoted description is then identified with its approximate counterpart in the Wye Valley; and the Wye Valley is thus by association elevated to the highest rank of legendary beauty. Thanks to Gilpin's initiative, Fosbroke can complete a task analogous to that undertaken a century and a half earlier by Sir John Denham, when he summoned Parnassus from ancient Greece to the Thames Valley.

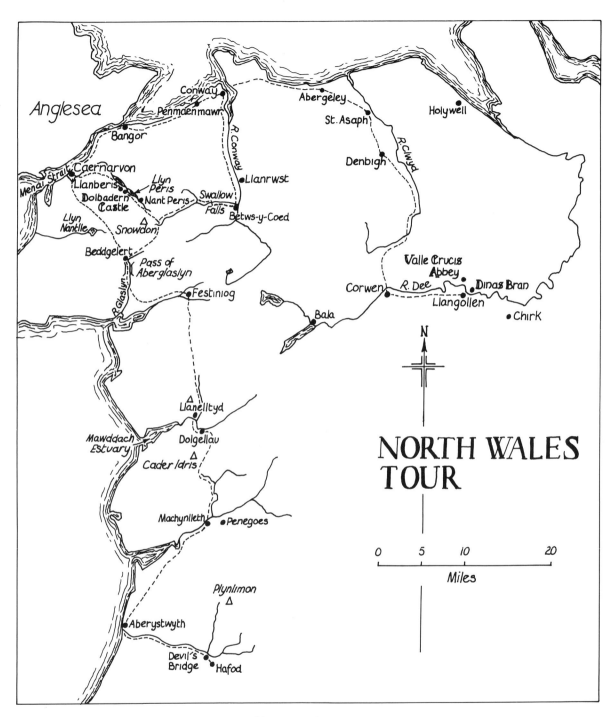

Map 2. North Wales

# VI

## The North Wales tour:
## mountains and bards

―――――――

'The Welsh tour has been hitherto strangely neglected', wrote Henry Wyndham in the account of his 1774 tour: 'while the English roads are crouded with travelling parties of pleasure, the Welsh are so rarely visited, that the author did not meet with a single party, during his six week's journey through Wales'.[1] Twenty years later, no doubt, tourists would have envied Wyndham his solitude. One reason for this reluctance to visit Wales was the relatively poor condition of the Welsh roads. A 1776 tourist reckoned that these roads were just one example of the fact that, on the whole, the 'Welsh are at least a century behind the English'.[2] The reactions of earlier travellers suggest that this estimate was too generous:

The Country looks like the fag End of the Creation; the very Rubbish of *Noah's* Flood; and will (if any thing) serve to confirm an *Epicurean* in his Creed, That the World was made by Chance.[3]

As we have noticed before, country which was unimproved, agriculturally or ornamentally, and which looked incapable of such improvement, had little appeal for the Augustan observer and often caused revulsion. The disgusted traveller quoted above expresses his horror in language reminiscent of Thomas Burnet's *The Sacred Theory of the Earth*, first translated into English in 1684, and extraordinarily influential for a century and a half. The 'very Rubbish of *Noah's* Flood' refers to Burnet's thesis that the originally smooth face of the Earth was destroyed, by God's anger in cooperation with natural physical forces, when the subterranean waters erupted through the Earth's crust and caused the great Flood. As the waters subsided, the debris of the crust settled into random heaps to form the present continents and great mountain ranges. The Earth now, according to Burnet, presents 'the Image or Picture of a great Ruin . . . the true aspect of a World lying in its Rubbish'.[4] It is little wonder that later travellers to North Wales so often referred to the *Sacred Theory*. The Snowdon peaks 'do altogether strongly excite the idea of Burnet, of their being the fragment of a demolished world', wrote Lord Lyttelton on his first visit to the region in 1756. By contrast, his road from Caernarvon to Bangor was blissfully antediluvian: 'fine shady lawns, perfumed so with honeysuckles, that they were a paradisetto'.

At a period when 'Capability' Brown was constructing so many private 'paradisetti' for the gentry, there was a singular interest in travelling to see the spectacular ruins of the antediluvian world, or, according to another theory, those places where it was thought Brown's divine counterpart had dumped Creation's unused raw material. Such a place was North Wales. The Sublime negligence – 'the very Rubbish' – from which the earlier travellers shrank was exactly to the taste of the later Picturesque tourist. For him, negligence on any scale was to be relished, after half a century of relentless 'improvements'. The landscape of North Wales had resisted the improver's hand just as its inhabitants, the true Britons, were supposed to have preserved their cultural integrity from the invasions of the Romans and, later, the English under Edward I.

One of the earliest travellers to be positively gratified by Welsh mountain scenery was Dr Thomas Herring, Archbishop of Canterbury from 1747–1757. He made his journey into North Wales in 1738:

The face of it is grand, and bespeaks the magnificence of nature, and enlarged my mind so much, in the same manner as the stupendousness of the ocean does, that it was some-time before I could be reconciled again to the level countries. Their beauties were all in the little taste; and, I am afraid, if I had seen Stow in my way home, I should have thrown out some very unmannerly reflections upon it; I should have smiled at the little niceties of art, and beheld with contempt an artificial ruin, after I had been agreeably terrified with something like the rubbish of creation.[5]

The last phrase is again clearly from Burnet. The most remarkable part of this response is Herring's contempt for Stowe, the garden which Pope seven years earlier in the *Epistle* to Burlington had glorified as 'a work to wonder at'. Herring's criticism suggests that the landscaped garden, in spite of the fact that it was freeing itself at just this period from formality of design, was already feeling competition from the more remote scenery of Britain. Ten years later, as we saw earlier (p. 55), one of the participants in Gilpin's *Dialogue . . . at Stow* recommended Lord Cobham to consider introducing some Lakeland scenery into his Stowe estate.

The Snowdon landscape, quite obviously, could not be 'improved'. When Joseph Hucks set out on his pedestrian tour of North Wales in 1794 with his undergraduate companion Coleridge, he announced that his chief object was 'to explore the hidden beauties of nature unmechanized by the ingenuity of man'. Snowdon had just this appeal:

> In this cold region, this infertile soil,
> The harvest scarce repays the ploughman's toil;
> The blasted mountains, and the naked rocks,
> But just with life sustain the climbing flocks.

The only thing to flourish in this grim environment, according to the poet, was an uncultivated moral integrity:

> Yet here old honesty, devoid of art,
> And gen'rous love springs native in the heart,
> Here health, content, and temp'rance close ally'd,
> With smiling mirth eternally resides.[6]

This consolation for the native was presumably one which only the touring visitor could fully appreciate. Joseph Cradock, whose *Letters from Snowdon* (1770) became widely known, disputed such facile idealization, from his own experience of North Wales:

Virtue, my dear friend, is not the inhabitant of uncivilized countries . . . The innocence of manners described by the poets, in the primaeval ages of mankind, had existence only in their own imagination . . . If we may define virtue to be a resistance, in a certain degree, to the force of our natural propensities [man in his natural state] knows not, nor acknowledges any such power.

But even this sensible philosophical assessment was susceptible to a little fanciful idealisation of rural charms, as we shall see later. David Solkin has argued that the growing interest in Wales from the middle 1760s onwards had much to do with contemporary events in England.[7] The idealisation of a remote, peaceful rural existence intensified at a time when there was conspicuous social unrest in the English counties. The Welsh peasantry were seen as enjoying a benign, quasi-feudal relationship with their local squirearchy, and thus remained uncontaminated by such mob grievances. Richard Wilson's Welsh landscapes of the 1760s, so Solkin argues, represent this essentially patrician view of an awesomely beautiful and benign landscape inhabited by a contented peasantry. These images in turn contributed to the growth of Picturesque tourism in Wales from the 1770s onwards and the discovery of a landscape very different from English scenery. Coleridge, writing to William Godwin in 1800, found he could best express his feelings about the quality of the landscape in North Wales by comparing it with the English Lakes:

As far as my memory will permit me to decide on the grander parts of Carnarvonshire, I may say, that the single objects are superior to any, which I have seen elsewhere – but there is a deficiency in combination. I know of no mountain in the north equal to Snowdon, but then we have an *encampment* of huge Mountains, in no harmony perhaps to the eye of the mere painter, but always interesting, various, and, as it were nutritive.[8]

The 'mere painter' shows a contempt for Picturesque criteria in evaluating scenery; but it was such criteria, nonetheless, which dominated conventional recommendations of North Wales:

> Ne'er shall the north [Scotland] with Cambria's beauties vie, . . .
> Claude's colours there, and Virgil's style are faint . . .
> Let Churchill's pen, and Rosa's pencil paint.[9]

Most later eighteenth-century travellers made a broad distinction between north-western and south-eastern Wales: between the awesome Sublimity of the one and the pastoral beauty of the other. Herring described his own journey in the northern regions as 'very romantic', 'most perilous'. Samuel Johnson was characteristically impressed by the more cultivated aspects: 'Wales, so far as I have yet seen of it, is a very beautiful and rich country, all enclosed and planted'.[10] The standard distinctions are summed up in the words of one 1791 tourist: 'The whole complexion of North Wales is bold and sublime . . . *sui generis*, singular in its kind, magnificent, striking, and superb'; by contrast, the 'beauties of South Wales . . . consist of picturesque landscapes, castellate ruins, and a fine country ornamented with verdure, woods, and agriculture'.[11] All in all, those who chose to make the tour of Wales knew they were to prepare for the full range of landscape experiences. The cost in terms of discomfort had to be reckoned with, but the dedicated pilgrim should not be deterred:

A man who has any taste for the romantic scenery of nature, or the beautiful and stupendous monuments of art, will lie among the drovers at Llantrissant . . . eat hard cheese at the Blue Boar at Caerphilly, or fast a whole morning in search of Lantoni abbey.[12]

Views of Welsh scenery had appeared now and again in paintings and engravings during the middle decades of the eighteenth century, notably in Richard Wilson's work and in Boydell's *Castles and Mountainous Views in Wales* (1749–50); but these scenes did not yet generate sufficient interest to persuade the tourist to travel in search of their originals, in spite of Wilson's recommendation that 'everything the landscape painter could want, was to be found in North Wales'. But by the time John Wolcot issued his advice to landscape painters the search for the Picturesque was well under way:

> Claude painted in the open air!
> Therefore to Wales at once repair,
> Where scenes of **true** magnificence you'll find.[13]

The first Picturesque tour in North Wales was in 1771. Sir Watkin Williams-Wynn, just about the wealthiest and most important man in eighteenth-century Wales, set out on his two-week tour in the late summer of that year.[14] He took with him Paul Sandby specifically so that the artist could record the scenery in watercolour drawings (fig. 28). The total company, consisting of '5 gentlemen, 9 servants and 13 horses', travelled west from Llangollen to Dolgellau, via Bala, then turned north to Caernarvon, crossed to Anglesey, and returned via Conway, Llanrwst and Holywell. The total cost of the tour was £111–7–6. Sandby took many sketches, several of which were made into aquatints for his *XII Views in North Wales*, published in 1776, and widely acclaimed.

Two years after Sir Watkin's tour, Thomas Pennant, the antiquarian topographer, travelled through the country. In his *Tour in Wales* (1778–81) he paid tribute to the 'fidelity and elegance' of Sandby's *Views*, which had begun to stimulate the public's appetite for travel into Wales. In 1769 Pennant had 'acquired that treasure, Moses Griffith', as his artist for the tours, and his books were illustrated with engravings from Griffith's original drawings. Pennant was primarily interested in the antiquities of Britain, and never claimed to be a connoisseur of scenery. Many subsequent Picturesque tourists were unfairly impatient at his apparent lack of sensibility:

28. Paul Sandby, 'Sir Watkin Williams-Wynn sketching' (1777).
National Museum of Wales, Cardiff

. . . this whole Countery is so wild & romantic in most respects, that even Mr. Pennant
(a very litteral & cold author) who gives as it were an inventory of every thing he sees
finds it impossible when he travils where *we have done*, to avoid taking a Poetical as well
as an Historical View of the morals and manners of old Britains.

But he was at the same time respected for his particular expertise. The lady just
quoted referred to those of her fellow tourists who had no '*minds Eye*' like
Pennant's, as 'mere Clod Pole travelers'.[15] Griffith was an appropriate choice of
illustrator for Pennant, as his work inclined more towards the 'Historical View'
than the 'Poetical'. He was quite scrupulous in topographical accuracy and could
manage architecture quite well; but his rendering of natural scenery, especially
rock, was clumsy. Donald Moore in his catalogue introduction to a 1979 exhibition of Griffith's work,[16] suggested that defective observation and poor artistic
technique were partly to blame for these deficiencies, but that the basic reason was
that nobody then understood how rocks had come into being. All contemporary
painters had this disadvantage, of course, though many were far more skilful than
Griffith. The stress on the importance for the painter of a scientific study of the
natural world made little impression until the publication of the first volume of
Ruskin's *Modern Painters* in 1843. Sandby himself, like Gainsborough, was content to base his painting of rock on small pieces of coal laid out on his studio table.
Many gentlemen of means over the last few decades of the eighteenth century

took with them a professional artist, so that their published Tours into North Wales could be embellished with engravings from watercolour sketches made on the spot. Henry Wyndham took the Swiss-born artist Samuel Hieronymous Grimm on his 1774 tour. Henry Wigstead took Thomas Rowlandson on his 1797 tour. Robert Fulke Greville, whose brother Charles had, together with Sandby, introduced the process of aquatinting into England, travelled with two painters in 1792: John 'Warwick' Smith and Julius Caesar Ibbetson. Tourists of more modest means tried to acquire some proficiency in sketching before they set out.

Joseph Cradock and Lord Lyttelton were among the first of those whose written accounts drew attention to the specific scenic beauties of North Wales: both have already been mentioned. Gilpin toured the country in 1773, but his *Observations* were not published until 1809, although, like his Wye *Observations*, his manuscript journals would have circulated fairly widely. Pennant remained the authoritative guide and informant on the antiquities. These records, together with Sandby's *XII Views*, meant that, by the 1780s, the Welsh tour could no longer be considered in Henry Wyndham's words so 'strangely neglected'.

### Llangollen – Corwen – Vale of Clwyd

'The Church & bridge – river & descending road w[th] the surrounding Mountains all Combine to give a complete romantic landscape'.[17] So wrote the young Turner of his first sight of the Vale of Llangollen during his 1792 tour. A 'complete romantic landscape' is just what Richard Wilson's 1770–1 oil, *Dinas Bran, from Llangollen*, depicts (fig. 29). Llangollen's natural beauty was completed, for Picturesque tastes, by its bridge and church, so useful as middle-distance features, and by the hilltop castle ruins of Dinas Bran. Sir Watkin Williams-Wynn, sponsor of the first Picturesque tour, owned an estate, Wynnstay, which was strategically positioned near the Welsh–English border, and commanded a magnificent view up the Dee valley to Llangollen. When that connoisseur of landscape gardening, Lord Lyttelton, visited the estate in 1755 he suggested that its owner should incorporate one particularly striking prospect to the west:

... if the park was extended a little farther, it would take in a hill, with the view of a valley, most beautifully wooded; and the river Dee winding in so romantic and charming a manner, that I think it exceeds ... any confined prospect I ever beheld.

It is probably this view which Sir Watkin commissioned Wilson to paint fifteen years later. Wilson gives it a mellow, Italianate rendering and incorporates as a striking background the Dinas Bran hill (fig. 30).

The Vale was a favourite entry point into North Wales, promising 'the most charming expectation of picturesque scenes and poetical indulgences of fancy'.[18] The river Dee ran through rich meadowland, 'such as love-sick poets paint', in John Byng's sardonic phrase, while above rose the steep and oddly conical castle hill, offering a useful nursery-slope preparation for the coming attempts at Cader Idris and Snowdon. That later parodist of the Picturesque, Thomas Rowlandson,

29. Richard Wilson, *Dinas Bran from Llangollen* (1770–1).
Yale Center for British Art, Paul Mellon Collection

30. Richard Wilson, *View near Wynnstay, the Seat of Sir Watkin Williams-Wynn, Bt.* (1770–1). Yale Center for British Art, Paul Mellon Collection

31. Thomas Rowlandson, 'Dinas Bran'.
National Library of Wales, Aberystwyth

had many falls on the way to the top, where he drafted a number of most delicate watercolours of views (fig. 31) from among the castle ruins.[19]

Llangollen bridge features in most sketches of the area. It was useful as both a middle-distance and foreground object. The broad piers forced the river to issue through the arches 'in a number of small falls, leaping from fragment to fragment, and presenting an appropriate fore ground to the charming picture, whilst the distant horizon is varied by the undulating contour of mountains'.[20] These small falls lent great animation to the scene, and were reflected on a larger scale in the more ponderous undulation of the mountain contours.

Coleridge's midsummer visit to the area was spoiled by the fact that the weather was intensely hot, so much so that 'we saw only what was to be admired – we could not admire'.[21] But some of the many who did admire were rendered quite inarticulate by its beauty:

. . . we hardly ever spoke! or if we did, it was only between long pauses that involuntarily we cried out sometimes all together, did you ever? – no never – [until] fatigued with our own barren exclamations . . . we all agreed to be *quite silent*.[22]

James Plumptre, the Cambridge classics scholar, was greatly excited by some open-air theatricals he saw in Llangollen in 1792. The company consisted of a prompter who sat on stage throughout, and two men who, with appropriate

32. George Cumberland, 'Valle Crucis Abbey', in his MS 'Tour in North Wales' (1784).
National Library of Wales, Aberystwyth

costume changes, assumed a variety of parts. The townsfolk were delighted, but Plumptre could not understand a word of the Welsh dialogue. After several enquiries he discovered that the purpose of this 'Tragi-comic-operatic Drama' was to ridicule the Methodists, taxes, and other contemporary grievances. It was the Methodists who were responsible for the suppression and near extinction of many such entertainments. This performance gave Plumptre 'a perfect idea of the rude and early ages of the drama'.[23] The travelling theatricals were called 'Anterlutes', according to Joseph Cradock, who saw a performance of *King Lear* during his 1770 tour. On that occasion, the stage was erected at the end of a barn and the 'green room' was, literally, that: 'a small enclosure made up of furze'. *King Lear* was scarcely recognisable as Shakespeare's play, partly because the roles of Lear's daughters were taken by brawny ploughmen.

A mile and a half to the north-west of the town is the ruined Valle Crucis Abbey, the surrounds of which were not always to the taste of the artist or tourist. On his 1773 visit Gilpin had specifically recommended some strategic tree planting to hide and reveal the ruins as the visitor walked slowly round the site. Whether or not the Abbey's owner, Sir Watkin, acted on his advice, the effect twenty-five years later was not wholly satisfying. Colt Hoare liked the correspondence between the delicate taper of the ash trees and the Gothic architecture (fig. 32), but still wanted a few trees removed to allow a better view of the fine western front.[24] The tempta-

33. Paul Sandby, 'View of the River Dee 3 Miles short of Bala . . .', no. viii in
*XII Views in North Wales* (1776). National Library of Wales, Aberystwyth

tion for the tourist to turn landscape gardener was acute in such circumstances:
'surely Browne never saw this place', thought John Byng, 'or he would have gone
wild to have handled it'. Brown would presumably have handled it with more
discretion than the designer of a startling green-and-white summer-house close to
the Abbey's east front:

. . . from this well-fancy'd retreat, the abbey is conceal'd by the apple trees in a cabbage
garden. What charming elegance! How worthy of Clapham or Hackney!!

It is surprising that Byng of all people should not have approved at least of the
motive for this summer house, which had been built for the convenience of those
who had brought cold meats with them and wished to dine in a secluded spot. To
Gilpin's disgust, the owner had added other ornamental touches. A small mountain stream had been diverted to a flight of stone steps, down which it fell into a
large square pond in front of the ruins. The pond was adorned with Chinese-style
railings, painted 'a lively green'.

   As for the scenery between Valle Crucis and Corwen, '*Connoisseuise in Prospects*
prefer it from it being terminated by so sublime an object as Cader Idris for a
*Back Ground*'.[25] This tourist was most likely recalling, or even consulting on the
spot, Paul Sandby's aquatint (one of the *XII Views*) with the very specific title
*View of the River Dee 3 Miles short of Bala with Cader Idris Mountain near Dolgelli*

34. Anon, 'View of some old hovels at Corwen. Augst the 10th 1802', and 'Cloudy view at Chirk Aug. the 4th 1802', from sketchbook Add. MS 24003. British Library, London

*30 Miles Distant* (fig. 33). Sandby's view, which includes himself perched on a rock sketching the scene, was taken a few miles south-west of Corwen. Corwen itself presented a striking contrast to the rich pastoral scenery of Llangollen. The poverty of its inhabitants was very evident; the dilapidation of its cottages made it look to one traveller 'as if it had lately suffered by a bombardment'.[26] Artists relished the rough, broken lines this scene offered them, as cliffs towered above the village, seeming to threaten further destruction. There is a telling juxtaposition of subjects in the 1802 sketch-book shown in fig. 34, where ramshackle, ancient Corwen is contrasted with the bold geometry of Telford's new aqueduct at Chirk, just a few miles away. As in the case of the Wye Valley ironworks, the Picturesque tourist generally shied away from such products of the industrial age. Exceptions could be made if there were stimulating contrasts to be exploited. Contemplating the aqueduct bridge on the Forth–Clyde canal, John Stoddart remarked that 'where objects of art enter into a direct rivalship, as it were, with the objects of Nature, and are of sufficient magnitude, and importance, to maintain the competition, the suspense, in which the mind is held, is of the most pleasing kind'.[27]

Heading north from Corwen, the tourist entered the Vale of Clwyd. Nearly everyone was enraptured with its gentle beauty. Lord Lyttelton compared it favourably with the landscaping of his own park at Hagley, but still preferred some of the scenery of Montgomeryshire; 'there is great beauty in this, but there is no

majesty; whereas there . . . the soft and the agreeable is mixed with the noble, the great, and the sublime'. Here is how the Vale appeared to Coleridge and Hucks, in Hucks's description, as their pedestrian tour took them to a point about five miles short of Ruthin:

. . . the vale of Clwyd, in all its beauty unfolded upon the sight: it appeared like a moving picture, upon which nature had been prodigal of its colours. Hamlets, villages, towns, and castles, rose like enchantment upon this rich carpet, that seemed covered with wood and enclosures; in the midst of it, . . . the town of Ruthin, partially appeared from the bosom of a most beautiful grove of trees; the vale on each side being bounded by a chain of lofty mountains, and far off, on a bold and rugged promontory, stood Denbigh, with its strong fortress, the undisputed mistress of this extended scene.

For all its enthusiasm, and naming of specific places, this is not a description which gives any distinctive beauty or vitality to the scene. One need only compare it with one of Ruskin's extended descriptions of a particular landscape in order to recognise how much the individual spirit of the place is missing. The details Hucks selects, and the way he arranges them in his description, indicate how closely he belongs to the older generalising traditions in landscape poetry and painting. Here are the framing mountain ranges, the town in the middle distance (with the clear echo of Milton's 'Boosom'd high in tufted Trees'), and the more remote, eye-catching ruin on a promontory. He is accommodating a particular scene to the conventions of landscape poetry and painting, as many tourists were to do, by explicit reference or otherwise. Here is an example from another tourist, again enjoying the Vale of Clwyd:

> I could not compare it to anything I had ever seen unless to some of the finest flemish landscapes – The Eye bounded by the loftiest Hills, the Vales having uniformly a fruitful Appearance finely wooded and watered, at once creates the most pleasing Astonishment.[28]

This tourist has not even bothered to reconstruct the view in words, as Hucks tried to do. He takes a short cut by his mention of Flemish paintings, so that the visually educated reader can call upon his own associations with a certain character of landscape. He then hurries on to describe the general aesthetic impact of the Vale with a formulary phrase.

The fact that the Vale prompted so many to invoke certain schools of painting did not necessarily make it an easy subject for the artist. Colt Hoare spoke for many when he complained that 'the Vale is in general *too wide* to furnish good subjects for the Pencil'. His own fastidious Picturesque tastes were eventually satisfied at Denbigh:

> I walked out, in search of the most advantageous points of view – and encircled the Castle ... I fixed my point at last from the Lime Stone Quarries on the road leading to St. Asalph – here, the Town appears to very great advantage – the ruins of a fine Castle at the summit – the modern church, and by its side, that of one in ruins [i.e. the never-completed Leicester's Church] a fine rich Country terminated by Mountains at a distance – with a very good and broken foreground – and the town covering the declivities of a steep hill, well blended with trees. The whole forms a rich and picturesque Scene – worthy the pencil of a Poussin, and similar in many respects to those he chose for his Pencil.[29]

Foreground road, middleground castle and town on a steep hill, and background mountain range suggest that Colt Hoare has in his mind's eye one of the Dughet Campagna landscapes popularised by the Chatelain engravings (e.g. fig. 35). The Vale thus acquires great dignity by association. The viewpoint is the key here. The scene's principal features are, after all, much the same as in Hucks's description of Clwyd from further up the valley: Denbigh Castle on its promontory, the rich countryside bounded by mountains, and the town 'well blended with trees'.

The Castle disappointed Mrs Thrale, when she visited it in the company of Dr Johnson in 1774. She had more the impression of an artificial ruin, and one does not travel all the way to North Wales from Streatham in order to see the sort of thing one could find in any of the large gardens in the Home Counties:

> The ivy has given one side more the appearance of a hedge than a wall, and the *tout ensemble*, as the Dilettants phrase it, is too delicately pleasing to afford one any of the images one expects from an old castle.[30]

Coleridge was also disappointed, but not by the ancient architecture:

35. Gaspar Dughet, *Landscape*.
Courtauld Institute, London

Two well drest young men were walking there – Come – says one – I'll play my flute – 'twill be romantic! Bless thee for the thought, Man of Genius and Sensibility! I exclaimed – and pre-attuned my heartstring to tremulous emotion. He sat adown (the moon just peering) amid the most awful part of the Ruins – and – romantic Youth! Struck up the affecting Tune of *Mrs. Casey*![31]

Both here, and in his regret that he found it too hot to admire properly the beauties of Llangollen, Coleridge shows a comic self-consciousness about his aesthetic duties as a tourist.

### Conway – the Welsh Bards

The scenery of the north-west coast offered little to detain the tourist, apart from a few curiosities such as the mixed bathing at Abergeley, where Hucks noted 'a dozen of both sexes promiscuously enjoying themselves in the lucid element'. A little further along the road to Conway he and Coleridge had an encounter which gave them both a cheering sense of superiority as tourists:

We met the Cantabs of my College, Brooke[s] and Berdmore – these rival *pedestrians* . . . were vigorously pursuing their tour – in a *post chaise!* We laughed famously – their only excuse was, that Berdmore had got *clapped*.[32]

On arrival at Conway the four of them, equipped with large sticks and knap-sacks set off for a hike, their appearance causing some excitement to the 'risible muscles' of the Welsh, who at other times, with some alarm, mistook them for Frenchmen. It was at Conway, six years later, that Samuel Rogers saw Joseph Farington and Sir George Beaumont, with their portfolios 'full of rocks and cataracts and ruin'd castles'.[33] These distinguished tourists were drawn to Conway, no doubt, because it was one of the most celebrated Picturesque scenes in Wales. 'Food for the pencil is to be found in abundance', Henry Wigstead wrote of the fortified town and its thirteenth-century castle high on a cliff overlooking the Conway estuary. 'Nor should I ever forget the wood opposite', wrote John Byng, dreamily playing the part of *L'Allegro*, 'beneath whose shade we reclin'd till the sun retir'd in roseate splendour; whilst by us pass'd homeward many a milk maid, from the hawthorn in the dale'.

Lord Lyttelton thought Conway Castle had the grandest appearance of any building he had ever seen; and he was convinced that Sanderson Miller, the designer of his own Hagley Hall as well as Hagley's mock-gothic ruin, 'would have fallen down and adored the architect'. But Gilpin, after granting that all the right ingredients for a Sublime and beautiful landscape – water, rising ground, woody banks, a castle – were assembled at Conway, judged that they were not assembled correctly for Picturesque taste. The artist, therefore, taking his view-point from the Conway Ferry, had to make some adjustments to the scene:

The best expedient to preserve truth . . . and yet to add as much composition as the natural arrangement of the materials will allow, is to introduce only a part of the castle near the corner of the picture; which would ease it of some of it's regular towers.

36. William Gilpin, 'View of Conway Castle, improved by planting a tree in the foreground, and
breaking the regularity of the scene', from the MS North Wales tour notebook, 1773.
Bodleian Library, Oxford

Conway Castle was too well preserved, that was the problem. There was too little
'vegetable furniture' on its towers to break the straight lines and add variety of
colour. The Picturesque problems of Conway lead Gilpin into a disquisition on
ruined castles and their uses in landscape painting. We realise here how excep-
tional Goodrich Castle on the Wye tour must have seemed in order to qualify as
'*correctly picturesque*': 'for we seldom see any castle, however meliorated by age,
and improved by ruin, which can, in all respects, be called a complete model'.
He then lists the special advantages for the artist of the ideal ruined castle:
'irregularity in it's *parts*,' the rich colouring of moss and weeds, and the ivy which
contributes to break up the severer lines of the building. Since Conway was deficient in the first and last advantages, it was better to relegate it to a side-screen.
The artist's next task, according to Gilpin, was to cut down part of the wood on
the opposite bank (the sylvan shades so relished by Byng). If this seemed to abuse
artistic licence, Gilpin could reassure the reader that 'As the wood, in fact, is
periodically cut down, this liberty is very allowable'. The final stage involves some
attention to the foreground, 'by planting a tree or two . . . and hiding part of the
regularity by their branches' (fig. 36).

This Picturesque obsession with composition and viewpoint is in marked contrast to the journal notes that the young Turner was taking of the Vale of Conway
in 1792. Here we get the sense that organised distances and side-screens are less

37. P. de Loutherbourg, *Cataract on the Llugwy*.
Victoria and Albert Museum, London

important than the movement in the landscape forms and the blending of colours – a sense of priorities expressed also in the rolling, unpunctuated form of Turner's prose description:

... here the swelling hills folding as it were over each other and beautifully gradating till they blend softly into the Horizon all blue and tender grey tints irradiated in the summit in the distances by the setting sun which bears the Hills in the foreground that overhang the River Conway quite in Shadow.[34]

An excursion of about fifteen miles up the river Conway brought the tourist to a number of celebrated waterfalls. One in particular, Swallow Falls, near the junction of the Llygwy with the Conway, was a favourite subject for the artists. De Loutherbourg's watercolour (fig. 37) accentuates the Sublime by introducing into the scene himself and his wife clasping each other, and the ancient guide to the Falls with his daughter.[35] The genteel tourists gesticulate with appropriate Pleasing Terror at the precipitousness of the Falls as if to compensate for the fact that the full drop cannot be represented in the picture.

'On a rock, whose haughty brow/Frowns o'er old Conway's foaming flood' Thomas Gray stationed his Bard, striking his lyre in defiance of Edward I's invading army:

> 'Hark, how each giant-oak, and desert cave,
> Sighs to the torrent's aweful voice beneath!
> O'er thee, Oh King! Their hundred arms they wave,
> Revenge on thee in hoarser murmurs breathe'.

*The Bard* was published in 1757. Hardly any of the later Picturesque tourists to these regions would have been ignorant of it; for it evoked in impassioned lyrical verse the spirit of North Wales, a landscape and culture romantically remote from lowland, sophisticated southern England. Some of the inspiration for Gray's Sublime figure appears to have come from John Parry, Sir Watkin Williams-Wynn's venerable harper. Parry visited London, and performed at Ranelagh Gardens in April 1746. He visited Cambridge in 1757, and, according to Gray:

Scratch'd out such ravishing blind Harmony, such tunes of a thousand years old ... as have set all this learned body a' dancing, and inspired them with a due reverence for *Odikle* [i.e. his Ode], whenever it shall appear. Mr. Parry (you must know) it was, that has put Odikle in motion again.[36]

Gray was already becoming interested in the possibilities for poetry of enlisting Celtic mythology as a lively, native alternative to the conventional Greek and Roman models: 'I think it would be still better to graft any wild picturesque fable absolutely of one's own invention upon the Druid-Stock'.[37] The 'Druid-Stock' was to become a very vigorous literary growth, as the Celtic Revival gathered momentum among English writers. Percy, Hurd, Shenstone, Gray and Mason were all 'Briton mad', according to the brother of Lewis Morris, who was initially the force behind the Revival.[38] The Revd Evan Evans published *Some Specimens of the Poetry of the Ancient Welsh Bards* in 1764. Twenty years later Edward Jones produced *Musical and Poetical Relicks of the Welsh Bards* with the clear echo of Percy's *Reliques of Ancient English Poetry* (1765) in its title and with a frontispiece engraving of Loutherbourg's painting of Gray's Bard.

The Druids had been exterminated in the Roman invasion of the first century B.C.; and popular belief attributed the persecution of the Bards, the inheritors and custodians of the Druidic tradition, to Edward I's invasion of Wales in the late thirteenth century. Hence arose the legend of the last of the Bards defying the English king, which Gray took as the source for his Ode. The Ode contributed much to the growing interest in Druidism and Bardic culture. William Stukeley's *Stonehenge, a Temple restor'd to the British Druids* (1740) had, as its title declared, firmly associated that enigmatic monument with the ancient British religion, an association reproduced in Thomas Jones' 1774 painting *The Bard*. Druids are frequently portrayed as resistance fighters against imperial Rome, in the literature of the period, in yet another expression of the national urge to emancipate a specifically British culture from classical authority. They are also cast as proto-Christians, devotees of the patriarchal religion or of a natural religion which exemplified the untaught worship of the natural world as God's creation. For the late-eighteenth-century tourist the spirit of Druidism was inseparable from Sublime mountain scenery and ancient ruins. The gaunt, blind bards seemed to be living links with the Middle Ages and earlier, the human equivalent of those remains of Gothic architecture scattered over Britain's wilder landscapes.

The painters seized on the subject of Gray's Ode. Among the more successful were de Loutherbourg, Fuseli and Thomas Jones in the eighteenth century, and Blake and John Martin in the nineteenth century. Paul Sandby's painting has not survived, and by all accounts this is a great loss: 'Such a Bard!' wrote Mason of Sandby's painting in November 1760, rapturously checking off the specific images in the poem against the picture: 'Such a headlong flood! Such a Snowdon! Such giant oaks! Such desert caves!'[39] Richard Bentley, the friend of Horace Walpole, produced a set of drawings for the poem, which greatly excited that connoisseur's admiration: 'Nothing but you, or Salvator Rosa, and Nicola Poussin, can paint up to the expressive horror and dignity of it'.[40] Joshua Reynolds, on the other hand, attempted it, and failed. 'Very Splendid Images will not always make a good Picture',[41] observed Samuel Rogers *à propos* Reynolds's experience. It may seem to us an oddly Romantic subject for Reynolds, until we remember that in its time the Ode was intended to be, and recognised as a legitimate subject for heroical history painting.

The Picturesque tourist was delighted to find a great number of bards, one per inn, almost, on the tour of North Wales. They seemed always to be ancient, and, allegedly, always blind. 'I suppose that they put out their eyes, when young, as they do those of bullfinches who are taught to pipe', mused John Byng. Their great age and apparent blindness, together with their priestly demeanour, pro-vided a fair guarantee that they would be revered and rewarded. Their music and

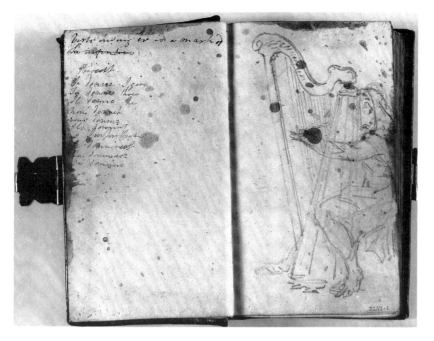

38. J. M. W. Turner, 'Harper seated playing a Harp', from a sketchbook in the Turner Bequest. British Museum, London

impassioned rendering of incomprehensible songs for the tourists made them 'the natural sons of Homer',[42] though they were equally able to please more trivial tastes with songs such as 'Dimples', or, with feudal enthusiasm, 'Sir Watkin's Delight'. Many a tourist delightedly remarked on the correspondence between their music and their native landscape as they played 'airs of the Country, as wild, and yet as harmonious as the beauties they are deprived from seeing'.[43] Gilpin, whose eye was always more sensitive than his ear, was also impressed: 'Their harps have an elegant form; and if their music is not exquisite, their appearance is picturesque'. Mary Morgan in 1791 was introduced to a blind bard in a village near Carmarthen, and was a little disappointed to find him dressed in a good cloth coat instead of loose robes, and with a neat head of hair instead of flowing locks. Her disillusionment was complete when she heard the following story of him:

A blind brother of the harp came to visit him, at which he was highly pleased, and talked much of taking him to Carmarthen, to *shew* him every thing that was worth *seeing* there. Mrs. H——, hearing of this, ordered that one of the servants should accompany them to direct their path. But the harper, disdaining this, walked off with his blind friend early in the morning. When they returned in the evening, the stranger declared himself well pleased with all he had *seen*, and in a minute manner described the places they had been at.[44]

In his 1739 travels, Dr Thomas Herring recorded a Picturesque scene which must have been repeated for tourists at nearly every Welsh inn, well into the nineteenth century:

> ... there came in a harper, who soon drew about us a group of figures that Hogarth would give any price for. The harper was in his true place and attitude; a man and woman stood before him, singing to his instrument wildly, but not disagreeably; a little dirty child was playing with the bottom of the harp; a woman, in a sick night-cap, hanging over the stairs; a boy with crutches, fixed in a staring attention, and a girl carding wool in the chimney, and rocking a cradle with her naked feet, interrupted in her business by the charms of the music; all ragged and dirty, and all silently attentive. These figures gave us a most entertaining picture.[45]

The description has a refreshing immediacy, even though Herring from the start establishes the scene as a typical Hogarthian 'genre' subject. Later tourists could summon the neighbourhood harper to perform at more or less any time of day or night and enjoy such a picture (fig. 38). Julius Caesar Ibbetson portrayed one of the most celebrated late-eighteenth-century harpers, John Smith, seated at his harp in a pyramid of enraptured adults and children, with Snowdon and Dolbadern Castle as the nebulous background.

On the eve of his ascent of Snowdon, Joseph Cradock and his clergyman companion hired not only a harper but a number of 'blooming country girls' to dance for them:

> It gave me infinitely more pleasure to hear this rustic concert, than the finest airs of an Italian opera; and to see these rosy rural nymphs direct their mazy steps, without the needless sumptuous apparel of luxury and pride, than all the ladies at St. James's, in their artificial beauty and attire.

After this tribute it is surprising to come across Cradock's later remarks suggesting that Edward I did a great benefit to Wales when he destroyed the 'vagabond poetical tribe' of Bards. The greatest contemporary threat to the survival of the harpers and dancers were the Methodists, who, as the Llangollen 'Anterlutes' dramatized, were much concerned to suppress all symptoms of what they regarded as pagan recreation. The tourists, on the other hand, had travelled far to witness and, by their charity, conserve precisely these vestiges of a pre-Christian culture.

Cynicism about the Bards developed in line with the waning of enthusiasm for the Picturesque. Mrs Barbauld, the eminent 'blue-stocking', wrote a bantering letter to Samuel Rogers while he was on his Welsh tour:

> Why do you bid me write who have nothing to communicate, where there are neither harps nor Druids? ... I have been trying in my own mind whether Miss Hagan with her fingers upon her harp will bear any comparison with an ancient Druid sweeping his with his flowing beard, but I find her so infinitely inferior in the sublime, that I am obliged to drop the similitude.[46]

The coastal road west from Conway soon brought the tourist to Penmaenmawr. The threat to self-preservation in negotiating the famous pass over this headland offered one of the most intense experiences of the Sublime in all Wales. The road was little more than a narrow ledge with a sheer drop down to the sea and a sheer cliff on the other side rising to 1500 feet. The schistic rock and débris of small avalanches added to the terror. Many tourists recalled Thomson's lines:

> ... with mighty crush,
> Into the flashing deep, from the rude rocks
> Of Penmanmaur heaped hideous to the sky,
> Tumble the smitten cliffs.[47]

The road was improved in 1772 (the year before Gilpin's visit) and a wall built on both sides. Dr Johnson travelled this way in 1774 and was greatly relieved at the increased security; but John Byng rather regretted the loss of the old horrors, 'where no two carriages could pass, where no wall above the sea was built, and where people might feel anxiety, without being deem'd timid; Now it is only a road to cross with surprise, transport, and wonder'. Mrs Siddons and her travelling companion paused here, along with a number of tourists, in order to absorb the wonders of Penmaenmawr. The great tragedienne refused to be upstaged by natural scenery:

A lady within hearing of us was in such ecstasies that she exclaimed, 'This awful scenery makes me feel as if I were only a worm, or a grain of dust, on the face of the earth'. Mrs. Siddons, turned round, and said, 'I feel very differently'.[48]

The threat of histrionic competition became a reality when Penmaenmawr took to the London stage. In the 1790s it was featured in the title of a Sadler's Wells spectacular, *Penmaenmawr; or The Wonders of Wales*. After the terrors of this pass, any landscape would be a relief, but Colt Hoare found Bangor positively 'riant': 'cultivation and population are well blended with the ruder features of nature which they tend to soften and animate'.[49] Anglesea, easily visible across the Menai Strait, proved to be more attractive in the imagination, as the ancient seat of the Druids, than in reality. The relatively flat landscape of the island had little interest for the Picturesque tourist who had just tasted and was soon to experience in full the sublimities of North Wales. Nonetheless the island's Druid monuments could excite pleasing Melancholy, as Cradock suggested by quoting several lines of Warton's celebrated poem to that Sublime goddess:

> When a smiling babe you loved to lie,
> Oft deep listening to the rapid roar
> Of wood-hung Menai, stream of druids old,
> That laved his hallow'd haunt with dashing wave

Caernarvon Castle, commanding the south-west end of the Menai Strait, was the most popular of all Welsh sites for the artist, if statistics are any guide. Between

1730 and 1850, 88 different views were published as prints.[50] Indeed there was strong competition only from Tintern Abbey, with 79 views. Richard Wilson's 1744–5 oil-painting *Caernarvon Castle* is one of the earliest views of the castle in its slightly adjusted natural setting. Its Picturesque rather than archaeological appeal is indicated by a gentleman sketcher in the foreground, whose work is being assessed in connoisseur fashion by his companion. Turner's 1799 watercolour of the Castle set at a considerable distance in an imaginary Claudean landscape, with a bearded harper in the foreground, is one of the most romantic and evocative images (fig. 39). Hucks was more immediately aware of the Castle as a relic of the disgraceful feudal period of British history. His is a good example of the political response to ruins discussed in the first part of this book. In contemplating these remains, he writes, we experience certain natural associations: 'the recollection of the feudal vassalage and slavery of former days, is accompanied by the pleasing circumstances of the relative prosperity and freedom which we now enjoy'. Such complacency is like the response to Caernarvon's rival, Tintern Abbey, where monastic ruins represented the enlightened overthrow of monkish 'superstition' and cloistered indolence.

In addition to the Picturesque and the political appraisals of Caernarvon, the tourist might subject it to the psychological test:

What can be the reason that this Gothic style of Architecture, is always productive of the Sublime? I remember Burke in his Treatise makes *Infinity* the principal source of it in buildings, & he instances in a Dome, etc. But it cannot proceed from this cause, as buildings of this kind are generally broken into so many minute parts. I believe the idea of Fear & danger they inspire, together with the gloom that attends them, is the chief source of our admiration & pleasure.[51]

This was in 1776. It is an indication of how strong Burke's authority in such matters remained, even though the tourist challenges one of the *Enquiry's* hypotheses. He realises that the formal aspects of the ruin do not supply a satisfactory explanation for the emotional impact of Gothic architecture; and he prefers to account for it by associationist fear and gloom, which are related to some of Burke's other effective causes of the Sublime.

In spite of its popularity with the artists, Caernarvon was not wholly pleasing in Picturesque terms. Like Conway, it was in too good a state of preservation: 'it does not produce those lively emotions in the mind, which edifices of this nature are apt to excite, from its wanting the fine circumstance of a mantle of ivy to relieve and soften down that broad face of stone which the extensive ruin presents to the eye'.[52] Turner's watercolour solved this by setting the castle in a distant haze. Paul Sandby avoided monotony by making the well-preserved section into a bold silhouette, contrasting it with the more distant, ivy-topped tower and the little modern cottage at its foot, and then 'animating' the foreground with sails, waggon and human figures.

As the tourist headed inland from Caernarvon he found, unfolding before him, increasingly awesome mountain scenery. Snowdon itself viewed from Lake

39. J. M. W. Turner, *Caernarvon Castle* (1799).
British Museum, London, the Turner Bequest

40. Paul Sandby, *Dolbadarn Castle and Llanberis Lake* (1764).
City of Birmingham Museum and Art Gallery

Llanberis was one of the most cherished subjects for the artist, notwithstanding Gilpin's dismissal of it as 'a bleak, dreary waste; without any pleasing combination of parts, or any rich furniture, either of wood, or well-constructed rock'. The only exception he makes is the view of ruined Dolbadarn Castle perched above the lake at Nant Peris, backed by Snowdon. This view, which seemed to epitomise the spirit of North Wales, inspired two of the earliest, distinctively Picturesque paintings of the Snowdon region: Richard Wilson's oil *Llyn Peris and Dolbadarn Castle* (1762–4) and Paul Sandby's watercolour *Dolbadarn Castle and Lanberis Lake* (1764) (fig. 40). Neither painter respects topographical accuracy. Wilson's landscape, based on a Dughet compositional structure,[53] is warmed by Claudean light. An even more curious hybrid landscape is his 1764–5 *Lake of Nemi or Speculum Dianae with Dolbadarn Castle* in which foreground figures from classical myth consort with Italian lake scenery, ornamented with a Welsh castle and backed by Snowdon. In their portraits of Dolbadarn Castle neither Wilson nor Sandby quite realises Gilpin's view of the lonely tower as 'an emblem of solitude'. That was left to Turner. The finest expressions of the desolate, Sublime spirit of this region were to come in his watercolour studies of the scene in the 1790s, culminating in the 1800 oil *Dolbadern Castle*, his Diploma piece for the Royal Academy (fig. 41). Here the very low viewpoint is topographically necessary in order to position the ruined tower on the high horizon where it is strongly silhouetted. Turner associates this 'emblem of solitude' with one of the heroes of Welsh history in some lines of his own verse:

> How awful is the silence of the waste,
> Where nature lifts her mountains to the sky.
> Majestic solitude, behold the tower,
> Where hopeless OWEN, long imprison'd, pin'd,
> And wrung his hands for liberty, in vain.[54]

The reference is presumably to Owen Goch, brother of Llewelyn the Last, who for a while led the resistance to Edward I's invasion of Wales. Owen was imprisoned in Dolbadarn for twenty years. Turner's subject, then, has an analogous relationship with the tradition of the last of the Bards, and is a celebration of the martyrs to Welsh liberty. But the ruined tower is the *prison*, not the embodiment of the spirit of liberty, even though in formal terms it occupies the same dramatic, cliff-top prominence as does the Bard in the various paintings of the legend. Turner's painting renders the scene in terms of his life-long preoccupation with the theme of the 'Fallacies of Hope': thus the hero pined futilely for his freedom over many years, and now not even his barbaric prison survives intact. Nature's desolate wastes dwarf human history, just as the Rosa-esque figures are dwarfed in the painting's composition. How different this is from Sandby's painting, where the confident, urbane tourists survey rather unintimidating mountain scenery in which Dolbadarn seems just an extra, tighter furl in the rock formation.

To the south of Llanberis, Pennant remarked on the noble view of Snowdon's summit from the western end of Llyn Nantlle: 'from this spot Mr. Wilson has favoured us with a view, as magnificent as it is faithful'.[55] This is a reference to Wilson's *Snowdon from Llyn Nantlle* (c. 1765–6), in which the warmly-lit foreground and middle distance feature pastoral and halieutic tranquillity around the un-ruffled lake. There is then an abrupt passage to the contrasted chilly, pyramidal form of Snowdon's summit in the background. The mountain crags seem here to form a protective barrier to this Arcadian idyll.

Gilpin, as we have seen, finds these mountain regions little suited to Picturesque taste. He foregoes what thousands were later to regard as the greatest experience in the North Wales tour, the ascent of Snowdon; and instead quotes at length Pennant's account of his ascent in 1773. Pennant reached the summit after a long, arduous climb on a hot August day:

A vast mist enveloped the whole circuit of the mountain. The prospect down was horrible. It gave an idea of numbers of abysses, concealed by a thick smoke, furiously circulating around us.[56]

This experience of climbing above cloud level befell many later tourists. They lost sight of the earth until the wind cut an opening in the cloud canopy and revealed briefly immense distances and depths. William Sotheby was struck by this weird play of mists and light:

> . . . all beneath
> By vaporous exhalation hid, lies lost
> In darkness; save at once where drifted mists
> Cut by strong gusts of eddying winds, expose
> The transitory scenes . . .[57]

The most thrilling description of such an ascent is by Wordsworth. He climbed Snowdon during his three-weeks' pedestrian tour of North Wales in 1791, and the experience was incorporated into *The Prelude*. Like many other tourists he planned to climb at night so as to be able to view the sunrise from the summit. He set off from the village of Beddgelert, and after contacting the shepherd, 'who by ancient right / Of office is the Stranger's usual guide', began the ascent on a warm night with low cloud:

> Thus might we wear perhaps an hour away,
> Ascending at loose distance each from each,
> And I, as chanced, the foremost of the Band;
> When at my feet the ground appear'd to brighten,
> And with a step or two seem'd brighter still;
> Nor had I time to ask the cause of this,
> For instantly a Light upon the turf
> Fell like a flash: I looked about, and lo!
> The Moon stood naked in the Heavens, at height
> Immense above my head, and on the shore
> I found myself of a huge sea of mist,
> Which, meek and silent, rested at my feet:

41. J. M. W. Turner, *Dolbadern Castle* (1800).
Royal Academy of Arts  London

42. John Skinner, 'The stone against which I rested half way up Snowdon', in his MS journal of a tour to Wales in 1835. Egerton MS 3113. British Library, London

> A hundred hills their dusky backs upheaved
> All over this still Ocean and beyond,
> Far, far beyond, the vapours shot themselves,
> In headlands, tongues, and promontory shapes,
> Into the Sea, the real Sea, that seem'd
> To dwindle, and give up its majesty,
> Usurp'd upon as far as sight could reach.
> Meanwhile, the Moon looked down upon this shew
> In single glory, and we stood, the mist
> Touching our very feet; and from the shore
> At distance not the third part of a mile
> Was a blue chasm; a fracture in the vapour,
> A deep and gloomy breathing-place through which
> Mounted the roar of waters, torrents, streams
> Innumerable, roaring with one voice.[58]

This extraordinary scene features as the climactic episode in the 'growth of a Poet's Mind' because it seemed to Wordsworth to represent the working of the 'mighty Mind', which, 'while it copes with visible shapes hears also / Through vents and openings in the ideal world / The astounding chorus of infinity'. Here the poetic imagination has transmuted a sensational tourist experience into a symbolic account of the way in which the Mind of Nature works upon 'the outward face of things, / As if with an imaginative power'; and this imaginative power is 'in Kind / A Brother of the very Faculty' towards which the Poet's mind is aspiring. The passage magnificently transcends the conventions of Picturesque tour descriptions and sententious moralising on scenic experiences. It bears the same relationship to those stereotypes as does Turner's *Dolbadarn Castle* oil to so many of its pictorial predecessors. Joseph Cradock's sentiments on his arrival at Snowdon's summit typify the stock quasi-Horatian moralising expected in the circumstances: 'the nearer we were to the etherial regions, the more our souls seemed to partake of their purity . . . O that it had been our lot to live among these mountains, un-envied and unknown!'.

Wordsworth's *Prelude* description does not wait for the dawn; but many tourists who trekked through the night (fig. 42) were well rewarded as the sun came up:

Never shall I forget the horror and the pleasure I then felt . . . [The sun] appeared to come forth from the ocean in fiery redness, and like a giant to run his course. A pure azure for a few minutes now displayed itself with refulgent beauty. The clouds were forming fast underneath, and the winds being brisk, soon carried them over head: and with such rapidity were they impelled from the great chasm of Llanberis that they seemed to rise like smoke out of a great furnace.[59]

To complete the Snowdon experience, all one then had to do was to record the visit, with name and date, on a scrap of paper, and wedge it under a stone, some-where on the summit for the amusement and respect of later tourists.

### Aberglaslyn – Vale of Festiniog – Cader Idris

The road south from Snowdon led through fine mountain scenery, particularly at Aberglaslyn Pass and the single-arch bridge thrown across the torrential Glaslyn. There had been a rainstorm the night before Robert Clutterbuck visited the scene, a circumstance greatly to the benefit of the Picturesque tourist: 'in the fervour of heightened expectation we considered the rain, which continued to fall without intermission, instrumental to our pleasures'.[60] The swollen river roaring through this narrow pass challenged the most Sublime landscape models: 'The romantic imagination of Salvator Rosa, was never fired with a more tremendous idea, nor has his extravagant pencil ever produced a bolder precipice.'[61] According to John Byng, even the venerable goats gazing down from these Rosa-esque precipices 'added lustre to the horror'.

The journey from the bridge over the mountains and into the Vale of Festiniog revealed a landscape 'shaken and overturned by the powerful operation of internal convulsion, and from which all animated nature has fled dispersed and alarmed'.[62] It seemed to Cradock 'the noblest specimen of the Finely Horrid, the eye can possibly behold . . . the last Approach to the mansion of Pluto through the regions of Despair'.[63] When Robert Fulke Greville toured Wales in 1792, with his artists Julius Caesar Ibbetson and John 'Warwick' Smith, the company experienced a tremendous storm on this road. Both Ibbetson and Smith (fig. 43) painted the

43. John 'Warwick' Smith, 'Actual Occurence, on the Steepest Ascent of the Mountain Road ...'.
National Library of Wales, Aberystwyth

scene in which the Greville phaeton is threatening to roll backwards down the steep path. The horses rear up at the lightning flash and, in one painting, a passenger is trying to wedge stone brakes behind the wheels. It is a fine exercise in the Sublime manner – dramatic contrasts in the lighting, sharp angles and precipices, the river below in torrent and the sense of the overwhelming power of the elements accentuated by the frailty of the phaeton and the figures.

The Vale of Festiniog was a most welcome relief after such travelling. It had already been much admired by travellers when Joseph Cradock arrived there in 1770. He suggested that its most pleasing quality was precisely 'the striking contrast, between this little vale and the horrid country round it'. Traditionally the Vale competed with Clwyd and Llangollen for Picturesque beauty, though John Byng thought it 'puff'd off beyond its deservings, by the pens of fanciful writers'. Wyndham recommended the Vale as a charming retreat for the painter, where nothing was wanting but fine weather and a serene sky 'to afford as rich studies as the neighbourhood of Tivoli or Frescati'.[64] Lord Lyttelton arrived there in July 1756 and described the country as the most perfectly beautiful of all he had seen. As in Wilson's painting of *Snowdon from Llyn Nantlle*, the high mountains enclosing the Vale 'seemed placed there to guard this charming retreat against any invaders'. To prove how healthy the Vale was, he mentioned the case of a Welsh farmer who died there not long before, at the age of 105, leaving behind him

44. Cornelius Varley, 'Cader Idris from Llanelltyd. N.W.' (1803).
Courtauld Institute, London

forty-four children by his three wives: '800 persons descended from his body attended his funeral.' In not quite the same breath, Lyttelton urged his brother the Bishop of Carlisle to settle there and renew his youth.

A journey of about fifteen miles to the south of the Vale brought the tourist to Llanelltyd at the head of the Mawddach estuary. The views here offered some exquisite compositions, with middle-distance bridge and towering mountain background. Here is one enthusiastic description of the tripartite composition, which compares interestingly with Cornelius Varley's 1803 view (fig. 44):

Setting myself down by the road side, I endeavoured to take the outline in order to assist my recollection hereafter. The Church and College of Llaneltid, standing on a gentle declivity, forming a beautiful foreground; the Bridge, the river, Mr. Vaughan's house, on a well wooded hill, with neat white cottages interspersed, occupy the middle distance; Cader Idris rises with unrivaled grandeur in the background.[65]

At nearly three thousand feet, Cader Idris was indeed rivalled only by Snowdon; and in many ways it was a more intimidating mountain, with its dark, slaty composition, sheer precipices and mysterious black lakes. 'Mr. Wilson, the English Claude, has conferred celebrity to this spot, by his pencil',[66] wrote one tourist, in reference to Wilson's *Cader Idris, Llyn-y-Cau* (c.1765–7) (fig. 45). Wilson's view was of one particular lake, 'overlooked by steep cliffs in such a manner as to resemble the crater of a volcano',[67] wrote Arthur Aiken. Craig-y-Cau, the sheer

45. Richard Wilson, *Cader Idris, Llyn-y-Cau* (c. 1765–7).
Tate Gallery, London

46. Anon, 'The Road leading to the top of Caer Idris. Aug. 12. 1802', from sketchbook Add. MS 24003. British Library, London

cliff which towers above the lake, 'from its spiry points and deep precipices . . . has assumed an appearance not much unlike the age-worn front of some antient cathedral'.[68] Wilson's painting was regarded as an excellent likeness, a tribute which will puzzle those who know the scenery. Wilson's view has caught the most distinctive features but drastically reduced scale and altered proportions, so that it looks more like a toy facsimile of a lunar landscape.

The climb to the summit was enlivened (sometimes made more arduous) by the local guides, who seem to have been eccentric characters, apart from the veteran Robin Edwards. It was presumably Edwards whom Henry Wigstead met, and who told him that he had taken Wilson, Gainsborough and most other artists over the last 30–40 years up to the summit (fig. 46). Another guide, who was obsessed with impressing his dignity on the tourists, was Edward Jones, a garrulous schoolmaster, who caused Bingley some amusement by his attempts to show off his learning and abilities as they trudged up the mountain. Thomas Clutterbuck was conducted by a Mr Pughe in 1798, who prided himself upon his genealogy which he traced back more than 300 years, and tried to persuade anyone who would listen (and halfway up Cader Idris there was little alternative) that he was related to all the Princes of Wales.[69] To Richard Warner he announced that his research had confirmed that 'his race had flowed in an uninterrupted stream for no less than three thousand years'.[70] This guide had renamed the Craig-y-Cau

143

47. Samuel Ireland, 'Market at Aberystwyth', from *Picturesque Views on the River Wye* (1797).
British Library, London

summit 'Pughe's Pinnacle' and was probably responsible for the stone-built hut
and fireplace there, providing a retreat for the tourists while they waited for the
dawn.

*Aberystwyth – Hafod – Devil's Bridge*

The road from Dolgellau to Aberystwyth passed through Machynlleth (two miles
west of Penegoes, the birthplace of Richard Wilson) and then went down past
Plynlimon to the coast. Near the end of the eighteenth century, the discovery of a
chalybeate spring promoted Aberystwyth's reputation as a fashionable spa, and it
became known, briefly, as the Brighthelmstone of Wales. The beauty of its natural
setting had been celebrated as early as 1749, in Richard Rolt's *Cambria*:

> The wide horizon circling to the view,
> Far as the visual ray can pierce, serene
> And blue, shines lovely
> . . . how thick the tawny fields
> Proud of their culmiferous crop? . . .
> The frondose woods how still? Save where the groans
> Of dying DRYADS sound, by the sharp axe
> Cleft to the vital core and crashing down.
> The sun-tann'd reapers range the furrow'd ridge.[71]

This description of strenuous rural activity is incompatible with one aspect of Aberystwyth much remarked on, the near proverbial laziness of its inhabitants: 'The Welsh Women appear to be the only people that are active the men are lazy, indolent and leave everything to be done by their wives so that, the Women are Men, and Men Women.'[72] To this laziness was to be attributed the notoriously insanitary conditions of the area. A 1738 visitor remarked that 'Necessary Houses are the only Places reputed needless here.'[73] Little had changed by the end of the century:

The people in the Country, not even opulent Farmers, never build any Temples to Cloacina, but sacrifice to that Goddess in the open air, the place generally appropriated for the Altar is the gable end of the House, and therefore it often happens that you are rudely taken by the Nose on your approach to it, and to compleat the business the Pig Stye is frequently attached to the other end.[74]

The only way for many to enjoy the North Wales tour was to keep administering the pomander or 'profuse libations of lavender water.'

From 1794 onwards Aberystwyth and its neighbourhood acquired a range of Picturesque associations. The most striking architectural feature of the town itself was the triangular embattled Castle House built by John Nash for Uvedale Price in 1794, the year of the publication of Price's *Essay on the Picturesque*. It is featured in the background to Samuel Ireland's 1797 picture of Aberystwyth market, with what looks like an 'Anterlute' in progress (fig. 47). This neo-Gothic summer residence stood appropriately near the few remains ('too ruinous for the pencil')[75] of the town's thirteenth-century castle. Price treated the precincts as a part of his garden, and introduced gravel walks among the ruins. With Price at Aberystwyth in the summer months, Payne Knight's cousin Thomas Johnes a few miles inland developing his grand estate at Hafod, and the Devil's Bridge and Falls of Mynach nearby, the area was rich in Picturesque interest, and a fitting conclusion to the North Wales tour.

The house and grounds of Hafod had been created in the mid-1780s deliberately to attract the tourists.[76] The owner Thomas Johnes had the advantage of the advice of both Uvedale Price and Payne Knight, who made frequent visits to the estate. John Nash was called in for consultation, and was probably responsible for the design of the two long wings of the Gothic mansion, though the architect commissioned for the house as a whole was Thomas Baldwin of Bath. The landscaping of the estate was on a colossal scale. Between 1795 and 1801 2,065,000 trees were planted. Garden and pasture were ornamented with peacocks and merino sheep. Miles of carefully calculated walks led across open mountain country, through grottoes and by waterfalls. It has been suggested that the Hafod scenery, natural and artificial, contributed to the imagery of *Kubla Khan*, as Coleridge and Hucks walked through its grounds in 1793. Samuel Rogers visited it in 1791, and in the following year, Robert Fulke Greville brought Ibbetson and 'Warwick' Smith for a few days' stay. Fifteen aquatints after watercolours

48. 'A Map of part of the Estate of Thomas Johnes Esq.: MP at Havod in the County of Cardigan', engraved by William Blake, from George Cumberland's *An Attempt to Describe Hafod* (1796). National Library of Wales, Aberystwyth

by Smith were published in James Edward Smith's *A Tour of Hafod* in 1810. Turner arrived here in 1798, and his graceful watercolour portrait of the house (if indeed it is Hafod depicted), backed by mountains half dissolved in mist, is one of the most evocative records.

Hafod was, literally, put on the map by William Blake in 1796 (fig. 48). He engraved a folding map of the estate, with dotted lines showing the walks, and stars marking the viewpoints, for George Cumberland's popular guide, *An Attempt to Describe Hafod* (1796). Cumberland had first visited Hafod in 1782. His travels over the next twelve years took him to the Alps, the Apennines, the Adriatic and the Rhine, 'where, though in search of beauty, I never, I feel, saw anything so fine, never so many pictures concentered in one spot' as at Hafod. This concentration of 'so many pictures' is the Picturesque tourist's highest praise, a way of quantifying natural beauty. Johnes had certainly taken great trouble in composing his pictures. He had himself superintended much of the re-landscaping, sometimes wading up to his waist in the river to find the right position for a viewing seat or grotto. Even a stretch of open grazing ground had been 'formed with due attention to picturesque inequality.'[77] Taking Hafod and its neighbourhood altogether, Cumberland finds 'Sweetest interchange of hill and valley, rivers, woods, and plains, and falls with forest crown'd, rocks, dens, and caves': Milton's Eden again – this time transplanted in deepest Cardiganshire.

From Cumberland's descriptions, one gathers that Johnes concentrated on offering the tourist thrilling grandeur, to a degree matched by scarcely any other landscaped estate in Britain:

. . . no language can image out the sublimity of the scenes; which, without quite arriving at a sentiment of aversion, produces, in the empassioned soul, all those thrilling sensations of terror, which ever arise from majestical, yet gloomy exhibitions.

The aesthetic calculations were of the finest: 'thrilling sensations of terror' which are *just* short of aversion exactly met Burke's prescriptions for the Sublime. The 'Robber's Cave' on the upper falls to the south-east of the house had precisely this sensational effect, as Benjamin Malkin experienced:

As we creep along the winding and slippery path, a dark hollow in the rock attracts our notice on the right; the din of falling water reverberates through the cave, and makes us hesitate about committing ourselves to its damp and gloomy recesses. By a simple but successful trial of art, the termination of the passage forwards seems to disappoint our hopes, when, on turning suddenly to the left, a rude aperture admits the light, and a sparkling sheet of water, in front of the aperture, urges its perpendicular fall from the rock above, into a deep hole below the cave.[78]

Malkin was disappointed to hear from his artist that this scene (which can still be visited) could not be adequately depicted: scale would be lost, and the chief sensation – the contrast between the dark station and the brilliant fall of water – was unmanageable on paper.

Since Burke had given Stonehenge as an example of a building which excites the idea of the Sublime, Johnes could properly include in the garden architecture of his Cambrian paradise an ancient temple or two. Cumberland found a superb site for 'a rude imitation' of a Druid temple on a smooth mound not far from the church of Eglwys Newyd, where 'a bard might indeed sit, and draw all his fine images from nature.' A Druid circle was, accordingly, built there.

A road led out of the estate to the north, and within three miles the tourist arrived at the Devil's Bridge and Falls of Mynach, where the Sublime and the Picturesque mingled in some of the finest scenery in Wales. Gilpin did not visit the area, but nevertheless was prepared to offer his authoritative advice on the best viewpoints, based on another published account of the scenery. This cavalier attitude quite exhilarated another tourist with contempt:

> Here ends a description of *the Devil's bridge*, curtailed and *picturesquefyed* from a foundling journal, that accidently dropped into the hands of a *Salisbury prebend*, who, though an original in sketching landscapes, has no objection to tint over the outlines of others, when it saves him the trouble of forming any of his own.[79]

For the Picturesque tourists there were at that time two bridges (the present, viable one was built in 1901) which spanned the narrow gorge from which the river Mynach falls some three hundred feet. Legend attributed the lower bridge, which some mistook for a natural formation, to the work of the Devil, completed in a single night. One 1778 tourist, while granting that it was 'most pleasingly horrible', wished that the 'cloven-footed Monarch' had employed the following day in making a good road to it.[80] The roads were bad enough, but access to the best viewpoints was even worse and necessitated hiring a local guide. This was usually the proprietor of the neighbouring Hafod Arms. An alternative guide, disconcertingly casual in her reception of the tourist, was a woman who lived in a nearby hut, built of dirt and weeds and with a tree growing out of it. This exquisitely Picturesque structure consisted of two apartments:

> . . . in one . . . I found a horse and a cow, and the other the whole family of pigs, ducks, dogs, cats, men, women and children . . . In one corner . . . sat the jolly damsel who was to conduct us to the bridge. She accosted us in broken English, begged we would be seated upon the bed, which served as a table and a chair to the whole family, and promised to attend us as soon as she had finished peeling her turnips. I assisted her in this operation, and we soon finished them all, upon which she dropped a thick woollen petticoat, put on her beaver, curtseyed, and said she was ready.[81]

The Falls and Bridge were best viewed, by Picturesque criteria, from below. The thickly wooded sides of the gorge added to 'the most awful sensations' inspired by the 'rocks, the variety of foliage, the gloomy horrors of the yawning chasm, constrasted by the white foam of the gushing torrents' which had worn the rocks into 'shapes strange and grotesque'. The eerie lighting in John Sell Cotman's 1801 watercolour captures the atmosphere more subtly than any other painting (fig. 49). In search of the right Picturesque viewpoint, Richard Warner clambered down the bank with his sketching materials, slipped and fell some fifteen feet. On his return

49. John Sell Cotman, *The Devil's Bridge, Cardigan* (1801).
Victoria and Albert Museum, London

to the Hafod Arms, 'horror was so strongly marked in my countenance, that my companions, for a few moments, scarcely recollected their brother tourist'.[82] The Bridge and Falls deterred even those who took the most elaborate precautions. We might end the North Wales tour with the spectacle of one imperious lady sketcher as she sallied forth from the Hafod Arms one morning:

... with a tin frame as a drawing board to keep her paper smooth, Cecily and Mark [maid and footman], following tandem, with each a portfolio under their arms ... to take the romantic views at the place ... Madam was too timorous to hazard her delicate frame in those situations necessary to answer her purpose. By the aid of Ropes etc. she did descend the steep at Devil's bridge but found the situation too damp to risque her health by tarrying to delineate.[83]

\*    \*    \*

The devotion to Picturesque principles, such as this lady exemplifies, the willingness to endure discomfort and even pain in order to 'take the romantic views', was something quite new in travel; and it is not surprising that other, less dedicated tourists (quite apart from the local inhabitants) were astonished by such antics as those of the lady sketcher. There was a sense of great achievement, of hardship overcome for people who had toiled up Snowdon or Cader Idris to see the dawn from the summit, or caught a heavy cold after an hour or two's sketching in the spray of a fine waterfall. There was too the particular attraction of being in places where, for good reason, few others had visited, of venturing beyond the pale of civilisation. The general verdict that Wales seemed at least a century behind England changed from being an insult and a deterrent to being a positive incentive for tourists by the end of the century.

Though it had its Sublime moments, the Wye Valley tour was not hazardous. North Wales certainly was. The search for the Picturesque may have been launched in the expectation of returning home safely with a bulging portfolio or an elegant journal fluent in all the fashionable descriptive vocabulary; but many returned with far more than could be expressed in Picturesque language. Of these a handful were inspired to fashion a new vocabulary. Wordsworth and Turner, as we have seen, both undertook the Picturesque tour of North Wales in their twenties and, in their poetry and painting, one can see their transcendence of the Picturesque conventions from which they started.

The Revd Richard Warner is representative of many who had trained themselves to regard the succession of landscape views as more or less correct compositions of various natural forms according to Picturesque principles. He had indeed served in Gilpin's Boldre parish in the 1790s and greatly respected his superior. But by the end of his Welsh tour he, like others, had begun to realise how a landscape with such awe-inspiring natural forms had 'a strong tendency to affect the human mind (naturally timid) with superstitious fears and whimsical notions'. The presence of the Bards, as reminders of an ancient religion, only reinforced this tendency. As a clergyman himself, Warner can hardly encourage this, but his curiosity is roused and his sympathetic interest engaged:

... nor do we feel ourselves inclined to reprobate the *mild superstition* ... It is a principle that arises from the feelings and affections of nature; and is, at all events, more amiable, than the cold *philosophism* of the present day, which disbelieves every thing, which contracts and petrifies the heart, deadens the affections, and destroys all the finer sensibilities of the soul.[84]

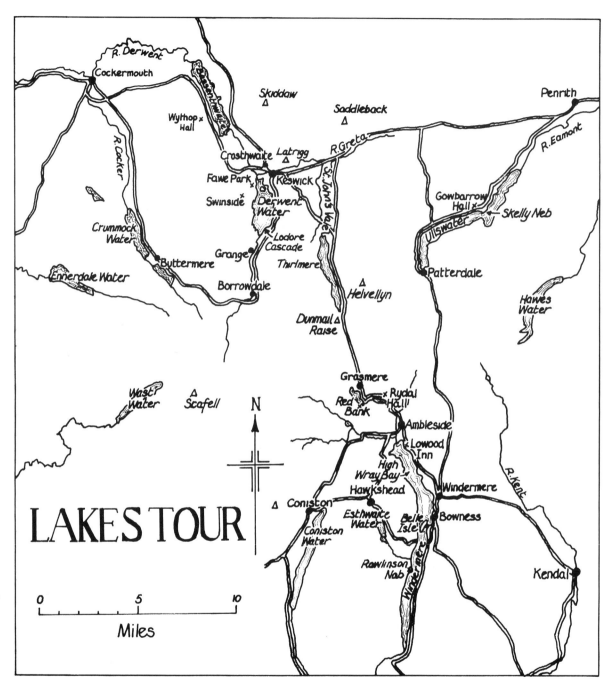

Map 3. The Lakes

# VII

## The tour to the Lakes

'There is a *Rage for the Lakes*', reported Hester Lynch Piozzi in 1789: 'we travel to them, we row upon them, we write about them, & about them'.[1] From the 1770s onward, the lake scenery of Cumberland and Westmorland was a serious challenge to the aesthetic supremacy of the European Grand Tour:

We penetrate the *Glacieres*, traverse the *Rhone* and the *Rhine*, whilst our own domestic lakes of *Ulswater*, *Keswick* and *Wyndermere* exhibit scenes in so sublime a stile, with such beautiful colourings of rock, wood and water, backed with so tremendous a disposition of mountains, that if they do not fairly take the lead of all the views in Europe, yet they are indisputably such as no English traveller should leave behind.[2]

In this competitive spirit Richard Cumberland dedicated his *Ode to the Sun* (1776) to the eminent portrait painter George Romney: 'Whilst you was engaged in contemplating those wonderful productions of ancient art, which ITALY is enriched with, I was tracing the ruder beauties of Nature in a domestic tour thro' the mountainous parts of WESTMORELAND and CUMBERLAND'.[3]

In the summer months, coaches of all shapes and sizes rattled along the shores of the Lakes, struggled up steep passes, and now and again, waited at the road-side while passengers jumped out to take a quick sketch of a bewildered shepherd. The Lakes themselves were scarcely less congested. Packed pleasure-boats loitered at viewpoints on Ullswater or Windermere, now and then firing off cannon to enable the tourists to listen to the succession of echoes, and then moving on to other vantage points. William Hutchinson recorded one such scene:

As a gentleman said to Robin Partridge the day after we were upon Windermere, 'Good God! how delightful! – how charming! – I could live here for ever! – Row on, row on, row on, row on;' and after passing one hour of exclamations upon the Lake, and half an hour at Ambleside, he ordered his horses into his phaeton, and flew off to take (I doubt not) an equally *flying* view of Derwent water.

It is not surprising that after some initial amusement, the natives of these regions became baffled and irritated by the search for the Picturesque. In his youth, Wordsworth lodged for a while near Derwentwater, 'under the roof of a shrewd and sensible woman, who more than once exclaimed in my hearing, "Bless me! folk are always talking about prospects: when I was young there never was sic a thing neamed" '.[4] The aural counterpart to Picturesque experiences – the cannon echoes – must have been even more vexing for the local inhabitants. The Earl of Surrey's boat on Ullswater, equipped with twelve brass swivel guns, would be taken out to a certain point on the lake just past Skelly Nab. Here the cannon would be aimed towards Gowbarrow Hall or a little above it, and discharged. After the immediate echoes had died, wrote Hutchinson:

> The sound of every distant water-fall was heard, but for an instant only; for the momentary stillness was interrupted by returning echo on the hills behind us; where the report was repeated like a peal of thunder bursting over our heads, continuing for several seconds, flying from haunt to haunt, till once more the sound gradually declined; – again the voice of water-falls possessed the interval.

Sometimes cannon fire could be alternated with martial music from two French horns, also taken on board. These echoes were subtly distorted as they played around different land forms and became translated into whole orchestras:

> ... here the breathings of the organ were imitated, there the bassoon with clarinets; – in this place from the harsher sounding cliffs, the cornet; – in that from the wooded creek, amongst the caverns and the trilling water falls, you seemed to hear the soft-toned lute accompanied with the languishing strains of enamoured nymphs; whilst in the copse and grove was still retained the music of the horns. – All this vast theatre, seemed to be possessed by innumerable aerial beings, who breathed coelestial harmony.

At the turn of the century Wordsworth expressed, through a character in one of his poems, the feelings of these Lakelanders who had been used to their country as a working country, which exacted too much time and energy from their lives to allow them the luxuries of tourism:

> These Tourists, heaven preserve us! needs must live
> A profitable life: some glance along,
> Rapid and gay, as if the earth were air,
> And they were butterflies to wheel about
> Long as the summer lasted.[5]

Such carefree travel was, partly, a reflection of the great improvement in the roads in the last third of the century. The threat of accident which could strand the traveller for hours amidst formidable scenery was a source of much terror. As a correspondent to *The Gentleman's Magazine* complained in 1752, the tourist is likely to spend most of his time 'considering how to steer the motions of his beast, and what to do in case he dislocates or breaks a limb, when at the same time he ought to contemplate with raptures the richest scenes of nature'.[6] For Defoe, travelling in the early part of the century, the country was 'the wildest, most barren and frightful of any that I have passed over in England, or even in Wales itself'.[7] But by the end of the century the tourists were becoming complacent about such formidable scenery. Good roads were introduced. Those in search of Sublime experiences now preferred the more daunting routes through the country: 'That you may see and have a faint idea of the Alps, and think you have performed as much as Hanibal, be sure to start as soon after nine a.m. as possible',[8] to cross Derwent Fells: in these remote regions Johnson Grant found no 'disturbing traces of cultivation . . . none of the pretticisms of inclosures'. Now it is cultivation rather than wilderness which disturbs the tourist. As on the other tours, the appearance of primitive simplicity, both in the face of the countryside and in the character of its inhabitants, beguiled the visitors. 'None can immerge themselves in this country of the lakes', remarked Ann Radcliffe, 'without being struck by the superior simplicity and modesty of the people'.

These later tourists, with their Hannibal aspirations, literally took the fells in their stride. On 5 August 1799 Coleridge climbed Scafell, notebook in hand: 'on a nice Stone Table am I now at this moment writing to you – between 2 and 3 o'Clock as I guess  surely the first Letter ever written from the Top of Sca'Fell!'[9] The character in Wordsworth's poem who deplored the invasion of these frivolous tourists was particularly struck by this kind of activity:

> Perched on the forehead of a jutting crag,
> Pencil in hand and book upon the knee, [Some]
> Will look and scribble, scribble on and look,
> Until a man might travel twelve stout miles,
> Or reap an acre of his neighbour's corn.[10]

It is difficult to tell from this whether the tourist is sketching or writing. Either way, he seems to be recording, *in situ*, after the manner recommended by Thomas Gray: 'Half a word fixed upon or near the spot, is worth a cart-load of recollection'.[11] The ascent of Scafell, Skiddaw or Helvellyn was as much a part of the Lakeland tour, as the ascent of Snowdon or Cader Idris was on the North Wales tour. But the conquest of mountains was not the chief attraction. The great feature on this Picturesque tour to Cumberland and Westmorland was lake scenery and extraordinary visual effects of the kind observed by Robert Southey:

It was a bright evening, the sun shining, and a few white clouds hanging motionless in the sky. There was not a breath of air stirring, not a wave, – a ripple or wrinkle on the lake, so that it became like a great mirror, and represented the shores, mountains, sky and clouds so vividly that there was not the slightest appearance of water. The great mountain-opening being reversed in the shadow became a huge arch, and through that magnificent portal the long vale was seen between mountains and bounded by mountain beyond mountain, all this in the water, the distance perfect as in the actual scene, – the single houses standing far up in the vale, the smoke from their chimneys – every thing the same, the shadow and the substances joining at their bases, so that it was impossible to distinguish where the reality ended and the image began. As we stood on the shore, heaven and the clouds and the sun seemed lying under us; we were looking down into a sky, as heavenly and beautiful as that overhead, and the range of mountains, having one line of summit under our feet and another above us, were suspended between two firmaments.

The lake as a great mirror (fig. 50) was inevitably a source of fascination for those who had developed the Picturesque habit of viewing natural scenery in the

Claude Glass. The Glass modified and reversed the landscape view, but it could not invert it as the lake so spectacularly did; and anyway no portable contrivance could compete with the scale of the lake mirror, as Gilpin noted:

If an artificial mirror, a few inches long, placed opposite to a door, or a window, occasions often very pleasing reflections; how noble must be the appearance, when an area of many leagues in circumference, is formed into one vast mirror; and this mirror surrounded by a combination of great, and beautiful, objects?

This was the great attraction of lake scenery, the value of which, according to Gilpin, 'arises rather from the idea of *magnificence*, than of *variety*':

A quick succession of imagery is necessary in scenes of less grandeur, where little beauties are easily scanned: but scenes, like these, demand contemplation. These rich volumes of nature, like the works of established authors, will bear a frequent perusal.

Although magnificence predominates, the painter – as distinct from the contemplative reader of these 'rich volumes' – will still wish for some animating variety in his scene. In this context Gilpin reminds his readers of the attractive fragility of these vast, natural mirror surfaces:

When the *whole* lake is tranquil, a gentle perturbation will arise in some distant part, from no apparent cause, from a breath of air, which nothing else can feel, and creeping softly on, communicate the tremulous shudder with exquisite sensibility over half the surface.

He judged that it was the effect of this kind of 'tremulous shudder', rather than the flawless mirror surface, which gave the most Picturesque form to the lake: 'it affords the painter an opportunity of throwing in those lengthened lights and shades, which give the greatest variety and clearness to water'. The variety of effects of light on water, especially on these large, land-enclosed stretches of water, fascinated Coleridge on his first arrival at Ullswater:

A little below PlaceFell a large Slice of calm silver – above this a bright ruffledness, or atomic sportiveness – motes in the sun? – Vortices of flies? – how shall I express the Banks waters all fused Silver, that House too its slates rainwet silver in the sun, & its shadows running down in the water like a column . . . the two island Rocks in the Lake . . . the one scarce visible in the shadow-coloured Slip now bordered by the melted Silver – the other nearer to me, likewise in the glossy shadow . . . How the scene changes – What tongues of Light shoot out from the Banks![12]

Most Picturesque descriptive prose seems leaden-footed by comparison with this exhilarated effort to catch the changing lights. Stylistically, Coleridge's description is remote from eighteenth-century conventions and much closer to later nineteenth-century developments in the pictorial or literary responses to natural scenery, to French Impressionism perhaps, or to Gerard Manley Hopkins' rapid notations of 'inscape'. Gilpin's prose always has a deliberate, measured construction, even when he is obviously excited by a landscape. This is analogous to his stress again and again on *composition* in painting, on the controlled coherence of

50. Francis Towne, *Lake Windermere*.
Yale Center for British Art, Paul Mellon Collection

the overall design in a landscape. But in the Coleridge passage we have lost any sense of the larger composition. He is not interested in side-screens or the relation between foreground and background, but in fugitive light effects. His prose responds to the task – 'how shall I express' – by collapsing formal syntax and discharging a volley of similes – 'like a column', 'melted Silver', 'tongues of Light' – knowing that at least some will strike the enchanting, elusive target.

Lake scenery was also rich in atmospheric variety. Gilpin had pointed out England's advantage in this respect over Italy's unrelieved clarity of distances: 'Our grosser atmosphere . . . exhibits various modes; some of which are in themselves more beautiful, than the most distinct vision'. James Clarke's *Survey of the Lakes* (1787) endorses this peculiar beauty: 'Clouds and vapours intersperse varieties of aerial scenery, that change as it were by magic, impressing on the objects within their effect a hue and cast of appearance that scarce seems earthly'.

Each of the great Lakes had its own peculiar character, which the tourist who was educated in the Picturesque would learn to associate with one of the three familiar masters of landscape painting, Claude, Poussin (usually Dughet) and Rosa. Thus, for example, according to Ann Radcliffe's analysis, Windermere was distinguished by 'Diffusiveness, stately beauty, and, at the upper end, magnificence'; and, like Coniston, its leisurely expanse, with no abrupt angles, and its border of grand but not thrillingly Sublime fells, suited it for the 'tender and elegant' touches of Claude's brush. William Hutchinson in his popular *Excursion to the Lakes* (1774) judged that Poussin's paintings 'describe the nobleness of Hullswater'. Now and again Ullswater was awarded to Claude, and Windermere to Poussin, but there was an impressive consensus on Derwentwater. Its fantastic wildness and romantic beauty could be rendered only by Salvator Rosa. These identifications offered a kind of guideline to the amateur painter as he selected and sketched his viewpoints.

The Picturesque tour of the Lakes was institutionalised with the publication of Thomas West's *Guide to the Lakes* in 1778, which was revised and enlarged by William Cockin, a Kendal schoolmaster, in 1780 and had gone through seven editions by the end of the century. West is catering specifically for those who practice the 'noble art' of landscape painting, 'in which the genius of *Britain* rivals that of ancient *Greece* and modern *Rome*'. The artist is invited to the Lakes to contemplate, 'in Alpine scenery, finished in nature's highest tints, the pastoral and rural landscape, exhibited in all their stiles, the soft, the rude, the romantic, and the sublime'. The *Guide* led tourists to specific viewpoints on the Lakes, known as 'Stations', which had been recommended by earlier visitors to the country, and in particular by Thomas Gray, Arthur Young, Dr John Brown and Dr John Dalton. The last two were among the first visitors to record their impressions of the Lakes in a Picturesque idiom. Dalton wrote a descriptive poem on the mines at Whitehaven, which was published in 1754. Towards the end of that poem he surveys Derwentwater, registering 'wonder and delight' at a scene which presented 'A pleasing, but an awful sight'. The other description, frequently referred to by later tourists, was a letter by Dr John Brown, written probably in 1753 and first published, in part, in 1767. Brown also concentrates on Derwentwater's scenery, declaring that it could only be done justice to by 'the united powers of *Claude, Salvator*, and *Poussin*'. Brown's letter is usually referred to as the first distinct evidence of a romantic and Picturesque response to the country of the Lakes; but we may also recall that rapturous tribute to the region in 1748, in Gilpin's *Dialogue . . . at Stow*.

In 1769 Arthur Young toured the Lakes. His principal object on this and his other tours was to record the 'present State of AGRICULTURE, MANU-FACTURES and POPULATION'[13] in Britain. But, as we shall see later, in his remarks on Derwentwater and Windermere, he had a very keen, educated eye for scenic beauty. In the same year, Gray visited the Lakes. The 'Journal' of his tour was published in 1775. Gilpin, who was born at Scaleby near Carlisle, made his tour in 1772, but his *Observations* on the Lakes were not published until 1786.

In tracing the Picturesque tour of the Lakes I shall take West's advice on the best route and make the approach from the south:

By this course, the lakes lie in an order more agreeable to the eye, and grateful to the imagination. The change of scenes is from what is pleasing, to what is surprising; from the delicate touches of *Claude*, verified on *Coniston* lake, to the noble scenes of *Poussin* exhibited on *Windermere-water*, and from these to the stupendous romantic ideas of *Salvator Rosa*, realised on the lake of *Derwent*.

### Morecambe Bay – Coniston – Windermere

The approach to the Lakes from Lancaster involved crossing the Morecambe Bay sands at low tide, an experience which 'cannot but suggest a series of ideas of a more sublime kind than those of rural elegance', noted William Cockin. Instead of observing, as West had recommended, the unfolding mainland scenery as the coach trundled across the sands, the tourist would find it much more stimulating to let his imagination loose on the fact that in a few hours time the whole expanse would be buried beneath fathoms of water. Ann Radcliffe entered 'these vast and desolate plains' early one morning in 1795, before the sea mists had wholly evaporated:

. . . it was sublimely interesting to watch the heavy vapours beginning to move, then rolling in lengthening volumes over the scene, and, as they gradually dissipated, discovering through their veil the various objects they had concealed – fishermen with carts and nets stealing along the margin of the tide, little boats putting off from the shore, and, the view still enlarging as the vapours expanded, the main sea itself softening into the horizon, with here and there a dim sail moving in the hazy distance. The wide desolation of the sands, on the left, was animated only by some horsemen riding remotely in groups towards Lancaster, along the winding edge of the water, and by a muscle-fisher in his cart trying to ford the channel we were approaching.

The description is finely managed: Mrs Radcliffe's long sentences slowly unroll like the heavy mists, and the figures, precisely caught in movement, are intermittently introduced to 'animate' the enlarging scene.

The first of the Lakes on West's itinerary was Coniston. Here he guided the tourist to three particular Stations along the eastern shore. The finest view, he thought, was to be taken from Station III, about half a mile south of Brantwood:

> After crossing the common, where grows a picturesque yew tree on the right hand, and a small peninsula rushes into the lake on the left, crowned with a single tree, enter the grove and pass a gate and bridge that crosses a small rivulet. – Look for a fragment of dark coloured rock on the margin of the lake, and near it will be found the best stand for the artist to take the finest view on the lake.

This view is composed as follows:

> Looking across the lake, by the south end that conceals *Coniston-hall*, and over the cultivated tract that rises behind it, between two swells of rocks, a cataract will meet the eye, issuing from the bosom of the mountains.

This is almost a direct line steadily ascending towards the background past an ancient Hall in the middle distance, buried in trees, then rising meadows, the rocky protrusions above them, the waterfall (probably from Leven Water, about 3 miles distant), and up and beyond into the 'bosom' of Coniston fells. From this angle, only one side-screen intrudes: 'on the right . . . wooded sloping rock, and over it the road [passing Brantwood] is catched slanting along'. The 'near-foreground' is a large expanse of lake; and in the far distance, 'behind the immediate mountains, the *Westmoreland* fells are seen towering to the clouds.'

It can be seen from this characteristic introduction to a Station that West is not really concerned to evoke, but simply to describe topographically. It is difficult from this description to see quite why the view is so fine, except that it contains all the proper Picturesque ingredients, properly disposed: ancient building barely glimpsed, pastoral land, mountain Sublimity, and water which in one place is fully animated, and in another tranquil. West has already identified Coniston with the 'delicate touches of Claude', and his choice of Stations presumably reflects this association. He describes the views on this lake as beautiful and Picturesque, but lacking the surprise or terror of the Sublime: the mountains are 'bold and steep without the projecting precipice, the overhanging rock, or pendent cliff.' These were to come as the other lakes were met in an ascending scale of aesthetic delight.

The journey from Coniston to Lake Windermere could include Esthwaite Water, the little lake which seemed to Ann Radcliffe to 'glide through the quiet privacy of pleasure-grounds; so fine is the turf on its banks, so elegant its copses, and such an air of peace and retirement prevails over it.' The *Vale of Esthwaite* was the title of Wordsworth's earliest topographical poem, modelled on Milton's *Il Penseroso*: 'Lone wandering oft by Esthwaite's [stream] / My soul has felt the mystic dream'.[14] The poem is a ragbag of moods and scenes with an insistent and rather shrill 'graveyard school' sensationalism, designed presumably as a lively contrast to the placid realities of Esthwaite. At the northern end of the lake was

Hawkshead: 'its milk-white tower, and several cots and groves which project this way, together with the overhanging trees, and mountains, form a most compleat group for the pencil of the Artist'.[15]

Windermere, the largest of all the Lakes, was impossible to absorb in one glance; and therefore the choice of Station was very important. West recommended five (fig. 51): one at each end of the lake's largest island, Belle Isle, one on Rawlinson's Nab (a promontory in the southern section of the lake), one at a point just above the Ferry house on the western side, and, his fifth Station, a panoramic view from the hill behind Bowness. James Clarke recommended another view, from a point on the lake just off the western shore, a little below High Wray Bay:

This situation is rather too low, but not much: I took a drawing there once, (but have lost it) some of the company fired a gun whilst I was making my draught, and it being a calm day, I catched the thin smoak as it had ascended about half way up the mountains, which had a very pretty effect.

Gilpin too enjoyed the views from a boat on the lake, but found them difficult to accommodate to Picturesque principles. The side-screens were either too massive and heavy, or too broken and insignificant. Gilpin's verdict on the view of the northern end of the lake, from a point near the lake's middle, was that it was 'rather amusing, than picturesque', and too extensive for the painter's use: 'yet it exhibited many parts which, as distances, were purely picturesque; and afforded an admirable collection of mountain studies for a painter'. But as his boat neared the northern shore at the outlet of the Brathay, the scenery reminded him of Berghem's paintings – meadows, cattle and, nearer the background, rock, 'generally left plain, and simple, almost without a single varying tint . . . while the cattle are touched with infinite force and spirit'.

Gray, West, Young and Gilpin each made a strong distinction between elevated viewpoints, which are not, generally, suitable for the artist, and the lower viewpoints (not too low, as Clarke warned), which suit well, largely because the artist there has a command of the foreground. This was the advantage of the Stations on Belle Isle. The island's various owners, from the middle of the eighteenth century onwards, took full advantage of its situation. From the grand panoramic viewpoint above Bowness, Young had viewed the island with complete approval, noting its 'most picturesque inequalities of surface', and its farmhouse on the water's edge, 'backed with a little wood, vyeing in simple elegance with Boromean palaces'.[16] But Hutchinson's closer inspection of the island a few years later registered horror at the 'improvements' being undertaken by its recent purchaser, Mr English, 'who is laying out gardens on a square plan, building fruit walls', and planning a mansion-house there (for the new mansion in its larger setting, see Frontispiece). Any tourist sensitive to the natural beauties of Windermere, he asserted, will be disgusted to see 'a Dutch Burgomaster's palace arise on this place, to see a cabbage garth . . . squared and cut out at rights angles'. But, as Clarke

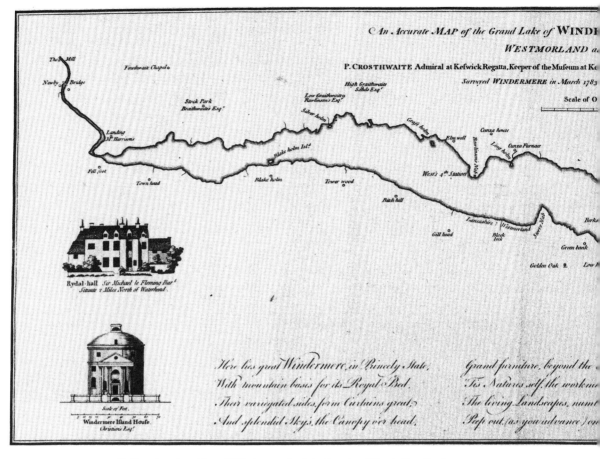

An Accurate MAP of the Grand Lake of WINDE

WESTMORLAND a

P. CROSTHWAITE Admiral at Keswick Regatta, Keeper of the Museum at Ke

Surveyed WINDERMERE in March 1783

Scale of O

Here lies great Windermere, in Princely State, Grand furniture, beyond the
With mountain basis for its Royal Bed. 'Tis Natures self, the workme
Their variegated sides, form Curtains great; The living Landscapes, numb
And splendid Skys, the Canopy o'er head, Peep out, (as you advance) on

51. P. Crosthwaite, *Map of Windermere* (1783), showing West's five Stations.
Dove Cottage, Grasmere

162

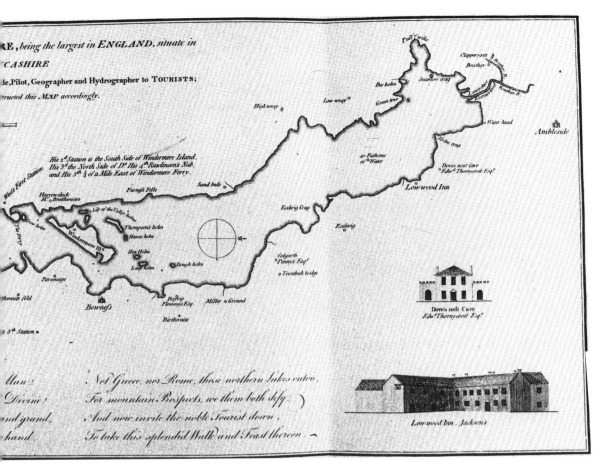

RE, *being the largest in* ENGLAND, *situate in*

CASHIRE

le, Pilot, Geographer and Hydrographer to TOURISTS;

rructed this MAP accordingly.

*His 2d Station is the South Side of Windermere Island.*
*His 3d the North Side of Do His 4th Rawlinson's Nab,*
*and His 5th ¾ of a Mile East of Windermere Ferry.*

West's First Station

Harrowslack
Mr Braithwaite's

Lily of the Valley

Thompson's holm

House holm

Hen Holm

Lady holm

Tom holm

Windermere Id

Parsonage

Furnels Fells

Sand beds

thwaite fold

Bowness

Bayard
Fleming's Esq.

Birthwaite

Miller Ground

Rough holm

Trentbeck bridge

Calgarth
Pennvs Esq.

Eelerig Crag

Eelerig

High wray

Low wray

Green tove

Bee holm

Seamew crag

Pull wike

Clappers gate
Brathay

Lancaster.

Waterhead Routher R.

to Water head

Holm crag

40 Fathoms
of Water

Doves nest Cave
Edwd Thornycroft Esq.

Low-wood Inn

Amblesude

& 5th Station

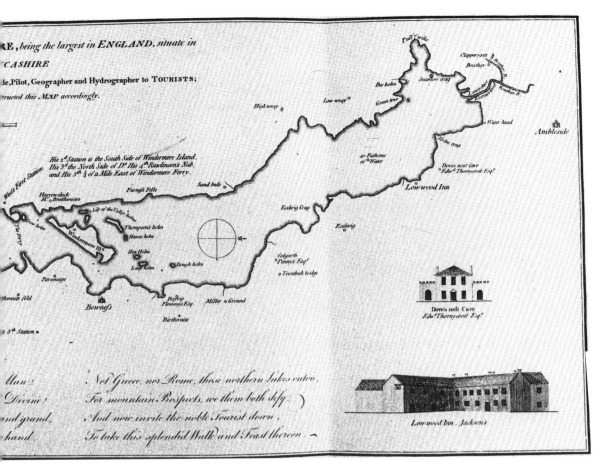

Dove's nest Cave
Edwd Thornycroft Esq.

Low-wood Inn. Jackson's

Man !

Divine !

nd grand,

hand.

Not Greece, nor Rome, these northern Lakes outvie,

For mountain Prospects, we them both defy:

And now invite the noble Tourist down,

To take this splendid Walk and Feast thereon.

52. John 'Warwick' Smith, 'Belleisle Lodge', from *Views of the Lakes in Cumberland* (1791–5).
British Library, London

and Grant protested, why shouldn't the island's owner have the convenience of vegetables from his own garden, rather than have to sail to the mainland each time? 'Grounds must not be laid out to please Gilpin, and other fanciful travellers through a country, but for the comfort of those in it' – an unobjectionable remark as long as it was realised that the comfort of the residents was to some extent economically dependent on their satisfying the tastes of the Picturesque tourists. Clarke considered that these Belle Isle 'improvements' actually enhanced the long-distance view of the island by introducing variety and contrast.

Mr English's mansion itself was designed so that it could command views of the lake in all directions, but its consequent form displeased many visitors: 'it wants only a little green paint and a label of Souchong or fine Hyson to make it exactly like a large shop tea canister',[17] complained William Gell. But Smith's illustration gives it the dignity of a Claudean temple in the landscape (fig. 52). The island's next owner, John Christian Curwen, was busy demolishing the formal gardens as Clarke was compiling his *Survey*. The new design, by Thomas White, was evidently a response to Picturesque tastes: 'Could the late accomplished and benevolent Gilpin now behold the lovely abode', wrote T. H. Horne in 1816, 'he would have the gratification of seeing the general outline, which he so ably sketched for its improvement, filled up in the most agreeable manner'.[18]

Windermere's most famous viewpoint was West's first Station, just above the

53. John Downman, 'Claife Station' (1812). Victoria and Albert Museum, London

Ferry point on the western shore. According to West, the great advantage of this Station was its command of nearly the full stretch of the lake:

To the north of this magnificent scene, a glorious sheet of water expands itself to the right and left, in curves bearing from the eye; bounded on the west by the continuation of the mountain where you stand, whose bold lofty side is embellished with growing trees, shrubs, and coarse vegetation, intermixed with grey rocks, that group finely with the deep green of yews and hollies. The eastern view is a noble contrast to this, adorned with all that is beautiful, grand, and sublime.

The viewpoint was already famous when Gray visited Windermere. Many subsequent writers told the story of how Gray had had to blindfold himself for the ferry journey across from Bowness, reserving his first view for his Claude Glass.[19] Wordsworth, in later life, admitted his boyhood enthusiasm for this view-point with its 'prospect of the islands below and the intermingling water'.[20] Magnificent side-screens and a glorious sheet of water over the middle distance are completed pictorially by the immediate surroundings of the Station, where, according to West, 'the trees are of singular use in answering the purposes of fore-ground, and of intersecting the lake'. The great scale of Windermere caused the artists some difficulty in this matter of finding the right foreground, a difficulty clearly expressed by William Green, whose drawings of the lake were etched and published in 1810:

... though the distances on Windermere are exquisite, as seen in nature; yet, by their remoteness from the eye, and the consequent monotony of the lines composing those distances, they generally require the aid of other objects with a view to destroy that monotony, and otherwise improve the intended picture.[21]

One notices again the use of that word 'improve', for Green is making the same sort of design adjustments on paper as the landscape gardener was doing on the great estates. When Green therefore takes his view on Windermere he is quite candid: 'The trees on the left were taken from the hedge-row on the right hand, with a view to benefit the composition'.

West, then, had chosen the site for his first Station with great care. Its slight elevation was nicely judged. A lower viewpoint down by the lake shore would be partially blocked by the little archipelago of islands off the Ferry point. Alternatively, some thought to try a viewpoint above the Station, but 'reaped no advantage from our labor; these giddy heights only adding horror to the scene without its former softened beauties'.[22] The local landowner, the Revd William Braithwaite, built an octagonal 'pleasure-house', later developed into a two-storey castellated summer-house on this Station, the ruins of which can be seen peeping above the trees in fig. 53.[23] The approach path led from the lake shore, through a neo-Gothic archway and spiralled up the hillside. For much of the last part of the climb the visitor had his back to the lake until he reached the rear of the summer-house which then strategically screened his view. A small staircase in this dark, apsidal rear of the building led to the upper chamber: the lower room was the lodge of the caretaker-cum-guide. The handsome upper room was the belvedere, furnished with a chimney-piece of Kendal marble and some elegant chairs and tables.[24] At the lakeside end of the room there was a bay with three windows, each commanding one of West's three prospects over Windermere:

... we were placed at the windows to enjoy them, whilst an Eolian harp poured forth its wild airs in perfect unison with the impressions created by the scenery ...[25]

Robert Southey visited the Station in 1802 and found further enhancements of the naturally Picturesque experience:

The room was hung with prints, representing the finest similar landscapes in Great Britain and other countries, none of the representations exceeding in beauty the real prospect before us. The windows were bordered with coloured glass, by which you might either throw a yellow sunshine over the scene, or frost it, or fantastically, tinge it with purple.

Each of these views is thus controlled into a Picturesque composition: it is framed, either by the rectangular frame of the window or by some foreground trees, and a variety of master-tints is available from the coloured glass windows.

The Windermere 'distances', which caused problems for the artist and obliged him to invent foreground trees and bushes in order to break up the monotony of a huge expanse of water, could nonetheless contribute in particular ways to

54. J. C. Ibbetson, *Langdale Pikes from Lowood* (c. 1800–6).
Yale Center for British Art, Paul Mellon Collection

enhancing the romantic experience of grand scenery. Let us take the situation of someone standing by the water's edge on Windermere. From this point the eye has a rapid and uninterrupted passage across the lake's surface to the opposite shore, where the first objects are already softened by being slightly out of focus, even for someone with excellent eyesight. There is no high-definition foreground to provide a starting point for the modulation of focus as objects recede into the distance. The tourist of 'sensibility' might translate this experience into the following terms: there are no immediate forms of hard reality, no foreground cottage or carbuncular tree to which the travelling eye can relate the distant softened landscape forms, where all cottages are neat, white dots and all trees are cushiony clumps; in short, without foreground there is no interference with the activity of a romantic, idealising imagination playing on vague, malleable forms. Such an experience was well described by Grant as he looked across Windermere from Lowood Inn, at which point there are no islands to intercept the view (fig. 54):

The opposite side . . . is just distant enough to have all its beauties prominent, and its asperities softened or concealed. Roads, that in reality are stony and difficult, appear waving, whitish lines, opposed to the dark woods on either side. A villa that, when approached, is cold and unsheltered, tapers to an obelisk, or a verdant knoll, a cottage damp with exhalations may sit like a water-nymph on the brink, or a hamlet, the residence of poverty, be a fair speckler of the mountain's brow.

'Distance lends enchantment to the view', as Thomas Campbell remarked in *The Pleasures of Hope* (1799). Campbell is following a long tradition of emblematic landscape poetry, in which the poetic viewer moralises upon the deceptions in distant views. John Dyer from his Grongar Hill viewpoint sees down in the Towy valley the tiny hedgerows, the 'streaks of meadow' and streams which look as if one could cross them with a single step:

> So we mistake the Future's face,
> Ey'd thro' Hope's deluding Glass:
> As yon Summits soft and fair,
> Clad in Colours of the Air,
> Which, to those who journey near,
> Barren, and brown, and rough appear.[26]

Grant concludes his meditations on the Windermere distances with just this kind of sentiment: 'Such is hope, as youthful fancy portrays it; thus, as we draw near, are the bright deceptions detected, and all our golden dreams at an end'.

### Ambleside – Rydal – Grasmere – Keswick

At Ambleside, at the head of Windermere, Pennant noticed 'The countenance of the people begins to alter; especially in the tender sex; the face begins to square, and the cheek bones begin to rise, as if symptomatic of my approaching *North Britain*'.[27] Ambleside developed rapidly in response to the invasion of the tourists.

55. Francis Towne, *Rydal Water* (1786).
Victoria and Albert Museum, London

56. Joseph Wright of Derby, *Waterfall at Rydal*.
Derby Art Gallery, Derby

James Plumptre in 1799 went to the inn he had visited two years earlier, and was astounded by the inflated prices.[28] He attributed the change to the patronage of affluent and sybaritic Londoners who wanted every comfort and were prepared to pay London prices for them. He went on to quote, approvingly, Gilpin's comments on the responsibility of the tourists for the corruption of the local people: 'giving them a taste for pleasures, and gratifications, of which they had no ideas – inspiring them with discontent at home – and tainting their rough, industrious manners with idleness, and a thirst after dishonest means'.

'A more interesting tract of country is scarcely anywhere to be seen than the road between Ambleside and Keswick',[29] according to Wordsworth, who spent most of his life in this part of the Lake District (fig. 55). The first stop was Rydal Hall, just over a mile above Ambleside, and the seat of Sir Michael le Fleming, fourth Baronet of Rydal. His grounds incorporated two fine waterfalls on Rydal Beck, for which he provided winding access paths, seats, and a summer-house. Of the two falls the upper was the larger, and in a situation rather too exposed for Picturesque tastes. Joseph Mawman and his companions, walking along these Rydal avenues in the full blaze of noon, heightened their pleasure by using Claude Glasses, 'the mellow tint of which softened the glare'.[30]

No such aids were needed to enhance the lower falls, which presented a *beau idéal* of romantic and Picturesque scenery (fig. 56). William Mason, the editor of Gray's *Memoirs*, was responsible for bringing this scene to the public's attention, in a footnote to Gray's Lakes journal:

Here Nature has performed every thing in little that she usually executes on her largest scale; and on that account, like the miniature painter, seems to have finished every part of it in a studied manner; not a little fragment of rock thrown into the bason, not a single stem of brushwood that starts from its craggy sides but has its picturesque meaning; and the little central stream dashing down a cleft of the darkest-coloured stone, produces an effect of light and shadow beautiful beyond description. This little theatrical scene might be painted as large as the original, on a canvas not bigger than those which are usually dropped in the Opera-house.[31]

The fact that the beautiful scene could be reproduced on canvas, almost life-size, is one important Picturesque qualification. Another is its shady situation: 'In every representation, truly picturesque, the shade should greatly overbalance the light', wrote Gilpin in his enthusiastic description of the scene. This shade, together with the noise of the falls, 'renders it peculiarly favourable to meditation and philosophic melancholy'. Grant enjoyed the way in which all the constituents of the scene 'are locked together in a conspiracy against the intrusive glare', unlike the upper falls. Among these constituents was a rustic bridge which crossed the stream just above the falls. Over this bridge passengers and cattle passed occasionally, and added just the right touch to the scenery. Mrs Cobbold was particularly delighted with the bridge, 'which, if I were a Landscape Painter I should certainly introduce into the view as its appearance does not exceed the simplicity of the Pastoral Ages'.[32] Once visitors had found their station for viewing these falls, it would have paid Sir Michael handsomely to have hired a rustic labourer, and to have launched him across the bridge, in loitering fashion, at just the right moment. As it was, the tourist had to rely on chance to complete his Picturesque scene. Joseph Budworth was very lucky: 'at the instant I am writing a man with his hayday dress, with a rake and a stone bottle, is passing over the bridge, the back shade makes his frame and dress so distinct I shall never forget the figure'.

Sir Michael had contrived the tourist's first view of the lower falls with great care:

... a little girl conducted us, round the house, by a winding path through a kind of rude plantation to a small rustic house of grey stone uncemented. The moment the door is pushed open, you see through the window before you, a cascade that appears to have been formed by the hand of a fairy.[33]

The contrast between the dark interior of this little seventeenth-century 'grotto'[34] and the green-tinted light bathing the scenery of the waterfall, which itself was perfectly framed by the large window, contributed to a sense that here was Nature adapting herself to art in such a way as fully to satisfy the Picturesque appetite. It was already a popular scene when Wordsworth consecrated it for English poetry by comparing it with one of the most famous streams of the classical world, Horace's 'fons Bandusiae', the little spring by his Sabine farm. In *An Evening Walk* the poet seeks shelter from the noon-day sun by a small cascade:

> Beyond, along the vista of the brook,
> Where antique roots its bustling course o'erlook,
> The eye reposes on a secret bridge
> Half grey, half shagged with ivy to its ridge;
> There, bending o'er the stream, the listless swain
> Lingers behind his disappearing wain.[35]

Wordsworth's description is a blend of the Picturesque conventions – the movement of the eye along a 'vista', the ivy-shagged bridge, and the 'listless swain' caught in meditation. It is derivative in many ways, a stereotyped description, and yet it is a description of a real place, one which Wordsworth knew well, and which, as his topographical footnote to the passage in his poem indicates, any of his readers who had made the tour to the Lakes would immediately recollect. When he eventually settled at nearby Rydal Mount, these falls legitimately became, symbolically, the poet's Bandusian stream. Wordsworth himself had by then become one of the objects of the Lakes tour. One visitor travelling past Rydal Water was able to boast that 'in this neighbourhood we happened to meet Mr. Wordsworth (Author of Lyrical Ballads) walking on the road side, with part of his family'.[36]

Wordsworth had moved to Rydal Mount from Grasmere. In 'Home at Grasmere' he described his first sight of the Vale, his settling there and his deepening love for it. The poem traces his maturing perception of landscape, from his first,

57. John 'Warwick' Smith, 'Grasmere Lake', from *Views of the Lakes in Cumberland* (1791–5);
the view is taken from near the Red Bank Station. British Library, London

tourist experience as a schoolboy when he beheld it from Red Bank,[37] a Station
to the south of the lake which West had recommended (fig. 57):

> The Station whence he look'd was soft and green,
> Not giddy yet aerial, with a depth
> Of Vale below, a height of hills above[38]

The Station is clearly approved as being neither a bird's eye prospect nor a very
low viewpoint. But once Wordsworth has come to know the Vale intimately, the
Station description gives way to a mystical perception of the landscape for which
he has to struggle to find the right words – 'a blended holiness of earth and sky'.

Thomas Gray had been one of the first tourists to be enchanted by Grasmere,
'one of the sweetest landscapes, that art ever attempted to imitate'. His first view
of it was from Dunmail Raise, on the opposite side of the Vale to Red Bank. He
loved its 'hanging enclosures, corn-fields, & meadows green as an emerald . . .
large farm-house . . . embosom'd in old woods, wᶜʰ climb half way up the mountain's side, & discover above them a broken line of crags, that crown the scene'.[39]
Dr William Maton recalled and commended this description as he surveyed the
Vale, but found more cultivation here than at most other lakes, 'on which account
perhaps it may be less pleasing to the picturesque eye'.[40] Gray had been delighted
by the fact that no 'flaring Gentleman's house' disturbed this 'little unsuspected

173

paradise'. But such houses were to come; for one of the consequences of the 'Rage for the Lakes' was the purchase of land and enclosure of commons in order to build houses which would command precisely these beautiful views. These houses, in their design, materials and situation were in strong contrast to the sequestered farms and cottages of the natives, who, as we have seen, had little patience or understanding of the new taste in 'prospects'. A good example of this incomprehension was reported by Grant as he travelled northwards through Grasmere:

We have met a poor, unrefined rustic, whose ideas of gain and fitness, were prevalent over those of the sublime and beautiful. He informed us of a Mr. Olive, who has lately purchased a sweet estate, and built a small dwelling-house, in a most delightful site, on the banks of Grasmere. 'He paid too dear for it, Sir; had I been in his place, I would have bought another estate among the mountains, at the same price, and twice the value; but Mr. Olive is a neat, nacky man like, and thinks it a *fine diversion* to look at the water coming down the fells, when there's a flood like, and that's all', with a sneer, 'that's all *he* has for his money'.

The rustic's contemptuous manner is matched only by the narrator's. They seem to belong to different worlds; or rather they inhabit the same world, but judge its benefits by wholly different criteria. Three quarters of a century after Gray had stood admiring Grasmere, Wordsworth was writing angrily to the editor of the *Morning Post*, invoking the spirit of his predecessor:

Were the Poet now living, how would he have lamented the probable intrusion of a railway with its scarifications, its intersections, its noisy machinery, its smoke, and swarms of pleasure-hunters, most of them thinking that they do not fly fast enough through the country which they have come to see.[41]

The new residents had chosen the Lake District primarily for aesthetic and recreational reasons, but to some extent their new wealth must have helped the depressed economy of the region: local shops were patronised, and local labour was needed to build their 'flaring houses'. Many of the owners were newly-rich industrialists from the northern cities, for whom undeveloped green landscapes must have had strong attractions. We may be thankful now that the Industrial Revolution's invasion of this landscape was mostly limited to these domestic developments. The invention of steam power came just in time for the Lake District, where the high potential for water power and other resources would otherwise have made it a valuable site for industrial development.

The road out of Grasmere rose steeply in its approach to the border between Cumberland and Westmorland, and entered some bleakly spectacular mountain country. The change in the landscape at this point prompted Gilpin to make a distinction between a '*scene of mountains*' and a '*mountain scene*'. In the former category the spectator is presented with a chaotic huddle of mountains, which it is the painter's task to form into pictures by '*imaginary combinations*'. The '*mountain scene*', on the other hand, is one in which Nature herself has made these beautiful '*combinations*'. One famous mountain scene was to be had from the sixth mile post from Keswick) where the road turns inland from Thirlmere by 'the Swirls'. The view is down towards St Johns Vale with Saddleback forming the background. This road alongside Thirlmere, with Helvellyn rearing up on the right, thrilled the tourist with the promise of Sublime landscapes. Hutchinson enjoyed the succession of pastoral images, which raised ideas of rural innocence, retirement, and love:

Neither did these images pass in the imagination only, for in this sequestered vale we met with a female native full of youth, innocence, and beauty; – simplicity adorned her looks with modesty, and hid her down-cast eye; virgin apprehension covered her with blushes, when she found herself stayed by two strangers; and as she turned her eyes for an instant upon us, they smote us with all the energy of unaffected innocence, touched with doubtfulness; – her lips, which in the sweetest terms expressed her apprehension, shewed us teeth of ivory; and on her full forehead ringlets of auburn flowed carelessly: a delicacy of proportion was seen over her whole figure, which was easy and elegant as nature's self.

– My companion, in a rapture, snatched out his pencil, and began to imitate; but the unaffected impatiency, and sweet confusion of the maid, overcame our wishes to detain her, and we let her pass reluctantly.

Such rustic beauties were a great attraction for the Picturesque tourist, especially when they seemed to conform to the model shepherdesses in traditional pastoral poetry. The most famous beauty of the Lakes was Mary Robinson, daughter of the innkeeper at the village of Buttermere. Joseph Budworth was responsible for giving the unfortunate girl full publicity when his *Fortnight's Ramble to the Lakes* appeared in 1792.[42] Mary was then incorporated into the Picturesque tour until she fell prey to the charms and subsequent marriage proposal of the forger John Hatfield, then masquerading as the Hon. Alexander Augustus Hope. Her sad story caught the public imagination in the early nineteenth century, no doubt, as Norman Nicholson suggests, because it seemed a kind of allegory of the corruption of pastoral innocence by city-bred evil.

The fallacies in such a simplified moral polarity were exposed by another famous human curiosity on the tour of the Lakes. At the southern end of Ullswater, in the village of Patterdale, there was a large old house ('that had once been handsome, and would still be so in a picture' Budworth suggested) known as the Palace of Patterdale. The 'King of Patterdale' was a disreputable old miser called John Mounsey, who held animals and humans in equal contempt. He could be cowed only by his 'Queen' (fig. 58), who squandered his wealth and her own reputation at the village inn.[43] For the price of a few drinks she would with great relish elaborate on the legendary vices of her husband. Here she made the spontaneous offer of her granddaughter's hand in marriage to Joseph Budworth's startled tour companion. This grotesque royal couple must have upset the romantic tourist's ideas about the Lakes' being the nursery of moral integrity; but there is little evidence of such disturbance.

Five miles on from Thirlmere the tourist reached Keswick, at the northern end

58. John White Abbott, 'Queen of Patterdale'.
Victoria and Albert Museum, London

of Derwentwater. Keswick in the 1790s was a town with a population of about 1000, and was enjoying considerable prosperity from the tourist trade. Colt Hoare insisted it was 'where every tourist to the Lakes should fix his Head Quarters for some days – the Inns are good – there are good horses – intelligent Guides, safe boats'.[44] The latter offerings were evidently a considerable improvement on Hutchinson's earlier experience of a 'nasty, leaky fishing-boat, with an impertinent, talkative, lying pilot'.

As for the 'intelligent Guides' to Derwentwater, two of the most experienced were rival owners of the town's two museums. Peter Crosthwaite, an ex-naval commander, opened his museum in 1783 and amassed a collection of bizarre curiosities, consisting more of gimcracks than antiquities:[45] a straw hat belonging to one who had sailed with Bligh on the *Bounty*, Aeolian harps at five shillings each, a collection of musical stones not quite in tune,[46] on which Crosthwaite would hammer out 'God save the King', a document showing sixteen different ways of spelling the proper name 'Braithwaite', and an assortment of coins, prints, Claude Glasses, maps, and other tourist aids. His house, as he boasted, was the loftiest in Keswick, commanding some fine views, and he had attached a number of little reeds to the windowsills through which one could look at the principal objects or Stations on Derwentwater. Crosthwaite's methods of attracting custom were regarded with some distaste. He would sit in the corner of his museum with a large drum. Mirrors were placed in every direction at the windows so that he could instantly see a promising carriage approaching, whereupon he would start thumping his drum in time with the museum's barrel-organ while his wife ran upstairs and pounded a large Chinese gong. However crude these methods, he was evidently very successful: in 1793, '1540 persons of rank and fashion' visited the museum.

His daughter was, by many accounts, more attractive than any of the other exhibits in the museum, and was the subject of a verse compliment published in one of the town's inns:

> When Nature commanded
>     Her beauties to rise
> On yon lakes and yon
>     Mountains She gaz'd
>     With surprise –
> But these charms now
>     Disdaining Her head
>     She does toss at
> And gazes along on the
>     Lovely Miss Cross
>     = thwaite[47]

Crosthwaite's maps of the Lakes were invaluable for the tourist. All the famous Stations were marked, and he had added a few of his own (fig. 59). One of his Derwentwater Stations, just below Latrigg, the hill behind the town, was marked by a cross cut out in the turf. He took the tourist boom very earnestly, and refused to sell any literature that at all disparaged the Lakeland tour (e.g. the Hon. Mrs Murray's *Companion and Useful Guide* and Plumptre's satirical operetta *The Lakers*).

Crosthwaite's rival was Mr Hutton, whose museum concentrated more on natural history exhibits. Hutton was an indefatigable guide to the local scenery, and prided himself on having accompanied West around Derwentwater when his Stations were being chosen.

## *Derwentwater – Borrowdale*

This accumulation of beauty and immensity tends not only to excite rapture but reverence; for my part I make an annual voyage to Keswick, not only as an innocent amusement, but a religious act.[48]

The Vale of Keswick was the most eagerly sought area on the tour to the Lakes. For both Gray and Pennant it was the Elysium of the North. It owed its early celebrity to two particular descriptions already mentioned: Dr John Dalton's *Descriptive Poem* published in December 1754,[49] and Dr John Brown's descriptive letter of 1753, part of which was published in 1767. Dr Brown, the 'Columbus of Keswick' as a contemporary called him, was brought up in Cumberland. In the 1730s and early 1740s he was tutor and drawing master to the young William

Gilpin. In the 1750s he came to know the Lyttelton family and their circle; and it was to Lord Lyttelton that he addressed his letter on Keswick.

Brown's *Description* established a descriptive model for many late-eighteenth-century tourists anxious to record their impressions of this scenery. He is clearly conscious of the difficulties of conveying the characteristic beauties of Derwent-water to a readership unfamiliar with so striking a landscape, and therefore employs several strategies. He begins by comparing it with Dovedale, a romantic region more accessible to those in the Midlands (the Lyttelton family for instance) and south of England, and therefore likely to be more familiar. But he finds Derwentwater far superior in both beauty and grandeur. Its chief advantage over Dovedale is in its juxtaposition of strong contrasts:

You will on one side of the lake, see a rich and beautiful landscape of cultivated fields, rising to the eye, in fine inequalities, with noble groves of oak, happily dispersed, and climbing the adjacent hills, shade above shade, in the most various and picturesque forms. On the opposite shore you will find rocks and cliffs of stupendous height, hanging broken over the lake in horrible grandeur, some of them a thousand feet high, the woods climbing up their steep and shaggy sides, where mortals foot never yet approached . . . a variety of water-falls are seen pouring from their summits, and tumbling in vast sheets from rock to rock in rude and terrible magnificence: while on all sides of this immense amphitheatre the lofty mountains rise round piercing the clouds in shapes as

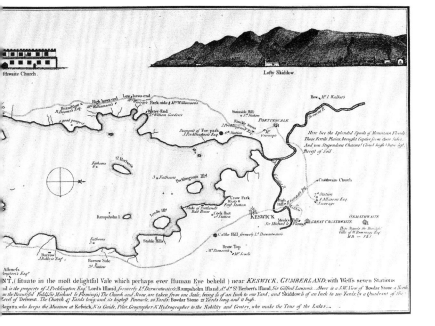

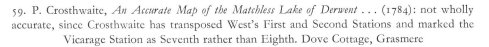

59. P. Crosthwaite, *An Accurate Map of the Matchless Lake of Derwent . . .* (1784): not wholly accurate, since Crosthwaite has transposed West's First and Second Stations and marked the Vicarage Station as Seventh rather than Eighth. Dove Cottage, Grasmere

spiry and fantastic as the very rocks of *Dovedale*.

In this, his first descriptive approach to the scene, he impresses on the reader the strong contrasts and vigorous movement in the landscape: 'rising', 'climbing', 'hanging', 'pouring', 'piercing'. His second approach is the analytical, when he brings into play the Addisonian terminology: 'the full perfection' of the Vale lies in its having united '*beauty, horror* and *immensity*' (whereas Dovedale has only horror). The original letter predated Burke's *Enquiry*: by the 1760s that 'immensity' would surely have become 'sublimity'. Brown however is not using the terminology with any very rigorous distinction.

His third descriptive tactic, in case the previous two are insufficiently evocative, is a resort to the Picturesque:

But to give you a complete idea of these three perfections, as they are found in *Keswick*, would require the united powers of *Claude, Salvator*, and *Poussin*. The first should throw his delicate sunshine over the cultivated vales, the scattered cots, the groves, the lake, and wooded islands. The second should dash out the horror of the rugged cliffs, the steeps, the hanging woods, and foaming water-falls; while the grand pencil of *Poussin* should crown the whole with the majesty of the impending mountains.

Subsequent tourists were to depend on a selection from these three approaches – the concrete (physical description and evocation), the abstract (the terminology of

179

eighteenth-century aesthetics), and the associative (the analogy with poetry or paintings); or they might combine all three as they try to convey the distinctive character of any grand landscape.

Dalton's poem attempts to describe what, in his Preface of about 1752, he calls 'the several uncommon, grand, or beautiful scenes of nature and of art'—precisely Addison's three categories. The most interesting and adventurous part of his poem is the description of the mines near Whitehaven, but for the later tourists it was his evocation of the scenery of Derwentwater which mattered most. Like Brown, Dalton is particularly impressed by the extraordinary contrasts in this landscape. He seems to take the view from near the head of the lake, by Lodore cascade:

> Horrors like these at first alarm,
> But soon with savage grandeur charm,
> And raise to noblest thoughts the mind:
> Thus by thy fall, *Lowdore*, reclin'd,
> The craggy cliff, impendent wood,
> Whose shadows mix o'er half the flood,
> The gloomy clouds, which solemn sail,
> Scarce lifted by the languid gale,
> O'er the cap'd hill, and darken'd vale;
> The ravening kite, and bird of Jove,
> Which round the aerial ocean rove, . . .
> Channels by rocky torrents torn,
> Rocks to the lake in thunder born,
> Or such as o'er our heads appear
> Suspended in their mid career,
> To start again at his command,
> Who rules fire, water, air, and land,
> I view with wonder and delight,
> A pleasing, though an awful sight:
> For, seen with them, the verdant isles
> Soften with more delicious smiles,
> More tempting twine their op'ning bow'rs,
> More lively glow the purple flow'rs,
> More smoothly slopes the border gay,
> In fairer circles bend the bay,
> And last, to fix our wand'ring eyes,
> Thy roofs, O *Keswick*, brighter rise,
> The lake, and lofty hills between,
> Where giant *Skiddaw* shuts the scene.

The metrical models are Milton's *Il Penseroso* and *L'Allegro*, perhaps via *Grongar Hill*. In effect, the thematic model is a fusion of the two Milton poems, since the Vale of Keswick combines both the gloomy grandeur of Milton's Melancholy, the goddess who dwells 'under *Ebon* shades, and low-brow'd Rocks', and the smiling fertile landscape of the goddess Mirth from *L'Allegro*. The presence of the first kind of landscape accentuates the pleasures of the latter kind, as Dalton's long sentence contrives to convey. This passage from his poem corresponds mainly to the first of Brown's descriptive strategies; but Dalton seems also conscious of a Picturesque completeness as he talks about the 'wand'ring eyes' being brought to rest, and the 'scene' closing with Skiddaw in the background.

All the early tourists were struck by the way in which Derwentwater assembled within a relatively small compass all the extremes of aesthetic pleasure in landscape. Notice how carefully Arthur Young balances the important antitheses in his general description:

The lake, the islands, the hanging woods, the waving inclosures, and the cascades are all most superlatively elegant and beautiful; while the rocks, clifts, crags, and mountains are equally terrifying and sublime.[50]

Gilpin quoted with approval another visitor's first reactions to the scenery – 'Beauty lying in the lap of Horror!' – as a phrase finely evocative of the way Derwentwater brought together, without reconciling, Beauty and Sublimity. Even Pennant was moved to invent a colourful simile for this scenery: 'Skiddaw … opens a pleasing front, smooth and verdant, smiling over the country like a gentle generous lord, while the *fells* of Borrowdale frown on it like a hardened tyrant'.[51] Some, however, like Ann Radcliffe found the combination too discordant:

The beauty of its banks … contending with the wildness of its rocks, gives opposite impressions to the mind, and the force of each is, perhaps, destroyed by the admission of the other … grandeur loses much of its elevating effect, when united with a considerable portion of beauty.

But it was just this contrast or tension which made Derwentwater the greatest attraction among the Lakes, especially for the Picturesque tourist in search of English equivalents to the scenery immortalised by the great seventeenth-century landscape painters.

After the tourist had taken a general survey of the lake, the next stage was to analyse each scene and isolate particular views which might individually be compatible with a Claude or a Rosa landscape. This was the particular endeavour of the Picturesque tourist, assisted by the established Stations around the lake to which he was directed by West's *Guide* or by the various guides from Keswick. Young complained of the difficulty of access to some of the best viewpoints (this was before the Stations had been established) and recommended developing Derwentwater into a kind of mid-eighteenth-century landscaped garden:

Winding paths should be cut in the rock, and resting-places made for the weary traveller: Many of these paths must necessarily lead through the hanging woods, openings might be made to let in views of the lake, where the objects, such as islands, etc., were peculiarly beautiful … It is amusing to think of the pains and expense with which the environs of several seats have been ornamented, to produce pretty scenes it is true, but how very far short of the wonders that might here be held up to the eye in all the rich luxuriance of nature's painting. What are the effects of a *Louis*'s magnificence to the sportive play of nature in the vale of *Keswick*![52]

Gilpin too felt that 'a nobler scene for improvement could not well be conceived',[53] but he was much more careful to specify how and to what extent such improvements should be made. The circuit round the lake should be made more accessible. It should be cleared of deformities; and it might be planted and decorated. All this was to be done with the utmost delicacy so as not to betray any formality: 'Nature always plants with much more picturesque beauty, than man [who] cannot put a twig into the ground without formality'. The best way to ensure that 'artificial woods', for instance, acquire a natural beauty is to plant profusely, wait for the trees to mature, and then axe selectively: 'The felling axe is the instrument, which gives the finishing touch of picturesque effect', rather as the mallet was recommended for improving Tintern Abbey's Picturesque appearance. As far as decoration is concerned, 'If the ruins of a castle, or abbey *could be* built, and stationed with verisimilitude, and propriety, they would undoubtedly be a great ornament'. Otherwise only a bridge or two of a rough natural kind would be admissible. A tottering Alpine bridge could be placed at one or two points, with a safe, serviceable bridge in its neighbourhood.

These recommendations by Young and Gilpin, together with Gray's meticulous descriptions of certain prime viewpoints on the lake, led to West's detailed directions to eight Stations around Derwentwater, three more than he had awarded to Windermere. But the development of Derwentwater for the Picturesque tour had some results which Young would surely have deplored and which Gilpin, in an addendum to his recommendations, censures strongly. Particularly obnoxious to most tourists was the 'tea-garden taste' of Joseph Pocklington (from a wealthy banking family in Nottinghamshire), the owner of Vicar's Island (now Derwent Isle) and of some land on the shores of the lake.

Vicar's Island, when John Leland saw it in the early sixteenth century, was 'ful of trees lyke a wylderness'.[54] When Hutchinson saw it first in 1773 it was mainly corn land: but 'on the eastern side a few sycamores formed a little grove, covering a hovel, which . . . gave the whole a picturesque appearance'. When Pocklington bought the island the cottage was demolished; 'and right in the middle, and upon the precise point of the island's highest elevation, rose a tall square habitation . . . like the temple of Aeolus, where all the winds pay him obeisance' (fig. 60).[55] This is Wordsworth expressing his disgust at the substitution of this brash mansion for the sequestered Picturesque cottage. It seemed to him to epitomise what had happened to the Lakes within a generation. The unwary visitor to the island, once Pocklington had developed it, might well have been amazed to find in so small a compass so many fascinating antiquities. Elizabeth Diggle and her aunt, hearing that there was a Druid temple on the island, hastened across from Keswick. They were escorted round the island by an elderly footman:

60. John 'Warwick' Smith, 'Pocklington's Island, Keswick Lake', from *Views of the
Lakes in Cumberland* (1791–5). British Library, London

I had walked half over the island without perceiving any signs of one. 'Till I heard my
aunt ask . . . if that was the Druid's temple, if his master had found it, in its present
state? I looked round & could see nothing but a few round stones set in a circle like
boys playing at Marbles. The man answered to the first question 'yes ma'am'; to the
second 'n . . . o ma'am, master had these stones put up to look like one that was found
near Penrith; but the Lake is always knocking em down', & well it may thought I.[56]

Pocklington also adorned his island with a small fortress and a boat house disguised as a Westmorland chapel. All these were scrupulously illustrated in a map
made by the loyal Crosthwaite.

Pocklington had appointed Crosthwaite Admiral of the Keswick 'fleet' during
the summer Regattas. This Regatta was a blend of country fair and grand spectacle, little to the taste of the more sophisticated visitor:

. . . conceive a number of people assembled to hunt a poor defenceless swine, with his
retro shaved, and soaped, by which alone he is to be caught, Feminines running for
Robes d'Chambre, and twenty sic like things . . .[57]

The naval encounter was the event which drew most attention. This involved an
attack on Vicar's Island under the command of Admiral Crosthwaite. The governor of the island's fort (i.e. Pocklington) returned a defiance to Crosthwaite's
summons to surrender, and in the first assault the fleet was successfully repelled.

The noise of cannon and musquetry on the lake, echoing again and again in the neighbouring mountains, stimulated the sense of the Sublime in the hundreds of spectators lining the shores. One was even moved to commiserate with Milton on his lost opportunity here: 'Had the poet who described the battle of the Gods seen a Regatta-day at Keswick, it would have very much enriched his muse for that subject'. The fleet's second attack was successful, the garrison capitulated, and the spectators dispersed to fireworks and a dance at the Assembly-room.

There were, over the years, other concessions to Picturesque tourism which would have won Young's approval, notably the clearance of Crow Park. Up to the middle of the eighteenth century this 'gentle eminence', as Gray called it, on the shore of the lake just below Keswick, was covered with massive oaks which had grown so close that one could go from one side of the wood to the other among the branches without ever setting foot on the earth. The land was sold in 1749, and the forest cut down over the next decade. This was how Gray found it in October 1769:

Walk'd to *Crow-park*, now a rough pasture, once a glade of ancient oaks, whose large roots still remain on the ground, but nothing has sprung from them. if one single tree had remain'd, this would have been an unparallel'd spot, & Smith judged right, when he took his print of the Lake from hence, for it is a gentle eminence, not too high, on the very margin of the water, & commanding it from end to end, looking full into the *gorge* of *Borodale*.[58]

Gray is referring to Thomas Smith of Derby whose, *View of Darwentwater &c from Crow-Park* was fairly widely known through engravings (fig. 61). Smith's scene is a startling one. The foreground, Crow Park, is littered with the stumps of the oak forest. Vicar's Island in pre-Pocklington state, with its corn sheaves and the sycamores clustered around the cottage, is clearly visible in the middle distance. Meadows and cottages adorn the western slopes: and at the far end of the lake, looking like the smoking jaws of Hell, is Borrowdale. A bucolic foreground is set against the strong sublimities of the background, thus illustrating Derwentwater's characteristic contrasts. Smith's rendering of Borrowdale is remarkable. The mountains look nothing like this from Crow Park, in either scale or form. Bellers's view (fig. 62) is closer to the truth. It has been suggested that Smith deliberately distorts shapes to satisfy contemporary tastes for chinoiserie – the mist-wreathed, conical mountains made to look like Chinese landscape forms.[59] It is also possible that Smith knew Brown's letter, and decided to stress more distinctly the 'horrible grandeur' of Borrowdale. Certainly he manages to convey Brown's description of the mountains as 'spiry and fantastic', adjectives which one would not think particularly appropriate to the scene.

James Clarke, in 1787, mentioned that Crow Park was soon to be laid to grass, 'and will then afford an excellent station for the landscape-painter: Mr. Hannan, (who was the first that I remember as coming for the purpose of drawing) admired this view the most of any in the country'. It was also Gray's favourite view, and accordingly included by West among his eight Derwentwater Stations. It may well

61. Thomas Smith of Derby, *A View of Darwentwater &c from Crow-Park* (1767).
King's College, Cambridge, Bicknell Collection

62. William Bellers, *A View of Derwent Water, Towards Borrodale* (1752).
King's College, Cambridge, Bicknell Collection

have become so celebrated because it was often the tourist's first lakeside view after finding accommodation at Keswick. Its low angle accentuated the distant mountains of Borrowdale and the high crags along the eastern margin. Gilpin's sketch of 'The general idea of Keswick-lake' is taken from much the same viewpoint (fig. 63). He tries, rather injudiciously, to divide the scene into side-screens and front-screen, and marks his disapproval of the Borrowdale end and the lines of the western mountains. Gray regrets the lack of any tree in Crow Park because it deprives the viewer of a foreground framing device. West's *Guide* also laments 'the frequent removal of the picturesque trees' on the lake's borders:

It is true, that the painter, by the creative power of his pencil, can supply such deficiencies in the features of his landscape; but the plastic power of nature, or the careful hand of industry, directed by taste and judgment, can only make up such losses to the visitors of the lakes.

Smith's Rosa-esque foreground tree is presumably due to the 'creative power of his pencil'.

Ann Radcliffe was impatient to take the view from Crow Park, but was disappointed on arrival. Her expectations had been too high, for, compared with the many eloquent descriptions she had read, and with her own earlier sight of the mountains bordering Derwentwater, she found the lake itself insignificant. Robert Southey, on the other hand, asserted, 'You do not wish it to be larger, the mirror is in perfect proportion to its frame'. Ann Radcliffe was in a minority which included the rather grumpy Morris Moule who felt that Gray, West and the other authorities were sometimes too lavish in their praise. He complained vehemently about the dangers involved in following some of their directions to choice viewpoints: 'Visitors of these places relying on their veracity ascend precipices which if he was to fall would dash him to Atoms'.[60] But these hazards were all in the game. Elizabeth Diggle boasted that she and her aunt had been up to their knees in mud to see the lake from a good point of view. Moule, who was clearly not such a devoted connoisseur of scenery, argued that there was no special aesthetic advantage in searching for the Picturesque in dangerous places, when most of the best views could be seen with comfort. He cynically suggested that the more recondite Stations were introduced only to detain the tourist longer in the country.

Half a mile to the north of Keswick was another of Gray's favourite viewpoints, the Crosthwaite Vicarage garden. On 4 October 1769 Gray arrived there a little before sunset:

[I] saw in my glass a picture, that if I could transmitt to you, & fix it in all the softness of its living colours, would fairly sell for a thousand pounds. this is the sweetest scene I can yet discover in point of pastoral beauty. the rest are in a sublimer style.[61]

How quickly aesthetic pleasure is given a commercial value! Gray's first sentence is paradigmatic of a sequence of responses which frequently occur to the Picturesque tourist:—(a) He finds a satisfying viewpoint for a fine landscape: (b) He turns away from it so that he can see it in his Claude Glass: (c) The landscape has now become a 'picture': (d) It now remains for the painter to 'fix' all that is 'living' within that mirrored scene, and transfer it to paper or canvas: (e) The end result is a commodity highly prized on the market. Gray's second sentence carefully distinguishes the pleasures of pastoral beauty from those of the Sublime, though, as we have seen in his appreciation of Grasmere, he has the true Picturesque tourist's delight in the variety and contrasts of a blend of beauty and sublimity.

The Vicarage-garden Station was still famous thirty years after Gray's visit. Dr William Maton, taking the view from here in 1799, was troubled by Gray's relish of what we might call a 'mixed mode' landscape. The development of his analogy with drama is an interesting reflection of the persistence of certain neo-classical canons of taste:

Why is unity in the drama . . . so indispensable to the attention & to the senses, yet the violation of it, in that great & rational source of agreeable sensation—landscape – not only ceases to give displeasure, but even becomes desirable and pleasing? I am quite unable to solve the difficulty, & perhaps may not escape the contempt of connoisseurs in landscape beauty for confessing that my own experience has never convinced me of the fact.[62]

Is 'landscape' properly described as a 'rational source' of pleasure? It is true that Picturesque theory was one attempt to rationalise the aesthetic response to land-scape, but it could hardly account for the full complexity of feelings and associations stimulated by scenery such as Derwentwater presented. The way to solve Maton's difficulty was to use the Claude Glass, which could at least give tonal unity to a 'mixed-mode' landscape. As an alternative, one could wait for Nature to harmonise the scene by taking the view under certain conditions of light. As Gray had managed to time his arrival at the Vicarage garden just before sunset, and had been rewarded for it, so West's *Guide* respectfully recommends following this example. The garden becomes his eighth Station, which 'ought to be an evening one', like Stations 6 and 5, on Fawe Park and Swinside respectively, 'when the last beams of the sun rest on the purple summit of *Skiddaw*, and the deep shade of *Wythop*'s wooded brows is stretched over the lake'. Station 7, on the other hand, from Latrigg, should be a morning view.

Sunset or moonlight views harmonised discordant elements and, furthermore, evoked a pleasing melancholy, in accordance with the tradition of night-pieces in poetry. Remember how Gray's famous *Elegy* opens with the 'knell of parting day', a time when pleasurable melancholy is released to wander freely through the twilight, and when shapes are indistinct and malleable by the imagination. Smells of grass and flowers arise as the day cools, and sounds seem amplified. Dr Brown concluded his *Description* with an invitation to a 'walk by still moon-light (at which time the distant water-falls are heard in all the variety of sound) among these enchanting dales' of Derwentwater. Such a walk 'opens a scene of such delicate beauty, repose and solemnity, as exceeds all description'. West, however, recommended timing such a walk just a little earlier:

63. William Gilpin, 'The general idea of Keswick-lake', from his MS Lakes tour notebook (1772).
Bodleian Library, Oxford

The setting sun tips the mountain's top with the softest refulgence; and the rising moon with her silver rays just continues in vision the glories of its base. The surface of the lake [becomes] a plain on which are pencilled by the moon, the faint outlines and shadows of the hills ... All now is in faint light, grave shade, or solemn darkness, which apparently increases the vastness of the objects, and enwraps them in a solemn horror, that strikes the mind of the beholder with reverential awe, and pleasing melancholy.

The tour around the lake from Keswick to Borrowdale began by skirting the eastern shore. The road ran between the shoreline, corrugated with little bays and promontories, and a succession of lofty crags and waterfalls on the left, until one reached the head of the lake at Borrowdale. It was important for the Picturesque tourist to discriminate among the many fine views on this three-mile journey. Gilpin's advice is authoritative:

The inexperienced conductor, shewing you the lake, carries you to some garish stand, where the eye may range far and wide. And such a view indeed is well calculated ... to obtain a general idea of the whole. But he, who is in quest of the picturesque scenes of the lake, must travel along the rough side-screens that adorn it: and catch it's beauties, as they arise in smaller portions – it's little bays, and winding shores – it's deep recesses, and hanging promontories – it's garnished rock, and distant mountain. These are, in general, the picturesque scenes, which it affords.

One such 'garish stand' is West's first Station, at the top of Cockshut Hill close to Crow Park. It afforded a view of nearly the whole lake and was much admired by Young and Gray. When they first knew it, it had been recently planted with trees. By the time Stebbing Shaw saw it in 1787 the young wood had grown into a forest, and the views were obscured. Its particular advantage was its commanding view of the cluster of islands in this northern part of the lake. Lord's Island and St Herbert's Island were a pleasing contrast to the overdeveloped Pocklington's Island. St Herbert's Island bore the remains of a real hermitage, which so stirred Hutchinson's imagination as he approached it that he apparently lost consciousness of his friend's presence in the boat:

I had shewn some distortions in my agitation through this whispered soliloquy ... my companion catched me by the arm and roused me, saying, 'The boatmen already think they have got a passenger that is frantic, and express by their looks their wishes to be rid of us'.

Pocklington was not to be outdone by authentic ruins. When he sold his island in 1796 he moved to Barrow Cascade Hall, about a mile further down the road from Cockshut Hill. There he built a white castellated hermitage and advertised for a hermit.[63] The wages were to be half a crown a day, and the conditions were that the successful applicant should talk to nobody for seven years, nor wash himself, nor cut his nails for that period. No one applied for the post. Sarah Murray declared that if she were a nymph of Derwentwater she would, like Niobe, weep herself to a statue at Pocklington's enormities.[64] He had an enthusiasm for white-washing everything within reach, his house, the adjoining rocks and even the trees. 'Pocklington shaved off the branches of an oak, whitewashed it, and shaped it into a obelisk – So Art beats Nature'[65] reflected Coleridge. The latches, hinges and nailheads of his gates were picked out in scarlet. As a final defiance he had a placard mounted at the entrance to one of his houses which read 'De gustibus non disputandum est', under which somebody inscribed 'As the man said when he kissed his cow'. His estate at Barrow included the fine Barrow Cascade, to which he made a few adjustments by altering the flow of water. By the early nineteenth century this cascade had been awarded four Stations of its own.

Lodore at the southern end of Derwentwater was one of the most famous natural wonders on the Lakes tour. The sound of the cascade, itself a herald of the sublimities of Borrowdale, was amplified by the mountain echoes. These echoes were commercially exploited by the proprietor of the Lodore Inn near one of the landing places at this end of the lake. To greet tourists off the boat with a sample of the aural Sublime, he would discharge a small cannon, and the echoes would rumble round the mountains for several seconds. Nine distinct echoes were counted on one occasion. There was, to begin with, a choice of two cannon available to the tourist, one at four shillings a firing and the other at two shillings and six pence. But, as Robert Southey sensibly argued, 'when one buys an echo, who would be content for the sake of saving eighteen pence, to put up with the second best, instead of ordering at once the super-extra-double-superfine?' Not many, evidently; for the smaller cannon rusted away through disuse until it became a hazard.[66]

The aural and visual Sublime were fully integrated at the cascade itself, which thrilled all who saw it in full spate:

How enviable we thought the peasants of this enchanting spot. And yet how little intelligible to them must have been the emotions that gave rise to our exclamations! . . . It far exceeded everything of the sort we had before seen. There is not a vestige of art. Nature has been so truly grand here in her workmanship, that she bids defiance to all attempts at improving the scene.[67]

In other words, we may be thankful that Lodore was not on Pocklington's property. The meticulous connoisseurship of the tourists at this site must indeed have baffled those 'enviable' peasants:

. . . the composition is picturesque to perfection – the torrent most finely broken, the impending cliffs richly trimmed with foliage. The fury with which the stream foamed, as it leaped from rock to rock, gave it an infinitely more striking appearance than it can present when there is a larger body of water – & it reached the ground, even in its present circumstances, with such a thundering violence, that the dreadful fragments hanging from the shaggy sides of the mountain seemed to totter in their holds, & the earth to tremble underneath . . . Sublimity & beauty are here united in the most happy and peculiar manner I have ever witnessed.[68]

The writer concludes by wishing he had the painter's skill here, where words fail.

Gilpin too is enraptured, even though he is reluctant to apply the term 'Picturesque'. This 'grand piece of natural ruin', he categorises as 'a single object' which 'wants no accompaniments of offskip . . . the greatness of it's parts affords scenery enough'. That is to say, the conventional requirement of the three distances can be dispensed with, and the 'nobility' of the cascade itself can fill the scene.

The view from the rocks at Lodore over Derwentwater (Dalton's view, it will be remembered) had, for the first time on this tour, the magnificent background of Skiddaw rising behind Keswick, and was acclaimed by Hutchinson:

Claude in his happiest hour never struck out a finer landskip; it has every requisite which the pencil can demand, and is perhaps the only view in England which can vie with the sublime scenes from which that painter formed his taste.

The only view in England to match a Claudean original: this is the highest praise that a Picturesque tourist can bestow. Farington naturally takes this famous view, and he supplies a foreground with framing trees, through which the river runs down to the lake (fig. 64). In the middle distance:

. . . the whole lake presents itself uninterrupted by any object but its own beauteous isles, and gradually diminishing, over the town of Keswick . . . the eye is carried thro' a surprizing avenue, formed by lofty Skiddaw and its opposite mountains [Cat Bells], and at length is lost over the delightful vale in which the lake of Bassingthwaite winds its woodgirt streams.[69]

Claude's landscapes are usually terminated by a chain of mountains, so that the eye meets a buffer, as it were, and returns to meander in the first two distances. But in the view from Lodore, the eye is exercised more strenuously by the 'surprizing avenue' which tempts it to further exploration beyond the confines of the scene.

The tourist was now at the threshold of Borrowdale, traditionally the most Sublime region on the tour to the Lakes. It had won its reputation mainly through the story of Gray's terrified refusal to venture further into the dale than the village of Grange, a mile up the road from Lodore. The two-arch bridge over the Derwent brought one to a village of little more than half-a-dozen houses, 'built apparently without mortar, and that so long ago that the stones have the same weather-worn colour as those which lie upon the mountain side behind them', thought Southey. Here Gray was given hospitality by a young farmer, Caleb Fisher: 'his Mother & he brought us butter, that Siserah would have jump'd at, tho' not in a lordly dish, bowls of milk, thin oaten-cakes, & ale'.[70] Gray was awestruck by the farmer's account of how he had plundered the eagle's nest the year before to carry off the eaglet. The young man clearly delighted in telling of his daring feats to the timorous poet. Seventeen years later, in 1786, the same farmer was encountered by another tourist, who received similar hospitality:

He said much of Gray's timidity, and told me he seemed to expect that every rock he saw, would fall on him. Some person whom he met there by accident, had given him Gray's tour.[71]

64. Joseph Farington, 'Skiddaw and Derwentwater from Lowdore Waterfall',
from T. H. Horne's *The Lakes of Lancashire, Westmoreland and Cumberland* (1816).
British Library, London

65.  Julius Caesar Ibbetson, *Castle Crag, Borrowdale* (c. 1812).
Abbot Hall Art Gallery, Kendal

In 1795 Thomas Clutterbuck was also entertained by Caleb Fisher; and Thomas Horne in 1816, nearly half a century after Gray's original encounter, met the 'garrulous old man', who still delighted 'to narrate to tourists the poet's fears, and the avidity with which the latter partook of his homely fare'.[72]

What had so terrified Gray might best be described by a medley of quotations:

Dark rocks yawn at its entrance, terrific as the wildness of a maniac; and disclose a narrow pass, running up between mountains of granite, that are shook into almost every possible form of horror. All above resembles the accumulations of an earthquake; splintered, shivered, piled, amassed . . . Huge and mishapen rocks were overhanging the road . . . Roots of old oak, hard as the rock, and in some parts seemingly engrafted in it . . . It looked like an entrance to the infernal regions, and the daemon of desolation might fix his empire unrivalled amidst the wreck of a universe . . . impending cliffs lifted high their embattled heads on the left, sharpened into a thousand points, and whitened with perpetual storms . . .[73]

'Oh Rousseau!' cried one visitor, 'what a Retreat was here for the Man of Nature'.[74] Borrowdale's forbidding barrier of cliffs insulated it from the social world (fig. 65). Before the middle of the eighteenth century, Clarke reported, the dale was 'hardly in a state even of civilization'. Agriculture was little understood, and the inhabitants were proverbial for general ignorance. Clarke observed that up to the last third of the eighteenth century a cart or indeed any kind of wheel carriage was totally unknown in Borrowdale. This was just the kind of primaeval culture and environment that the tourists came to see, bringing with them their paraphernalia of associations with a pastoral Golden Age, fashionable Sublime aesthetics and visual prejudices founded on Italian landscapes. Robert Southey arrived with high expectations.

[Guide books and journals] told us of tracts of horrible barrenness, of terrific precipices, rocks rioting upon rocks, and mountains tost together in chaotic confusion; of stone avalanches rendering the ways impassable, the fear of some travellers who had shrunk back from this dreadful entrance into Borrodale, and the heroism of others who had dared to penetrate into these impenetrable regions: – into these regions, however, we found no difficulty in walking along a good road, which coaches of the light English make travel every summer's day.

The first carriages to become familiar in Borrowdale were, ironically, those of the tourists. It was their visits which contributed most to the disappearance of what they had come in search of in the last decades of the century.

Map 4. The Highlands

# VIII

## The Highlands tour and the Ossianic Sublime

Scotland was unfortunate in having attracted Samuel Johnson as one of her first English tourists. Many later eighteenth-century tours to the Highlands were undertaken specifically for the pleasure of challenging or endorsing Johnson's censorious commentary on Scotland's people and landscape when it was published in 1775 as his *Journey to the Western Islands of Scotland*. Johnson, in his judgement of landscapes as in so many other areas of his criticism, belonged to the Augustan tradition, and this tradition could allow little to admire in Scotland:

An eye accustomed to flowery pastures and waving harvests is astonished and repelled by this wide extent of hopeless sterility. The appearance is that of matter incapable of form or usefulness, dismissed by nature from her care and disinherited of her favours.

In this view he was supported by many travellers from the south, who, like William Gibson, were intimidated by the 'deep valleys, dusky moors, vast lochs and scowling mountains, enveloped frequently in fogs and . . . reverberating only to the roar of torrents, or the moaning winds'. The Highlands were regarded as 'destitute of every object most welcome to man's social spirit'. Another member of Johnson's circle, Oliver Goldsmith, was by nature rather more responsive to country scenery; but even so his first experience of Scotland was most discouraging. He arrived at Edinburgh in September 1753, and wrote to a friend:

Shall I tire you with a description of this unfruitfull country? where I must lead you over their hills all brown with heath, or their valleys scarce able to feed a rabbet? Man alone seems to be the only creature who has arrived to the natural size in this poor soil; every part of the country presents the same dismall landscape, no grove nor brook lend their musick to cheer the stranger, or make the inhabitants forget their poverty.[1]

As far as Johnson was concerned the most conspicuous deficiency in the Highland landscape was the lack of trees, particularly trees of any maturity. As he approached Banff, he recorded that he had now travelled 200 miles of the country, and seen only one tree not younger than himself: 'A tree might be a show in Scotland as a horse in Venice'. This lack of trees he attributed to an habitual improvidence and laziness in the Scots, who attached no importance to conservation or cultivation, and had denuded their own landscape: here as elsewhere in Johnson, moral, economic and aesthetic judgements were inseparable.

Johnson was by no means the first visitor to point out the lack of trees. An English officer stationed in Scotland in 1699 observed that 'had Christ been betrayed in this Countrey (as doubtless he should, had he come as a Stranger) Judas had sooner found the Grace of Repentance, than a Tree to hang himself on'.[2]

Later travellers were, as often as not, unfair to both Johnson and Scotland on this contentious matter; for, towards the end of his *Journey*, Johnson shows himself to be fully aware of and sympathetic towards the problem of afforestation in Scotland:

Plantation is naturally the employment of a mind unburdened with care ... and at leisure to derive gratification from the prospect of posterity ... It may be soon discovered, why in a place, which hardly supplies the cravings of necessity, there has been little attention to the delights of fancy, and why distant convenience is unregarded, where the thoughts are turned with incessant solicitude upon every possibility of immediate advantage.

Ground sown with trees cannot be used for pasture or crops, both of which yield quicker returns for a struggling economy. In addition, the scarcity of trees was matched by the scarcity of inhabitants in the Highlands.

Both the host nation and her English tourists reacted strongly to the negative criticism in Johnson's *Journey*. 'He set out under incurable impressions of a national prejudice, a religious prejudice, and a literary prejudice',[3] concluded John Knox, who travelled to the Hebrides in Johnson's footsteps in 1786. Hester Piozzi was later sent urgent invitations to come to Scotland, specifically so that she might contradict her illustrious friend's disparaging account.[4] John Lettice, a Sussex clergyman and poet, set out for the Highlands with the published intention of repairing the damage done by Johnson, and 'of rendering the *moral* as complete as the *civil union* betwixt the English and the Scots':[5] and that doughty traveller, Mary Ann Hanway, left for Scotland only a few months after the publication of the *Journey* with the task of vindicating the Scots and their country from 'those illiberal aspersions' under which they had laboured so long. In one of her many combative flourishes she remarked that she thought it a pity Johnson had not contented himself with *writing Ramblers*, instead of *taking* a ramble. Johnson's comments on Scotland only exacerbated existing tensions between the English and the Scots which dated much further back than the Jacobite uprisings. To increase their chances of a hospitable reception on their pedestrian tour of Scotland, a London lawyer, John Bristed, and his companion dressed as American sailors and cultivated American accents, sometimes shifting into Irish when it seemed more expedient (fig. 66).

By the 1790s Johnson was of little importance as a precedent for the tourist to the Scottish Highlands. Picturesque taste had usurped his authority. Moreover, the Ossian cult and the appetite for the Sublime in landscape drew tourists into Highland regions which had bewildered and depressed Johnson. Even the supply of trees had improved by then. 'I never remember to have seen richer groves of

66. 'The Author and his companion in the Highlands', frontispiece to John Bristed's *Pedestrian Tour through parts of the Highlands of Scotland 1801* (1803). British Library, London

oak, beech, and birch, or finer single trees, in any part of England', remarked Henry Skrine, the barrister and tireless traveller, in 1795.[6] All those trees Johnson had dismissed as being younger than himself were now, twenty years later, reaching maturity.

The great stretches of barren mountain country and moorland which the Highlands presented to the traveller, had no equal on any of the British tours. Mrs Piozzi thought that Scottish prospects excelled all others for Picturesqueness.[7] According to Farington, her opinion was endorsed by the great master of landscape painting:

Turner thinks Scotland a more picturesque country to study in than Wales. The lines of the mountains are finer, and the rocks of larger masses.[8]

But Gilpin had considerable reservations. 'On entering Scotland', he wrote, 'what makes the first impression on the picturesque eye are those vast tracts of land, which we meet with intirely *in a state of nature*'. There were good foregrounds – broken knolls, ragged rocks, winding roads – but the '*Scotch distance* rarely exhibits any diversity of objects'. Fully aware of these serious deficiencies in a landscape which had 'too much the appearance of dead life' and which induced a kind of mental despair, John Dalrymple recommended various ways in which the mid-century Scottish landowner could 'improve' his Highland estate.[9] It was particularly necessary to introduce into the garden the sights and sounds of life – very white cottages, plenty of trees and turbulent cascades. But apart from these oases of 'improvement', the best that Johnson could say about the Highlands was that such desolate regions do exist and are indeed 'one of the great scenes of human existence', and that he who refuses to see them is a lesser man.

Johnson had little of that taste for the Sublime which Scottish scenery above all could satisfy, and to which his distinguished contemporary Thomas Gray seems to have been precociously susceptible: 'Since I saw the Alps, I have seen nothing sublime till now'.[10] Gray made his tour to Scotland in 1765. When he got back to London, he tried to sum up the effect on him of such a landscape:

[the mountains of the Highlands] are extatic, & ought to be visited in pilgrimage once a year. none but those monstrous creatures of God know how to join so much beauty with so much horror. a fig for your Poets, Painters, Gardiners, Clergymen, that have not been among them: their imagination can be made up of nothing but bowling-greens, flowering shrubs, horse-ponds, Fleet-ditches, shell-grottoes, & Chinée-rails.[11]

Johnson and Gray are not as far apart in their reactions as they might seem: both willingly acknowledge an enlargement of the mind consequent on such scenery, though for Johnson it is primarily the moral sense that is enlarged. This was a good enough reason for visiting a country which, even forty years after Johnson's tour, could still be considered 'beyond the limits of *civilized travel*'.[12] But, as we have seen on the other tours, *'civilized travel'* for pleasure had for decades specifically searched out the remains of a remote, barely civilised past. It was perfectly logical to ask, 'If all our *European* Travellers direct their Course to *Italy*, upon the account of its Antiquity, why should *Scotland* be neglected, whose wrinkled surface derives its Original from the Chaos?'[13] This same tourist of 1699 was vitriolic about the barbarity of the Scots. He suggested the people derived their name from 'the word σκοτὴ (Darkness)', and he meant the darkness to be applied both to their 'gross and blockish understandings' and to their gloomy country. A year after the '45 uprising a letter of advice 'to a young Gentleman' to dissuade him from journeying to Scotland claimed it was more likely for the Pope to turn Protestant than that an educated man could 'ampliate his understanding by grazing in the *Caledonian* Forest':

Some are of Opinion that, when the *Devil* showed our Saviour the Kingdoms of the Earth, he laid his Thumb upon *Scotland* . . . because it was not likely to be any Temptation.[14]

But there was no dissuading the tourists who began to visit the Highlands in increasing numbers from about 1760 onwards. In 1759 Lord Breadalbane noticed 'it has been the fashion this year to travel into the highlands, many have been here this summer from England, I suppose because they can't go abroad': and in 1773 he recognised that the Highlands tour was becoming *le bon ton*.[15] In spite of this, the Highlands were nowhere near as congested as the Lake District. Even in July 1798, in the heyday of Picturesque travel, Dr Thomas Garnett, the physician and natural philosopher, reported that during the first three weeks of his tour in the Highlands he never met a single traveller.[16] The loneliness of the route was in itself an experience of the Sublime. Mary Ann Hanway wrote to her sister that for days she had been 'travelling through places so gloomy, that was I to attempt to describe them, it would give you the vapours for this month to come'. It was fortunate that these roads, even in the Highlands, were remarkably good, and many a tourist paid tribute to the man held to be mainly responsible for this, General Wade. Wade superintended the building of roads and bridges through the Highlands in the 1720s, built partly to connect the line of English forts established after the 1715 Jacobite rebellion. He became the subject of some extravagant accolades, as in this 1764 Dedication for a poem on the 'Genius of Scotland':

> And see, where bursting from a Gothic night
> Half her brave race emerges into light; . . .
> By THEE! her genius raised, with glad surprise
> See cultured groves, and cheerful villas rise.
> Pleased she beholds the golden harvests nod,
> And the bold arch controul the swelling flood;
> O'er wastes the traffic-crowded causeway stretch,
> And spreading hedges fence the grateful beach.[17]

Even such a sober authority as the current *Red Guide* to Scotland is inclined to credit Wade with having done more to make Scotland known to the outer world than had Johnson or Walter Scott. The forts themselves, Fort Augustus, Fort George, and Fort William, became useful staging posts for English tourists who had been upset by some of the more squalid accommodation in the Highlands:

Here is great store of Fowl, indeed, as foul Houses, foul Streets, foul Linnen . . . They have good store of Deer. . . . dear Lodgings, dear Horse-Meat, Dear Tobacco.[18]

The poorer people were regarded as little more than savages, content to live in filth and degradation. Mrs Piozzi found it convenient to blame this on France's traditionally close links with Scotland – 'The Love of Dirt is another Continental Taste'[19] which the people have adopted. Wade's military roads and the presence of the forts, together with the erosion of clanship and slow improvements in agriculture were thought to have brought the Highlands quickly from the middle ages into the eighteenth century. An additional civilizing influence was the steady stream of tourists from England. 'All the world is travelling to Scotland' exclaimed Elizabeth Diggle, who made her tour in 1788. But not all the world had the courage to penetrate the Highlands. The story was told at the Inn at Luss on Loch Lomond of two English travellers who were alarmed by the thick mists as they set out one morning. One observed to his companion that he was sure the sun never shone in the Highlands; 'the other being of the same opinion, they immediately turned their horses round and hastened back to the sun-shine of the Seven Dials, and the clear atmosphere of Exeter-Change'.[20] Scottish bad weather was notorious. John Stoddart, the journalist, told of a disappointed traveller at an

Inverary Inn who had been confined there for several days by the wet. In desperation he asked his landlord if it always rained in Scotland. 'Hoot na!' answered the landlord with great simplicity, 'it snaws whiles'.

The weather was part of Scotland's distinctive character, as one of her most eminent scholars and poets, James Beattie, was careful to point out. His celebrated analysis of his country's character appeared in a 1762 essay 'On Poetry and Music, as they affect the Mind', and it is worth quoting at some length:

> The highlands of Scotland are a picturesque, but in general a melancholy country. Long tracts of mountainous desert, covered with dark heath, and often obscured by misty weather; narrow vallies, thinly inhabited, and bounded by precipices resounding with the fall of torrents; a soil so rugged, and a climate so dreary; as in many parts to admit neither the amusements of pasturage, nor the labours of agriculture; the mournful dashing of waves along the firths and lakes that intersect the country; the portentous noises which every change of the wind, and every increase and diminution of the waters, is apt to raise, in a lonely region full of echoes, and rocks, and caverns: . . . objects like these diffuse a gloom over the fancy . . . cannot fail to tincture the thoughts of a native in the hour of silence and solitude. [consequently . . .] their poetry is almost uniformly mournful, and their views of nature dark and dreary.[21]

A 'picturesque' *but* 'a melancholy country': Beattie suggests the two are not quite compatible. Gilpin respectfully quotes part of this passage, and admits that all the objects described by Beattie are 'circumstances of a melancholy cast' and 'not entirely of the picturesque kind': yet 'they are nearly allied to it; and give a tinge to the imagination of every traveller, who examines these scenes of solitude and grandeur'. These scenes of melancholy grandeur found no more popular expression than in the Ossian poems. Whatever side one took in the controversy over their authenticity, these poems accompanied nearly every Picturesque tourist into the Highlands, and provoked rapturous recitations by the sides of waterfalls, or on the mountain tops. An example of 'Ossianic Mania' is given in the travel letters of Anne Grant, a lady of exquisite sensibility:

> . . . every blast seemed to touch a viewless harp; and every passing cloud, brightened with the beams of the moon, appeared to my mind's eye a vehicle for the shades of the lovely and the brave, that live in the songs of other times.[22]

Both in cadence and imagery these 'songs of other times' distilled the influence of the landscape and the climate, and their primitive idiom was a thrilling contrast to the polished social poetry of the Augustans and their successors. Anna Seward, who, as a child, had grown romantically fond of Derbyshire countryside and 'the Salvatorial style' in poetry and painting, confessed how this 'early-acquired predilection steeps my eyes in the dews of pensive transport, when they stray over the pages of Ossian.'[23] Ossianic poetry appealed to a taste already stimulated by Welsh Druidic mythology and some poems by Gray and Collins. Since the interest in Ossian was such a strong motive for this tour, it may help to give a brief recapitulation of the controversy.

James Macpherson, a young Scottish schoolmaster, published a collection of poems in 1760 entitled *Fragments of Ancient Poetry, Collected in the Highlands of Scotland, and Translated from the Gaelic or Erse language*. The popularity of the book was such that he received funds for two journeys into the Highlands and Western Islands to research further into Gaelic poetry. He collected versions of some of the traditional songs of the region, and in 1761 published *Fingal, an ancient epic Poem, in six books*, and two years later *Temora*. *The Works of Ossian, The Son of Fingal*, which combined *Fingal* and *Temora* and added several other poems, was published in 1765, and went through some 25 editions in the next 30 years. That these poems, purporting to be translated from ancient Gaelic originals, were largely inspired forgeries is now generally accepted. Dr Johnson was at the head of those who, in Macpherson's day, publicly denounced them as spurious, and he was challenged to a duel by their author. But Macpherson also had some impressive supporters, notably Hugh Blair, Professor of Rhetoric at the University of Edinburgh, who contributed a 'Critical Dissertation' to *The Works of Ossian*:

. . . poetry, which is the child of imagination, is frequently most glowing and animated in the first age of society. [for the people of this society] Their passions have nothing to restrain them: their imagination has nothing to check it. They display themselves to one another without disguise . . . in the uncovered simplicity of nature. As their feelings are strong, so their language, of itself, assumes a poetical turn. Prone to exaggerate, they describe everything in the strongest colours; which of course renders their speech picturesque and figurative.[24]

Much of this reads like an anticipation of that other famous vindication of a new kind of poetry reflecting the passionate nature of a simple community – Wordsworth's Preface to *Lyrical Ballads*, just over thirty years later. In both cases the poetry is seen to owe much of its tenor to the influence on that society of a Sublime natural environment. Elizabeth Montagu writes to Lord Lyttelton in 1760 to thank him for sending a copy of the recently published Ossianic *Fragments*:

I hear Lord Marchmont says, our old Highland bard is a modern gentleman of his acquaintance; if it be so, we have a living poet who may dispute the pas on Parnassus with Pindar and the greatest of the ancients, and I honour him for carrying the Muses into the country, and letting them step majestic over hills, mountains, and rivers, instead of tamely walking in the Park or Piccadilly.[25]

The Scottish Highlands, as Beattie suggested, cast their sombre influence over the poetry of Ossian. The discovery of a British Homer was just what that nationalistic age wanted: 'We meet with no Grecian or Italian scenery; but with the mists, and clouds, and storms of a northern mountainous region'.[26] A few of the less exclamatory lines from the opening of 'Carthon: A Poem' will give a sufficient taste:

A Tale of the times of old! The deeds of days of other years! . . . The murmer of thy streams, O Lora, brings back the memory of the past. The sound of thy woods,

Garmallar, is lovely in mine ear. Dost thou not behold, Malvina, a rock with its head of heath? Three aged firs bend from its face; green is the narrow plain at its feet; there the flower of the mountain grows, and shakes its white head in the breeze. The thistle is there alone, and sheds its aged beard. Two trees, half sunk in the ground, show their heads of moss. The deer of the mountain avoids the place, for he beholds the gray ghost that guards it: for the mighty lie, O Malvina, in the narrow plain of the rock.[27]

The bardic tone of this highly rhythmical prose was a refreshing sound, especially to the English ear, beginning to tune itself to the Sublime. The tourists carried with them *The Works of Ossian*, 'acknowledged by every lover of the *beautiful* and *sublime*, to contain in them the most animating and lofty ideas, calculated to inspire the mind with heroic courage and virtue'[28] (fig. 67). But cultural and economic change in the Highlands since 1745 had, to many of the older generation of High-landers, destroyed this Ossianic spirit forever. The Revd J. Michell, touring with the Duke of Somerset in 1795, encountered a 'firm Fingalian' who told him that Ossian and his bards had been exiled by high rents and potatoes: 'The first pre-cludes them from attending to anything but the claims of their landlords; and the last, by securing them against scarcity, have inspired them with ideas of gain, to which they were entire strangers'.[29] Gone too were the initiation rituals through which the aspiring young chieftain of a clan had to pass to prove his manhood – skill in hunting, and courage in cattle-stealing:

The solemnities in the inauguration of a chief are no more. The voice of the bard is silent in the hall. The deeds of other times are no longer recounted as incentives to emulate their forefathers.

The deeds of other times were recited instead in London drawing-rooms. 'The system is altogether changed; and the manners of civilized Europe are rapidly prevailing in the remotest corners of the Highlands and Western Islands'. A fading culture begins to acquire an antique value. It is an irony we have already noted, that those most curious about a primitive culture were also those most influential in erasing it. By the turn of the century, only the inhabitants of the Western Islands were thought to have retained faithfully this folk culture: 'as they are inferior to their neighbours in every branch of modern improvement, so they excel them in these relics of former excellence'.[30] James Plumptre, for his part, was thoroughly sceptical about the vaunted Ossianic inspiration to virtue. He regretted having forgotten to pack his Cowper and taken only Ossian as his pocket companion through the Highlands: 'Ossian is at most only a Poet: Cowper is a poet and a Christian'.[31] In the journal of his tour into Scotland he included an Ossianic parody, 'Empti-Ponchin: A Gaelic Fragment', which tells in epic terms of his chilly reception at a Highland inn.

The Highland landscape, mountainous and misty, permeated by the spirits of Fingal and Ossian, was the greatest incentive after the mid-1760s to make this formidable tour of Scotland. John Stoddart describes an evening spent in con-versation with the Duchess of Gordon at her cottage in Kinrara: 'our time was

67. Alexander Runciman, 'The blind Ossian, singing and accompanying himself on the harp',
a design for the ceiling of Penecuik House.
National Gallery of Scotland, Edinburgh

passed with authors most interesting in such a situation – with Ossian, the painter of Highland scenery – with Burns, the still more animated painter of Scottish feelings: nor should I forget Mr Price's Essay on the Picturesque, which served as a text-book to all our discussions on local improvement'. Burns himself toured the Highlands in 1787 and gave a representative summary of the objects most likely to be sought by the tourist: 'I have done nothing else but visited cascades, prospects, ruins and Druidical temples, learned Highland tunes and pickt up Scotch songs, Jacobite anecdotes, etc these two months'.[32] In the 1790s Londoners could catch a taste of Scottish scenery when *Harlequin in Hebrides*, was put on at Sadler's Wells. The lavish sets included 'A *Highland Laird's* Chamber', 'A *Highland* Village' and 'A dark, rocky Cavern on the Coast of Scotland'.[33]

Robert Heron, who wrote an authoritative topographical guide to Scotland in the early nineteenth century, toured the Highlands in 1792 and in his *Observations* sums up why this had become a very fashionable summer tour within the previous ten or twelve years:

The celebrity of Dr Johnson's name rendered the English curious to learn something of a place which he had visited as a scene in which he might contemplate nature in her grandest, wildest aspects, and human society in its rudest, simplest form . . . – About the same time, or earlier, Mr. Pennant, after the publication of his British Zoology, was induced to make the tour of Scotland, and presented a large and pleasing account of it to the Public . . . In addition to the writing of these two travellers, the progress of Gardening and of Landscape-painting in England, contributed to persuade English company to visit the wilder scenes in Scotland in the Summer months.

Heron adds to these incentives the great abundance of game, good accommodation and roads, and the fact that the appeal of the English summer resorts was exhausted.

There were two Scottish tours recognised over this period. What might be called the 'Long Tour' followed the north-eastern coastline up to Aberdeen and round to Inverness, then down by Loch Ness and Ben Nevis with perhaps an excursion to the Western Islands, especially Iona and Staffa, and then back to Glasgow. This is more or less the route followed by Johnson and Boswell. The other tour was undertaken by those who came to Edinburgh for reasons of health or amusement:

[they] generally visit Glasgow, Loch Lomond, and Inverary, on the West; or Perth, Dunkeld, Blair, and Taymouth, on the North. Many gentlemen visit all these places; and this is called *The Short Tour of Scotland*.[34]

Gilpin's tour was Edinburgh–Stirling–Perth–Dunkeld–Taymouth–Killin–Loch Awe–Inverary–Loch Lomond–Glasgow and the Falls of the Clyde (the latter site was described but not actually visited). This route, with one or two changes, is the one we shall follow in this chapter.

The most favoured entry point into Scotland from England was across the border into Gretna Green. This was the celebrated resort of those who, as Henry Skrine delicately put it, 'seek a speedier introduction to Hymen than their own country will allow'.[35] According to Scottish law, runaway couples could be married without parental consent here and within a few minutes of their arrival across the border. The 'glowing females of the present generation are not to be tyed down by either prudish or prudential duties', wrote Mary Ann Hanway with shrill irony: 'No, forsooth, liberty! dear liberty is the TON; and, so, heigh for a chaise and pair, and Gretna-Green'. Since parents were often in hot pursuit, such speed and convenience were well worth the fee of two guineas or so; and if there was no time for the ceremony, as Pennant remarked, 'the frightened pair are advised to slip in bed, are shown to the pursuers who imagine that they are irrecoverably united, retire, and leave them to "consummate their unfinished loves" '.[36] The village blacksmith, fisherman or joiner generally performed the ceremony, and many a tourist plied the old blacksmith with whisky to induce him to tell his store of anecdotes. Gilpin recommends Gretna Green as the greatest seminary in Europe for apprentice novelists: 'A few months conversation with the literati of this place, will furnish the inquisitive student with such a fund of anecdotes, that with a moderate share of imagination in tacking them together, he may spin out as many volumes as he pleases'.

The novelist who had least need of such steamy contemporary material, Walter Scott, became inseparably associated with the countryside to the south of Edinburgh, particularly with the river Esk and the Lothians. Of the Esk he wrote 'no stream in Scotland can boast such a varied succession of the most interesting objects, as well as of the most romantic and beautiful scenery'.[37] This romantic scenery included the fine castles of Dalhousie, Roslin (fig. 68) and Hawthornden (the retreat of Ben Jonson's friend the poet William Drummond). The last two castles especially were favourites with the Picturesque tourist. Robert Burns and Alexander Nasmyth, the distinguished Scottish landscape painter, walked to Roslin Castle from Edinburgh one fine morning in 1786. Nasmyth made a pencil sketch of Burns (fig. 69) standing beneath the great Norman arch of Roslin, meditating on 'the eternal renewal of youth and freshness of nature, contrasted with the crumbling decay of man's efforts to perpetuate his work'.[38] John Stoddart, who toured the Esk country with Scott in 1800, recommended the lowest possible viewpoint for this much sketched ruin by wading down the stream itself near to the foot of the castle crag which then appeared 'at once beautifully wild, and awfully sublime', with its ruined towers faintly seen between the branches.

Edinburgh itself, according to Gray, was 'that most picturesque (at a distance) and nastiest (when near) of all capital Cities'[39] – another example of how a discreet distance improves objects. For Gilpin the castle itself was Edinburgh's only Picturesque object, provided it was viewed from the bottom of its rock. This was

68. Paul Sandby, *Roslin Castle, Midlothian* (c. 1770).
Yale Center for British Art, Paul Mellon Collection

69. Alexander Nasmyth, 'Part of Roslynn Castle: the figure is Rt. Burns' (1786).
Scottish National Portrait Gallery, Edinburgh

where Joseph Farington chose his angle for his delicate pen and wash study of the
castle from the Grass Market (fig. 70). Farington had been commissioned by John
Knox, the philanthropist and book-seller, to make some drawings for a book on
the Picturesque scenery of Scotland (a project prematurely terminated by Knox's
death in 1790). He arrived in Edinburgh during the very wet June of 1788 and, as
weather permitted, began exploring good viewpoints. There is some discrepancy
between the dates in his tour journal and the precise date, 'June 28th 1788' on the
Grass Market drawing. Here, anyway, is his account of the growth of the drawing:

Thursday July 3rd – Rose at four o'clock and went to a situation under the Castle leading to the Grassmarket and drew in the first outline of a view of the Castle which is
intended for one of the subjects in Mr. Knox's publication . . .
[July 8. To Grassmarket] where I proceeded with my view of the Castle and penned
it in . . .
[July 10. To Grassmarket] and tinted from nature the Castle, Rock and Cottages.
[July 19. Confined indoors by rain] I employed myself in going over some of my outlines with a Pen in order to correct and fix them.[40]

The few days' pause in Edinburgh before setting out for the Highlands enabled
the tourists to reflect on the social conditions of the Scottish people and compare
life in the capital with that in one of the great English cities. The English visitors
seem to have been obsessed by one particular characteristic:

70. Joseph Farington, 'Edinburgh Castle from the Grassmarket' (1788).
National Gallery of Scotland, Edinburgh

The Master of the Hotell asked us if we did not think Edinburgh arrived at the zenith of elegance. No says I, nor never shall, 'till I see the chambermaid of such a house as this in shoes and stockings.[41]

Every tourist, it seemed, had to register shock at the shoelessness of the Scottish women: 'Oh! how unlike fair England's feet / In glossy shoe so trim and neat'.[42] Some were particularly hard on the elderly women of the city, who were regarded as the personifications of the 'wayward Sisters' in *Macbeth*:

The old women far exceed in Ugliness, our English Hags. It is not easy to conceive the sublime extent of their Ugliness, augmented by the Effects of the Weather, Climate, Rags, & Poverty.[43]

But many of the younger women, if their shoelessness could be overlooked, were distinctly attractive: the lack of any head covering except a ribbon in their hair gave them a 'very pretty simple picturesque appearance' thought Elizabeth Diggle. But their casual improprieties astonished the more genteel English tourist. Sir Nathaniel Wraxall, a baronet and the author of some notorious political memoirs, was transfixed one morning as he looked out of the window of his inn:

. . . a young Woman, very well dressed in white, but without Shoes or Stockings, came out of a House not far distant; & squatting down on the side of the 'Burn', quite un-concealed, proceeded to perform her Devotions to Cloacina in the most expeditious

Manner. Having dispatched her Sacrifice, she shifted her situation about a Foot on one Side, continuing still however in the same attitude for a few seconds, when she rose, let drop her cloathes, & returned very quietly to the House.[44]

The lack of lavatories was generally deplored in this elegant, euphemistic manner: 'the Goddess C-ac-n has no worshippers, the inhabitants sacrificing universally to the rustic deities'.[45] The common people of Scotland, like the Welsh, were thought to be more than a century behind their English counterparts in terms of behaviour. However there was a distinction to be made between the Low-landers and Highlanders, one that was, surprisingly, more favourable to the latter. The Highlanders 'a manly, bold, and hardy race, are courteous in their manners, civil in their address, and hospitable to the utmost extent of their little power'; whereas Lowland manners 'cannot fail to disgust a stranger'.[46] Picturesque tastes, in theory, always preferred the human ornaments in a landscape to be rugged and dishevelled. But such preferences were severely tested when the tourists confronted the reality at close quarters, when distances no longer lent enchantment to the view. Their predicament resembles that fine balance required by the Sublime, between exposure to real danger and the titillation of danger perceived from a relatively safe position.

If the tourist and sketcher had been baffled, like Gilpin, with the Picturesque problems of Edinburgh, he was to be perplexed still more by three sites in the next stage of the tour up the right bank of the Forth to Stirling. The first problem was Hopetoun House. This enormous house, superbly situated overlooking the Forth, had been developed over the first half of the eighteenth century, latterly by the Adam brothers. But its majestic classical lines were anathema to Picturesque tastes. Gilpin recommended the distant view only, when the regular building was connected with an irregular object: 'The horizontal lines of the house, and the diverging lines of the hill accord agreeably'. He goes on to make the point that the artist who has to paint a modern house is usually obliged to break up its regularity of line 'at least with a few branches of trees, if he have nothing else at hand'. Gothic architecture or ruined classical buildings were, by comparison, tailor-made for the painter. More pictorial problems occurred at the ironworks along the banks of the Forth. John Stoddart was reminded of the paintings of Joseph Wright of Derby, though he regretted that Wright had selected only the most glowing and violent effects of industrial scenery, when there were subtler contrasts to be explored.

But the greatest challenge for the Picturesque connoisseur was the prospect to the south-west from Stirling Castle, by far the finest view in Scotland, according to Pennant. The principal object was the river winding for miles in great sweeping loops down the Firth of Forth. 'It is exceedingly grand, and amusing', granted Gilpin, but 'it is not indeed picturesque'. It could not qualify for this because it was a bird's eye view. We have encountered this paradox already on tours in search of the Picturesque: the view from Ross churchyard, the Vale of Clwyd in North Wales, and Windermere from West's fifth Station, were all magnificent views but unsuitable for the painter. The most interesting discussion of the Stirling Castle view occurs in John Lettice's *Tour*. He much admires the prospect, and at the same time acknowledges that Gilpin would not allow him to call this Picturesque. It is nevertheless 'a magazine in which ten thousand landscapes and pictures may be found by the tourist or painter', even though no landscape painter would have chosen this particular viewpoint:

Most objects should be near enough the painter's eye, to define their form, colour, and characters. A certain familiarity must subsist between him and the fore-grounds of the scene he paints. His business is to produce pleasure upon fixed principles. Grand conceptions of nature; surprise, admiration, elevation of mind; reflections upon art, cultivation and human power, and numberless sentiments and associations of ideas, will affect, and charm, a spectator on first surveying so glorious an horizon, which no rules of verbal description, drawn from the art of painting, could ever enable him to communicate to a reader.[47]

The Picturesque objection is really that there is only one distance to this whole scene, an infinitely receding background. But Lettice's objection is to those 'fixed principles' of Picturesque description which are too limited and inflexible to be able to convey the full emotional impact on the spectator of such a grand view. Mental elevation, reflections, associations – these are all non-visual, or perhaps post-visual responses stimulated by the view, and Picturesque vocabulary has no resources for these. Lettice's objection is endorsed by John Stoddart when he also considers the view from the Castle: 'To make painting the standard of those pleasures which landscape can afford, is, however, to set Art above Nature, the handmaid above her mistress'. Elsewhere in his *Remarks* he distinguishes the Picturesque tourist from 'the man of nature and feeling'.

The road east from Stirling followed the River Devon for some of the way, with Picturesque opportunities at the Rumbling Bridge, for those with steel nerves. Sarah Murray tried to sketch the scenery: 'but in the attempt I was several times obliged to shut my eyes, and take fast hold of the rock on which I sat, lest I should drop from it into the whirling foaming stream.'[48] She had been told at Kinross that the Bridge and Falls were not worth a visit – 'so little do the common people of that, or any other country, discriminate what is, or is not worth seeing'.[49]

The Picturesque tourist was much more at home with Loch Leven. Gilpin walked out from Kinross one evening when a light mist was rising from the lake and stealing up the hillside, 'blending both together in that pleasing ambiguity, through which we can but just distinguish the limits of each'. To enhance his view still more, the foreground was 'improved by picturesque figures' of fishermen dragging in their nets, the contents of which Gilpin enjoyed at supper that night. But for him, Loch Leven was of more historical than Picturesque interest. Mary Queen of Scots escaped from her castle-prison on the lake's island in 1568, with the aid of the infatuated young George Douglas. All the tourists knew of this romantic story. Gilpin described a narrative outline for an appropriate allegorical painting of the episode, with the God of Love, torch in hand, laughing triumphantly as he steers the boat and its lovely passenger across the lake to safety.

Loch Leven's scenery gave some hint of the Highland landscapes to come. Another foretaste was enjoyed by James Plumptre when a party of Highlanders arrived at his Kinross inn, upon which 'the well known lines involuntarily escaped our mouths "What are these so wither'd and so wild in their tire?"' He promptly bought a copy of *Macbeth*, 'to enjoy properly the enchanted and poetic ground we are soon to tread'.[50] Plumptre later on his Long Tour did trace some of the historic sites mentioned in the tragedy, and up at Cawdor Castle, scene of the 'sanguinary inhospitalities of Macbeth', in Gibson's phrase, when he was shown what purported to be the room and bed where Duncan was murdered, 'could not refrain from instantly assuming the King's posture and by the help of imagination felt a dagger plungd into my breast by my friend'.[51] In the neighbourhood of Cawdor was the 'blasted heath' where Macbeth met the witches. Dr Johnson, like many other tourists, solemnly recited the appropriate speech from the play as he and Boswell travelled over the heath. The site was, by general agreement, 'judiciously chosen, for all the old women, of the lower classes, in this part of the country, have the appearance of midnight hags. They only want the cauldron and the broomstick to compleat them for the stage'.[52] In 1825, John Skinner was shown the exact spot – a clump of trees – where the encounter with the witches took place. It was known in the neighbourhood that the local Laird had inadvertently sold this hallowed spot along with some other property, and that when he discovered his folly, he had repurchased the clump, 'although every stick in it must have cost him a guinea at least'.[53]

### Dunkeld – Blair

The first *Macbeth* scenery, back on the Short Tour, was about fifteen miles north of Perth at Birnam, with the ruins of Duncan's Castle and the site of Birnam Wood. The baldness of Birnam was a great disappointment: 'there is no wood upon it now' reflected Plumptre, 'as I suppose it never returned from its march with Malcolm's Soldiers to Dunsinane'.[54]

From now on, Highland scenery was enriched with both Shakespearean and Ossianic associations. Dunkeld, the town next to Birnam, was reckoned to be the entrance to the Highlands, the place to pause and tune one's sensibility to the Sublime experiences which lay ahead. Robert Heron arrived as evening was coming on, and as the neighbouring scenery was tinged with gloom:

I began to reflect that I was entering the land of Ossian's heroes; the land which presented those few simple, grand, and gloomy objects which gave a melancholy cast to the imagination of the poet, and supplied that sublime, but undiversified imagery which forms one of the most peculiar characteristics of ancient Gaelic poesy.

The brooding evening landscape was augmented by a ruined Cathedral in the grounds of the Duke of Atholl's estate. All in all, as Gibson reflected, Dunkeld 'composed a landscape well worthy the pencil of a Salvator or Poussin'. This was no longer Claudean scenery.

Robert Heron rose next morning to make his tour of the Dunkeld region. Rain was falling heavily. He attended church and listened to a grim sermon on the prospects of a future state of retribution. 'The combination of all these circumstances wrought my mind into a calm, solemn and pensive frame, suitable to the character of the scenery'.

The Duke's grounds extended a little to the west of Dunkeld along the river Bran, and included a number of fine waterfalls. The first of these, a fall of about forty feet, won the highest praise from Gilpin, after he had censured the fussy formality of the cultivated flower borders on the approach paths:

The two rocky cheeks of the river almost uniting compress the stream into a very narrow compass; and the channel, which descends abruptly, taking also a sudden turn, the water suffers more than common violence from the double resistance it receives from compression and obliquity ... This whole scene, and it's accompaniments, are not only grand; but picturesqueley beautiful in the highest degree. The *composition* is perfect: but yet the parts are so intricate, so various, and so complicated, that I never found any piece of nature less obvious to imitation.

This, one of the finest Picturesque sights in Britain, could not long remain unexploited. In 1757 a small summer-house was built for the third Duke of Atholl on a ledge overlooking the falls. It was called the 'Hermitage', even though its architecture and interior decoration were in the elegant neoclassical style of the period. At some later point, the large bay window which gave onto the falls was paned with coloured glass, so that, as Mary Ann Hanway describes, through the red part of the window the waterfall 'appears to be sheets of liquid fire rolling down the rock like the lava of mount Etna'. Or, through the green panes the water was turned into 'a lava of liquid verdigrease'.[55] Gilpin disliked these gimmicks, and suggested that if coloured glass had to be used it should be optional – for example, sections of glass hung up in frames with handles.

What was designed to enhance much more often disgusted the tourists. Robert Heron, whose melancholy mood had been carefully nurtured by dismal weather, ruins, glimpses of Highland scenery, and a particularly pessimistic sermon, greatly relished the natural scenery of the Bran falls, 'that wild sublimity which calls home the powers of the mind from lighter excursions'. But it was impossible to sustain this in the Hermitage:

The glaring gaiety of the room was of a character inconsistent with that of the objects around it. It dispelled the solemn awe, and pleasing melancholy ... yet not so entirely as to introduce in their room, its own airy cheerfulness; and the consequent effect was, that the imagination and the feelings were harrassed and disgusted between the two.

As the Ossian cult swept through Britain, the Hermitage was adapted and renamed 'Ossian's Hall'. It is important to realise that the approach to these falls, usually under the conduct of the Duke's gardener, was so contrived that the falls

71. 'The Hermitage, Dunkeld', from James Cririe, *Scottish Scenery* (1803).

themselves were always obscured until the very last minute. Their mysterious roar grew distinctly louder, until one was inside the Hermitage and suddenly looking straight down over them from the bay window (fig. 71). The main idea behind this was to heighten the Sublime experience by delay and suspense. The Ossianic modification to the building must have added one more tantalising preliminary to what was already an elaborate aesthetic adventure. From the approach path, the visitor was ushered into a dark, gothicised vestibule. Immediately opposite the door there appeared a painting (by Charles Steuart) of Ossian as an ancient blind bard seated 'in an attitude of enthusiasm' his shield and lance beside him and his harp in the background, singing to a group of enraptured women. William and Dorothy Wordsworth visited Ossian's Hall during their 1803 Scottish tour. Dorothy recounts how, while they were contemplating the picture of Ossian in the gloom of the vestibule, a lever was surreptitiously pulled by the gardener and the painting suddenly flew back into the walls –

. . . and lo! we are at the entrance of a splendid room, which was almost dizzy and alive with waterfalls, that tumbled in all directions – the great cascade, which was opposite to the window that faced us, being reflected in innumerable mirrors upon the ceiling and against the walls.

The sudden burst of light and noise after the gloomy seclusion of the vestibule, and the frenetic swirling movement reflected in the mirrors were a triumph of staged Sublimity exploiting extreme contrasts. Some idea of the sensation can be gained even today. The Hall has been partly restored. The painting of Ossian has long since disappeared, though a tall, narrow cavity in the wall shows where it was concealed and a small aperture in the side wall of the vestibule is the site of the lever mechanism. Even without these accessories the few steps from the dark vestibule into the viewing chamber can be quite thrilling. The chamber with its apsidal ends seems to act as an amplifier, so that the roar of the falls in full spate is suddenly very loud.

To a connoisseur like Elizabeth Diggle even the different styles of the vestibule and viewing room seemed significant: 'I conceive both these apartments are meant as emblematic of the ancient & modern times'. The mirrors set into walls and ceiling must have replaced the coloured panes of the bow window. To Robert Heron the effect made the room seem 'more like a *boudoir* than a hermitage', but others were delighted. Some of the mirrors were tinted so that the reflected water looked like flames, or like boiling oil, and the ceiling mirror 'gave it the Appearance of a white Smoke ascending with great Velocity through an opening above'.[56]

After their initial shock, Wordsworth and his sister burst out with laughter at the Duke's 'distressingly puerile' contrivances. Wordsworth later wrote a verse 'Effusion' on the Dunkeld Pleasure-Ground disparaging such 'baubles of theatric taste'. He suggested that Ossian would be more fittingly commemorated with a rough granite statue on the banks of the Bran, and he adds a Ruskinian qualification – 'uncouth the workmanship, and rude! / But, nursed in mountain solitude'.

Half a mile up river from the falls was (and is) an arrangement of large boulders, known as 'Ossian's Cave', a structure rather more appropriate to the Ossianic era than was the Hall.

The Ossian motif was not as alien to the Dunkeld region as many thought. About twelve miles to the south-west was Glen Almond. In the 1740s some of General Wade's soldiers working on the military road to Inverness, which was to pass through the Glen, raised a huge stone which lay in their path. Beneath it was found a coffin composed of four grey stones and containing burnt bones. This celebrated find became known later as Ossian's Grave and was an object of pilgrimage and general curiosity in the later eighteenth century.

### *Blair Atholl – Taymouth*

'D'you know Frank how many days it took to make the World?', asked a soldier during a march through Glen Garry in the Forest of Atholl. His friend replied six. 'Then by God . . . this country must have been the work of the 6th day for it seems to have been made *in a Damned* hurry'.[57] The Short Tour went no further north on this side than the Duke of Atholl's estates at Blair, so had only a peep into dreadful Glen Garry before turning south-west.

By contrast to the Glen, the road from Dunkeld to Blair through Strath Tay was a beautiful tour of gentle Highland scenery:

Hills to the skies no signs of living creatures, clouds half down the hills, rivers at bottom, rocks & woody banks, & for variety a highlander leading a cow to feed: take these well together & you produce a highland scene according to the most approved receipts.

The Picturesque recipe for a Highland scene, given by Elizabeth Diggle, is illustrated in a comparison recently made by James Holloway between two versions of a Strath Tay landscape.[58] The first is a 1747 drawing by Paul Sandby (fig. 72). Thirty years later Sandby's view was engraved and slightly altered to take account of changes of taste (fig. 73). As Holloway remarks, 'by 1780 the view was not thought to be sufficiently "Highland" and several additions were made to dramatise the landscape; the mountains were heightened and their outlines made more rugged, fir trees and a kilted onlooker were introduced'.

Blair Castle was one of the great showpieces of the north. Here Wordsworth and his sister were exhausted by the obligatory three hours' walk through the pleasure-grounds: 'Having been directed to see *all* the waterfalls, we submitted ourselves to the gardener, who dragged us from place to place, calling attention to, it might be, half-a-dozen (I cannot say how many) dripping streams'. Miles of gravel walks led by waterfalls, woods, rustic temples, orchards and flower gardens. The formal gardens were decorated with brightly painted statues ('the product of Hide-park corner', thought Gilpin), including Harlequin and Columbine, and a stucco representation of a favourite old game-keeper pointing his gun at passing tourists. Blair Castle itself had undergone recent changes. The Duke had grown

72. Paul Sandby, *Strath Tay* (1747).
National Library of Wales, Aberystwyth

frustrated by the frequent exploitation of the castle's strength (it was the only securely fortified residence in a large wild area of the Highlands) and he removed the towers and battlements and three of its storeys so that it could never be properly garrisoned again. Gilpin remarked that 'the picturesque eye regrets the loss . . . and is hurt at seeing a noble castle transformed into an ordinary house'.

Three miles beyond the castle were the Falls of the Bruar, on behalf of which Burns wrote his 'Humble Petition' to the Duke of Atholl to clothe its naked banks with trees to add variety, beauty, and shade to an already fine series of waterfalls.

> Would then my noble master please
> To grant my highest wishes,
> He'll shade my banks wi' tow'ring trees,
> And bonnie spreading bushes.[59]

The 'tow'ring trees' chosen by the Duke to accede to Burns's wishes, were mainly larch and fir. The Wordsworths wished they had been Scotland's native trees – birch, ash, mountain-ash; but they agreed that by about the middle of the nineteenth century the present trees would be a worthy monument to Burns's memory. As with the Bran at Dunkeld, the Duke had organised gravel walks on both sides of the Bruar, thrown a bridge or two across the river and built some rustic viewing-huts. The river Tilt, closer to Blair Castle, also had some fine cascades, ornamented again by the Duke:

73. After Paul Sandby, *Strath Tay* (engraving).
National Library of Wales, Aberystwyth

I had often, like others, experienced the pleasures which arise from the sublime or elegant landscape, but I never saw those feelings so intense as in Burns. When we reached a rustic hut on the river Tilt, where it is overhung by a woody precipice, from which there is a noble waterfall, he threw himself on the heathy seat, and gave himself up to a tender, abstracted, and voluptuous enthusiasm of imagination.[60]

This strong emotional response contrasts sharply with Gilpin's remarks on how overrated these falls were. The great mistake made by these falls, he claims, is in the 'circumstance of their falling *into the river* [which] makes them appear smaller by bringing them into comparison with a greater stream'. He also censures the York Cascade (over which the Duke had placed an elegant, but quite incongruous Chinese bridge) for not falling correctly – the fall being too broken and 'frittered'.

The Duke's gardening activities in the midst of these wild landscapes presented a familiar aesthetic dilemma. How much 'improvement' could properly be undertaken in such scenery? Once certain 'stations' were publicised, affording the best view of a fine landscape, it seemed both reasonable and desirable to make the access to those stations as comfortable as possible without jeopardising the natural integrity of the viewed landscape. But in practice it could never be so simple. In Sublime scenery particularly, much of the Sublimity arose from the sense of difficulty, even peril, in negotiating a way into the landscape. But when precipices or roaring falls are approached by gravel walks and viewed from within

219

rustic huts – no matter how close one is – a clear division is made between the spectators' security and the landscape. It is at this point that Picturesque considerations can come into play, as a condition of the relative detachment of spectator from spectacle.

### Taymouth – Killin

> Admiring Nature in her wildest grace,
> These Northern scenes with weary feet I trace;
> O'er many a winding dale and painful steep,
> T'abodes of covey'd grouse and timid sheep,
> My savage journey, curious, I pursue,
> Till fam'd Breadalbane opens to my view.[61]

For Burns the Taymouth estate presented an opulent paradise, with its palace, wood-fringed lawns, carefully shaped hills, bridge designed by Robert Adam, and the neat little village of Kenmore. He stayed at the inn just outside the Park gates and wrote these lines over the parlour chimney piece. His arrival was a particularly refreshing experience after the long trudge through barren and wild Highland scenery. Gilpin thought that 'Perhaps no country in the world abounds more with grand situations, especially in the highland parts of it, than Scotland: and perhaps none of the Scotch nobility have a greater variety of noble situations, than the earls of Breadalbin'. The compliment came as the conclusion to his most unfavourable remarks on the Earl's 'improvements': 'nothing could show a more thorough inattention to every idea of beauty and taste'. His main complaint was the formality of design: none of the long walks seemed to show off the surrounding scenery properly. The Wordsworths too complained of bad taste – 'banks being regularly shaven and cut as if by rule and line'.

In spite of these strictures some tourists, like Burns, were thrilled to find something resembling a Claudean landscape in the heart of Rosa-esque scenery. As Robert Heron remarked,

On this principle, is it, as I should suppose, that the tour of the Highlands of Scotland has become fashionable. Here is much of the wilder scenery of nature. But, these wild scenes are interspersed with various spots of ornament and cultivation; which set them off by contrast.

Burns' poem enumerates most of the conventional components of a Claudean landscape, but leaves them unorganised. In all probability he was responding specifically to the most celebrated viewpoint on the estate. A short walk from the village inn down the right bank of the river Tay brought one to an artificial mound on which was a Temple of Venus, more prosaically known as Maxwell's Temple. The prospect viewpoint was a grass platform on which one stood facing west:

The immediate fore-ground is an uneven lawn, and shrubberies leading down to the town of Kenmore, and the river; then come the town, the church, the bridge, and the

74. W. H. Watts, 'Loch Tay', from Thomas Garnett's *Observations on a Tour through the
Highlands* [etc] (1800). British Library, London

wide expanse of the lake [including] a small island . . . covered with trees, through which
peeps a ruin [of a twelfth-century priory]. The part of the road to Kielin, on the north
side of Loch Tay . . . makes no inconsiderable figure in the landscape, as from the bridge
it winds up an almost perpendicular crag, chiefly covered with firs . . . Beyond that crag
sweep away to the west, mountain upon mountain . . . till all is lost behind the towering
points of Benmore, in the centre of the utmost distance . . . In short, the view is a complete landscape of lake and alpine scenery, mixed with the haunts and habitations of man,
and all in style.[62]

This 'complete landscape' contains the proper three distances carefully distinguished in this description: the broken foreground, the middle distance with
bridge, church and ruin beside river and lake, and the background of soaring
mountains. To enhance the Picturesque experience the Temple, rather incongruously, housed a large prospect glass on a moveable stand, so that the individual
components of the scene could be examined more closely. Both the Watts and
Campbell views are taken from this position (figs. 74 and 75). Gilpin's view, also
from the Temple, has managed to expunge all traces of man – there is no village
or church tower, no bridge and no mountain road. Gilpin's other viewpoint was
much closer to the lake. It was taken from the rising ground in the precincts of
Kenmore Church and offered one of the grandest examples of lake scenery he had
ever known:

75. Alexander Campbell, 'Taymouth' ('Sketched on the Spot'), from Campbell's *A Journey from Edinburgh through parts of North Britain* (1802). British Library, London

On the right, a lofty mountain [bearing the winding road to Killin] falls into the water, and forms a grand promontory. It's lines at the base are finely broken by a wooded island [the ruined priory was perhaps screened by trees from this angle]. Another promontory projects from the opposite shore, and both together form the water into a spacious bay. Between the two promontories the distant mountains recede in perspective; and the lake goes off in the form of another bay.

Plumptre evidently had his Gilpin with him (as well as his *Ossian* and his *Macbeth*), for he went to this Church viewpoint specifically to compare what he saw with the Gilpin aquatint, and complained, quite unfairly, that Gilpin falsified the scene. Gilpin had indeed excluded from his background the prominent Ben Lawers clearly visible to Plumptre: but, as Gilpin had to stress again and again, his drawings were meant not to be exact topographical records but rather to give '*the character of the country*'.*

The grounds of Taymouth, though too formal in design for most Picturesque tourists, displayed a wide variety of garden architecture: several small temples, a seat called Aeolus, properly if uncomfortably exposed to the four winds, a sham fort, a small summer-house on a swivel base, and a Druid circle.

*In his 'Account of the Prints' in *Observations* on the Highlands, Gilpin stressed that 'when I have seen a line out of place, I have a great propensity to correct it by one that is more picturesque'.

On the southern side of Loch Tay was a site much valued by Lord Breadalbane, and perhaps designed to rival the Duke of Atholl's Ossian's Hall. The main object was a waterfall on the river Acharn. As at Dunkeld, great care was taken to forbid the tourist a view of it until just the right station was reached. An area in the neighbourhood of the falls was fenced off and kept locked. Once inside this, you were conducted into a very dark subterranean passage which led into the 'Hermitage', an octagonal cell with a three-sided bay window facing the falls across the steep ravine. The walls of the room were covered with moss and shells. Various stuffed animals – wildcat, goat, fox – hung on the walls, and more animal skins adorned the upholstery. There were baskets of artificial fruit, and a library of wooden books covered with old leather backs. 'It might make a vermin room for some sportsman', thought James Plumptre, 'or suit a *London Hermit*, but not one who had retired from the world and its vanities'.[63] But the view through the window was a triumph. The remains of the Hermitage and passage are still visible.

The ride from Kenmore to Killin, a ride of about fifteen miles along Loch Tay, was disappointing as an experience of lake scenery. There was a uniformity in the lake which made it appear more like a river of unequal dimensions than a lake with a variety of broken promontories, bays and islands. But the area bordering Loch Tay was the most populous in the Highlands and the signs of life along its shores pleased many a tourist who had grown depressed by the desolate countryside. Elizabeth Diggle enjoyed her evening ride as 'the sun gilded the mountains a thousand ways, the birds sung, the highlanders peeped out from their wretched huts with merry faces to stare at us, & looked so happy I could not pity them for living in such places'. One charming experience of Highland hospitality happened to Richard Sulivan on the same journey from Kenmore to Killin. He and his party had started out late from Taymouth and the moon was high as they rode along the shores of the Loch. At one point they heard the sound of a voice singing and went to investigate. They found a seventeen-year-old girl and her two small brothers sitting on the grass. Around them stood the cattle, apparently charmed by the girl's songs. When she stopped, Sulivan and his friend urged her to continue, but she refused:

. . . neither will I continue with my song unless you oblige me in my desire, and drink a little milk; the only refreshment I have to offer. The request was too courteous to be evaded; the heart-strings melted at the touch. We instantly complied, and emptied the vessel which she presented to us. Now then, says she, I will begin again, my cows too will thank you for your goodness; we are constant friends; they love their mistress; nor will they murmur at contributing to her happiness. Thus saying, she turned to the one that was nearest to her, and placing herself at her side, began an air that rivetted us to the spot: the night was, however, stealing on a pace; her parents expected her home; she therefore arose and blest us.[64]

Sulivan's bucolic encounter was matched by a scene which confronted the Wordsworths during their evening ride through Glen Dochart, just beyond Killin, and made them much regret that they were not painters:

76. William Gilpin, 'Castle of Dochart upon an island in the Lake', from the MS Highland tour notebook, 1776. Bodleian Library, Oxford

Two herdsmen, with a dog beside them, were sitting on the hill, overlooking a herd of cattle scattered over a large meadow by the river-side. Their forms, looked at through a fading light, and backed by the bright west, were exceedingly distinct, a beautiful picture in the quiet of a Sabbath evening, exciting thoughts and images of almost patriarchal simplicity and grace.

On Glen Dochart Gilpin pronounced, 'The imagination was interested but not the eye'. But Loch Dochart certainly did interest his eye, with its varied shoreline and wooded island adorned with the ruins of a castle: 'The great picturesque use of islands, in these situations, is to break the tedious lines of such promontories, and mountains, as they fall into the water'. His original sketch of the scene was much altered for the published aquatint (figs. 76 and 77). The magnified castle island now slides into the picture from the right as a wing or side-screen, and the promontory behind it has been made to drop much more steeply into the lake. The 'rules of composition' have virtually invalidated the topographical record.

The waters of the river Fillan, which runs into Loch Dochart, were famous for their curative powers, especially in cases of insanity. The patient was walked twice round a neighbouring cairn on which he would have to place a small amount of money as an offering.[65] He was then immersed three times, bound hand and foot, and confined for a night in a ruined chapel nearby. If he was found loose the following morning he was pronounced cured, but if still bound, incur-

77. William Gilpin, 'Loch Dochart', aquatint from *High-Lands* (1789)

able. The prescription was gruesome enough to unbalance any sane person.

*Glencoe – Loch Lomond*

The tourist who reached Crianlarich, about ten miles west of Killin, had a choice of several routes: north to Glencoe, west to Dalmally and on down to Inverary, or south to Loch Lomond and home by Glasgow. As we near the end of the tours we might bring closer together the experiences of Sublimity and Beauty in Highland landscape terms by branching up to Glencoe and then returning directly to Loch Lomond. Glencoe was the undiluted Sublime. Awesome natural scenery was enhanced by grisly historical associations and Fingalian legend. As every tourist knew, it was the site of the savage massacre of the Macdonalds in 1692, and it was the fabled birthplace of Ossian himself.

The entry into the Glen from the desolate wastes of Rannoch Moor was, and still is, a very formidable experience. High up at the head of the Glen 'a person feels as if he were placed among the ruins of the world':

Just at the cataract at the south-side of the glen, under which the water dashes after its fall, are huge towers upon towers of solid rock, forming a multitude of steps to the greatest height, and all in a drizzling state . . . Adjoining this extraordinary weeping mass, is a continued range, of a mile in descent, of other crags equally perpendicular and high;

225

in most of which appear caves and arched passages, with pillars, like the communication from one ile to another, high up in the sides of Gothic cathedrals . . . The whole mass, to an eye below, appears like an immense and inaccessible ruin of the finest architecture, mouldered, defaced, and become uneven by a vast lapse of time, and inclemency of weather, which has variegated its native grey, by ten thousand soft tints, that nothing but time and weather can produce.[66]

A number of tourists echo this sense of Glencoe as a giant architectural ruin. The appeal of this idea has much to do with the Picturesque theorist's relish of the dilapidation, by time and weather (if not by the mallet), of formal buildings, which, it may be remembered, both Price and Gilpin describe with some care. Addison had remarked that 'we find the Works of Nature still more pleasant, the more they resemble those of Art'. Just as buildings in ruin are assimilated into Nature, so certain striking natural objects can seem to aspire towards the condition of artifacts.[67] Unusual rock formations such as Matlock Tor in Dovedale, or the southern range of prominent crags here in Glencoe known as the Three Sisters, strongly suggested the original work of a designing hand. One of the most interesting contemporary examples of this sort of issue came as a result of Joseph Banks's published discovery of the basaltic grotto, Fingal's Cave, on the island of Staffa. Banks and others argued from the evidence of the extraordinary geometrical formations of the rock that the Greek temple builders, far from imposing an alien, artificial symmetry on Nature, had simply been copying Nature's own exquisite precision. The argument was part of the challenge to the prevailing belief that the asymmetry of Gothic architecture most authentically expressed nature's organic forms.[68]

Many tourists felt they were better able to describe Glencoe when they could resort to associations with architecture:

We turned suddenly into the famous valley of Glenco, which presented on our left, and those standing almost in an even series, and perpendicularly, the terminations, or (will you rather allow me to call them?) the gable ends of five enormous mountains.[69]

The imagination which chooses thus to interpret the forms of Nature as the devastated remains of human enterprises can quite as easily resort to animism, especially when confronted with such gigantic and mysterious phenomena as Glencoe could present. Here is one susceptible tourist, John Stoddart, entering the Glen from the western end:

As it was about ten o'clock in the morning of the 5th of September, and I was at a very considerable distance from the base of the hill, its height and steepness may be easily conceived. Its face was wholly of rock, almost literally perpendicular: and it rose, like a huge black wall, from the margin of a small lake, formed by the river. While I was gazing at this object, proceeding slowly, and getting more abreast of a narrow opening between this and a nearer hill, a pointed rock, which rose to a height far beyond both, came gradually into view. It seemed to lean forward, to the opening of the glen, and having a round patch of snow on its front, looked like a one-eyed Cyclops, bending from an embrasure in this gigantic rampart.

This experience, where the awe-struck imagination almost instinctively animates landscape forms, resembles Wordsworth's experience recorded in the first book of the *Prelude*, where he steals a boat and rows out onto moonlit Ullswater. In both cases the spectator's own movement gives the illusion of the purposeful movement of mountains as his slowly changing angle of vision discloses new views. It is an experience that most people have had, and in its anthropomorphizing tendency is akin to the analogy of the crags with ruined architecture. If the sophisticated tourists could betray such tendencies, it is no wonder that they became more sympathetic to those primitive cultures that ascribed divine powers and personalities to the forms and forces of Nature. In such surroundings as Glencoe it hardly taxed the sympathetic imagination at all to believe in the world of Ossian. The 'huge black wall' just described was Black Rock, rising from beside Loch Triochatan. According to legend, this was the birthplace of Ossian whose Cave was a deep recess in the Rock. Down the flanks of the huge crags near the head of the Glen, innumerable mountain torrents ran into the river Coe, which the swelled into Loch Triochatan. The Coe is the river 'Cona' of *Ossian*: 'Their sound was like a thousand streams that meet in Cona's vale, when after a stormy night they turn their dark eddies between the pale light of the morning'. The fabled river issued from the Loch to run on down the Glen, past the remains of the huts of the Macdonalds and the Laird's neat white house, site of the beginning of the massacre, and eventually out into Loch Leven.

From Glencoe's Sublimity to Loch Lomond's pastoral beauty was the most exciting contrast on the Short Tour of the Highlands:

> Still on thy banks so gaily green,
> May num'rous herds and flocks be seen;
> And lasses chanting o'er the pail,
> And shepherds piping in the dale[70]

The author of these lines, Tobias Smollett, spent much of his early life in the Lomond area and is commemorated there by a pillar with a Latin inscription partly composed by Samuel Johnson and censured as 'miserably bad' by Coleridge. Smollett had known the area before the middle of the eighteenth century. By the end of the century numerous printfields and bleach fields had usurped the pasture lands. While this was greatly to the benefit of the local economy, 'at the same time . . . the innocent simplicity of manners will be banished', wrote Dr Garnett in nostalgic pastoral mood: 'the love of gain, which has a strong tendency to contract the heart, and banish social affections, will, as well as other vicious propensities, take their place'.[71] But the tourist's determination to indulge pastoral fantasies at Loch Lomond was not to be shaken by social reality, as Mary Anne Hanway once again proves:

78. John Skinner, 'Woman in the Corn field August 30 . . . Reapers in a field near the road',
in his MS tour notebook of 1825, Add. MS 33685. British Library, London

I write this from a place, my dear Lady Mary, of which I am (to use a woman's word) *extravagantly* fond, being one of those rural, and romantic spots which the Arcadian swains were poetically supposed to enjoy in the Golden Age.

One of the closest approximations to Smollett's 'lasses chanting o'er the pail, / And shepherds piping in the dale' was experienced by one notable tourist as he travelled along Loch Lomond's shore, and 'Passed a female who was reaping alone: she sung in Erse as she bended over her sickle; the sweetest human voice I ever heard: her strains were tenderly melancholy, and felt delicious, long after they were heard no more'.[72] The tourist was Thomas Wilkinson, whose 1787 tour journal was read by his friend Wordsworth; and this sentence became the source for one of the best-known poems in the language, 'The Solitary Reaper' (see fig. 78).

Loch Lomond was the last experience of Highland scenery on this tour, or the first, of course, for the tourist beginning at Glasgow. 'The number of the mountains', wrote Thomas Newte, 'their approximation to one another, their abrupt and perpendicular elevation: all these circumstances taken together, give an idea of a country *consisting* of mountains without intermission, formed by Nature into an impregnable fortress'.[73] The mountains of the Highlands were judged to be very different from those of the Lakes, 'where an appearance of plenty gladdens the sympathetic heart, as much as the romantic prospects which they afford, amuse the imagination'.[74] Towering over all other mountains was Ben Lomond, 'like *Saul* amidst his companions' in Pennant's much quoted phrase. In addition to its majesty, it was also highly Picturesque, its sides properly broken, 'rugged and varied with bossy projections like incrustations and warts over its whole surface . . . a Painter would hardly venture to delineate so perfect a Form lest he should be suspected of exaggeration'.[75] The ascent was not too difficult. The main hazards were rain and storms, hazards which only enhanced an already Sublime experience. Mary Anne Hanway, who could find no companion for the ascent, was told of a lady who walked up to the top in the morning and returned to dinner without appearing tired. 'I think I hear some fine lady amongst my own countrywomen', she reflected, 'who affect to be tired to death with a couple of turns in the Mall, exclaim, Oh! what horrid, indelicate creatures must those women be that could *form* such a plan, much less *execute* it!'

Those who stayed at the inn at Tarbet, and were preparing themselves for the ascent, were amused by a 1771 didactic poem written on a window pane. The poem offered good advice to the more impetuous climber: 'Oft stay thy steps, Oft taste the cordial drop, / And rest, Oh! rest, long, long upon the top'.[76] Provided he had not too often tasted the cordial drop on the way up, the tourist who reached the top could be rewarded with an immense prospect if the weather was fine: 'a scene, not, indeed picturesque, for it defies the pencil; but nobly poetical, as it excites the sensations of true sublimity', according to Stoddart. A little written record on a scrap of paper tucked into a crevice at the summit would then be left for future climbers to consult, and the conquest of Ben Lomond was complete.

Gilpin found Picturesque scenes in the upper reaches of the Loch, but thought the southern lacking in unity of composition: there were no background mountains and the lake surface was too broken by the number of islands. Since it failed as a *picture* therefore, he decided to examine it as a *map*, and set out for the famous viewpoint on Inch Tavannach. Tavannach was so close to the shore that it seemed like the far border of a small lake. Within this little lake was a small tree-covered island which captivated Dorothy Wordsworth as she came to a point about two miles south of Luss:

How delightful to have a little shed concealed under the branches of the fairy island! . . . It was but like a natural garden . . . I thought, what a place for Wm. he might row himself over with twenty strokes of the oars, escaping from the business of the house.

It is remarkable how many tourists were inspired by fantasies of rural retirement at about this point on Loch Lomond. Perhaps it was due to the transitional nature of the landscape itself, pastoral lake scenery on the border of the Highlands. Anne Grant had ideas of establishing a 'fashionable' nunnery – a Protestant one, she quickly added – here at Luss. 'Do not mistake me,' she went on; 'I would not altogether intend this for a place of penance and mortification, but rather as an asylum from the levity and dissipation of the age'.[77] There were, in fact, asylums on Loch Lomond, though not of a kind to suit Anne Grant. On one of the many islands was a madhouse:

I know of no situation so fitted for it – secluded from the gay busy hum of men – ban'd from society by the loss of the noblest powers of the Soul – to retreat & dwell unknown among the wonders of nature, must surely temper madness itself – if not it can never become the object of dread, or of Ridicule – here the Tears of Dotage might flow from Marlborough in silence, and Swift might drivel in oblivion.[78]

The lunatic is literally insulated from society. Other social misfits also reluctantly found refuge on the Loch here. Inch Calloch, once a real nunnery, was converted to a kind of prison for prostitutes who were confined here by their relatives, often to the end of their lives, which in quite a number of cases was reached very soon after their enforced landing on the island: the bodies of suicides were washed to the shores of the Loch. The island became something of a tourist attraction:

We landed . . . and had not proceeded far, before we perceived a number of females retiring in haste to a house of mean appearance: their dress was dirty & negligent, and their countenances as far as we could discern pale & wan with care.[79]

The temptations to a voluntary retirement on the shores of Loch Lomond made even Gilpin yield to a little 'reverie' after he had completed his survey from the top of Inch Tavannach rock:

We may conceive of the happiness of a few philosophical friends, retiring from the follies of life to such a scene as this; and settling themselves in the separate islands . . . Their happiness would consist in the refined pleasures of intercourse, and solitude. The visionary does not consider the many economical difficulties and inconveniences of a plan . . . Among the amusements of this happy people, it would not be the least to improve their little territories into scenes of simplicity and beauty – academic groves, Elysian fields . . . The intrusions of a tattling world would be totally excluded: while books, and elegant amusements, would be a sovereign antidote against the howling of winds, and the beating of waves. – But enough of these idle reveries, which belong not to terrestrial things.

### The Falls of Clyde: Conclusions

The Highland tour was over. The abrupt thrust of the rock of Dumbarton, five miles to the south of Loch Lomond, seemed like a strange, delayed echo of the mountain sublimities now left behind (fig. 79). There was however one more grand scenic sensation, which brought the Short Tour to a fitting close, and which brings the present search for the Picturesque to its conclusion. This involved following the river Clyde up from Dumbarton, through Glasgow, past the ruins of Bothwell Castle to Lanark, the town with the new cotton mills. Here the river's course included a series of spectacular waterfalls, Bonnington Linn, Cora Linn and Stonebyres Linn.[80] Sarah Murray discovered 'one of the most enchanting walks of half a mile that can be met with on the face of the earth',[81] on the path between Cora Linn and Bonnington Linn. It followed along the top of the cliff through

79. William Gilpin, 'View of Dunbarton-castle at a distance', aquatint from
*High-Lands* (1789).

dense woodland, with occasional glimpses of the Clyde rushing furiously among
the broken rocks below. Most of these glimpses had been judiciously cut by the
proprietors of the estate, Sir John and Lady Ross. While these two developed
the aesthetic potential of the falls, the New Lanark cotton mills a few hundred
yards downstream were noisily harnessing the Clyde's hydraulic power. The two
worlds lived side by side: refined patrician pleasure-grounds, and the new age of
mass production and experimental socialism.

Bonnington was the furthest upstream of the falls. Here the water forced its
way down several different channels in a large semi-circle of cliffs, rather than
concentrating its fall as at Cora Linn: 'From a rock hanging over the Clyde, on
which a small bastion has been built, is a very good though somewhat distant
view of this fall'. Dr Garnett is very likely referring to the viewpoint on the right
bank, about a quarter of a mile from the falls, chosen by Paul Sandby for his
watercolour drawing of about 1750 (fig. 80). Garnett decided that Bonnington's
scenery was not Picturesque because of 'a lumpish hill' in the background which
would be much improved by planting some trees. The hill is clearly visible in
Sandby's drawing, as is the conical dovecote above the falls. This building was
later adapted for Picturesque tastes into a 'Foghouse', which meant that the whole
of the interior was lined with moss, something like a restrained version of the
Hermitage at Acharn Falls on Loch Tay. But before this adaptation, which probably

231

80. Paul Sandby, *Bonnington Linn* (c. 1750).
National Gallery of Scotland, Edinburgh

made little alteration to the exterior, a painting by Jacob More had already converted the dovecote into a ruined tower as architecturally more consonant with the Sublime scenery of the falls. Dorothy Wordsworth wished that the Foghouse could be moved to a better site, further away from the main path. She was also one of the few to complain that these walks, with their occasional openings onto the river were injudiciously managed: 'You were prepared for a dead stand, by a parapet, a painted seat, or some other device'. She dislikes the artificiality here and the lack of continuity of movement, when each opening brings one to a halt on the cliff edge, from which one returns to join the path again. She also regrets the loss of that excitement of discovery, of which she had complained while being conducted through the pleasure-grounds of Blair Atholl. The same objection could apply to West's Stations (the term is synonymous with Dorothy's 'stand'), which are enforced pauses in a tour. The movement of unfolding scenery is formally arrested at a point where the composition of landscape features most closely corresponds to a landscape painting. Gilpin's movement through a landscape is directed towards finding particularly satisfying viewpoints, whereas Dorothy Wordsworth wants to dissolve these established viewpoints back into the movement of the tour and recover the pleasures of accidental discovery.

About half a mile downstream from Bonnington the Clyde twists sharply to the right beneath the ruined Cora Castle on its left bank. Within another 200 yards the gorge widens and makes a larger sweep to the left. At the beginning of this turn are the 90-foot stepped falls of Cora Linn:

As you advance you hear a sullen noise, which, soon after, almost stuns your ears. Doubling, as you proceed, a tuft of wood, you are struck at once with the aweful scene which suddenly bursts upon your astonished sight . . . this great body of water, rushing with horrid fury, seems to threaten destruction to the solid rocks that enrage it by their resistance. It boils up from the caverns which itself has formed, as if it were vomited out of the lower regions. The horrid and incessant din with which this is accompanied, unnerves and overcomes the heart.[82]

Cora Linn was one of Britain's most Sublime experiences, as tourist after tourist testifies. The essence of the Burkean Sublime was its irrationality: it seized hold of the mind before the mind could begin consciously to organise any response. The first experience of Cora Linn quite destroyed Picturesque calculations:

Your organs of perception are hurried along and partake of the turbulence of the roaring waters. The powers of recollection remain suspended by this sudden shock; and it is not till after a considerable time, that you are enabled to contemplate the sublime horrors of this majestic scene.[83]

'Recollection' here means not so much recall or memory but the orderly gathering together again of the mental faculties after their dispersal under shock. Only then can one 'contemplate' the scene, control and direct one's response, and begin to describe it in words or paint.

The task of verbal description was immense, especially for the tourist who was fastidious about choosing just the right terms of appraisal for such a magnificent scene. This predicament is comically illustrated in Dorothy Wordsworth's account of Coleridge's exchange with a fellow tourist, as they stood to enjoy Cora Linn:

C., who is always good-natured enough to enter into conversation with anybody whom he meets in his way, began to talk with the gentleman, who observed that it was a '*majestic* waterfall'. Coleridge was delighted with the accuracy of the epithet, particularly as he had been settling in his own mind the precise meaning of the words grand, majestic, sublime, etc., and had discussed the subject with William at some length the day before. 'Yes, sir', says Coleridge, 'it *is* a *majestic* waterfall'. 'Sublime and beautiful', replied his friend. Poor C. could make no answer.

Contemplation and appraisal were assisted by the provision of observation seats by the path overlooking the falls. Behind and above these cliff-edge viewpoints was a pavilion (the building is still there) which commanded a broad sweep of the falls and the village and mills of New Lanark. As at Dunkeld, the owners of the estate had mounted mirrors in various positions around the interior. The large mirror, angled to reflect the scene as a whole, enabled the timid to view Cora Linn without danger – 'which is hardly otherwise to be approached, for fear of giddiness, arising from the unusual scene'. The approach to the falls from the opposite bank, in the grounds of Corehouse, took one past Cora Castle to a rather lower

81. J. M. W. Turner, *The fall of the Clyde, Lanarkshire : Noon – vide Akenside's Hymn to the Naiads*
(1802). Walker Art Gallery, Liverpool

82. J. M. W. Turner, *The Falls of Clyde* (c. 1835–40).
Lady Lever Art Gallery, Port Sunlight

viewpoint, difficult of access. From here Jacob More, the 'Wilson of Scotland', painted his much esteemed *Cora Linn* (1771). Later Picturesque tastes lowered the viewpoint still further, at some hazard to the artist's life. Turner's 1802 water-colour (fig. 81), based on sketches made during his 1801 Scottish tour, is taken from near the foot of the falls. As his title reference to Akenside indicates, he has placed among the rocky débris a group of Naiads, the tutelary deities of rivers and springs. The composition was modified seven years later when it was etched for Turner's *Liber Studiorum* and included in his 'Elevated Pastoral' section, where the presence of the Naiads quite clearly gives the landscape a heroic status in neo-classical terms. Turner's oil painting of the late 1830s is a radical reinterpretation of Cora Linn (fig. 82). No longer are the recognisable forms of landscape clearly delineated and strategically lit within a stable and conventional composition. Classical figures and Scottish topography are now dissolved in brilliant torrents of colour. The old mode has been almost reversed in this near visionary rendering of the celebrated Picturesque site: 'light modified by objects',[84] in Thomas Hardy's fine phrase.

\*  \*  \*

The Clyde Falls thus offer a paradigm of Picturesque experiences and of the tensions within the Picturesque prescription. We can watch this in the changing emblematic status of the Bonnington Foghouse, in Dorothy Wordsworth's impatience with Stations, and in the range of viewing positions, from the safe, purpose-built belvedere high above the Falls down to an alarmingly close exposure to the Sublime. We can trace it also in Turner's Cora Linn portraits, which look backwards and forwards: backwards to explicit neoclassical allegory, forwards to the explosive, near-abstract treatment of his later years. With Dorothy Wordsworth and Turner what begins as a routine tour in search of the Picturesque ends with a recognition of the extent to which the dynamic qualities of the natural world are repressed by Picturesque controls. Both are impatient to dissolve rigid Picturesque conventions in order to regain the aesthetic initiative, to discover for themselves spontaneous beauties and natural energies.

The late-eighteenth-century search for the Picturesque ends with the recognition of its limitations. As a way of perceiving the natural landscape it was too restricting. It was exclusive first in social terms. Its pleasures were available principally to the leisured connoisseur élite, whose full aesthetic engagement with a wild landscape and its inhabitants entailed a corresponding moral detachment. It was not the Regency satires – in Jane Austen and Peacock, and in Combe and Rowlandson's *Dr. Syntax* – which brought an end to that first phase of the Picturesque. It was more the increased pressure on the social conscience of early Victorian liberal humanism and Evangelical zeal. The capacity for a purely aesthetic, formalist enjoyment of scenes of rustic decay could not be reconciled with humane sympathies. Ruskin recorded in his diary one Picturesque experience in which moral and aesthetic judgements resumed that old antagonism which Gilpin had avoided by urging the suspension of the moral sense:

I had a happy walk here this afternoon, down among the branching currents of the Somme ... a few mere stumps of pollard willow sticking out of the banks of soft mud ... boats like paper boats ... for the costermongers to paddle about in among the weeds ... wallflowers and geraniums, curiously vivid ... seen against the darkness of a dyer's back yard ... the water still working its way steadily over the weeds, until it narrowed into a current strong enough to turn two or three mill-wheels, one working against the side of an old flamboyant Gothic church, whose richly traceried buttresses sloped into the filthy stream; – all exquisitely picturesque ... I could not help feeling how many suffering persons must pay for my picturesque subject and happy walk.

The diary extract is quoted in a footnote to Ruskin's discussion 'Of the Turnerian Picturesque' in *Modern Painters* (Volume IV, 1856). Here he distinguished two types of Picturesque, the higher, Turnerian, and the lower Picturesque. The lower is the heartless 'surface-picturesque', the old, detached, formalist delight in disorder and ruin enjoyed by the man 'incapable of acute sympathy with others'. The higher Picturesque, exemplified in Turner's work, is one in which the painter 'has communion of heart with his subject'. He may portray dilapidated windmills and crumbling abbeys, but he will infuse into his picture noble moral sympathies. It would be hard to imagine a more radical challenge to the aesthetic premises of late eighteenth-century Picturesque than Ruskin's emphatically ethical criteria, which were largely endorsed in mid-nineteenth-century England. Dickens paid a visit to the slums of Naples in 1845 and reported back: 'I am afraid the conventional idea of the picturesque is associated with such misery and degradation that a new picturesque will have to be established as the world goes onward'.[85] In his Christmas book for that year, *The Chimes*, he returns to the attack. The gnarled labourer Will Fern addresses a gathering of the prosperous bourgeoisie at Bowley Hall:

'Gentlefolks, I've lived many a year in this place. You may see the cottage from the sunk fence over yonder. I've seen the ladies draw it in their books a hundred times. It looks well in a picter, I've heard say; but there an't weather in picters, and maybe 'tis fitter for that, than a place to live in'.

The Picturesque, in these terms, simply perpetuated social divisions. Poor Will Fern's weatherbeaten cottage must have been an asset to the Bowley Hall estate (fig. 83). It reminds us of the way patrician taste more directly controlled and exploited Picturesque experiences in the later eighteenth century. A number of the finest sights were on private property: Sir Michael le Fleming's summer-house view of Rydal Falls, Braithwaite's elaborate development of West's First Station on Windermere, the Duke of Atholl's 'Ossian's Hall', and Sir John and Lady Ross's organisation of the Clyde Falls tour.

But the élitism of the Picturesque was ultimately less important than its other limitations, in particular its restriction of the potential range of responses to the

Trotty found him in the street. His voice was deeper and more husky, and had a trembling in it now and then; but he never raised it, passionately, and seldom lifted it above the firm stern level of the homely facts he stated.

" 'Tis harder than you

83. Clarkson Stanfield, illustration to Dickens's *The Chimes* (1845)

natural world. In 1789 Hannah More told Horace Walpole of her experience of 'sailing down the beautiful river Wye, looking at abbeys and castles, with Mr Gilpin in my hand to teach me to criticize, and talk of foregrounds, and distances, and perspectives, and prominences, with all the cant of connoisseurship, and then to *subdue* my imagination, which had been not a little disordered with this enchanting scenery'.[86] Her complaint was echoed a few years later, when Wordsworth recorded his impression of the Alps in *Descriptive Sketches* (1793), to which he subsequently added a revealing note:

I had once given to these sketches the title of Picturesque; but the Alps are insulted in applying to them that term. Whoever, in attempting to describe their sublime features, should confine himself to the cold rules of painting would give his reader but a very imperfect idea of those emotions which they have the irresistible power of communicating to the most impassive imaginations.

Turner and Dorothy Wordsworth would have well understood this frustration.

We have already on many occasions in this book come across tourists similarly straining at the Picturesque leash. Doubts about the meaning and application of the term multiplied almost as soon as it gained currency. For this reason alone it is misleading to think of a distinct Picturesque phase or period. Christopher Hussey's pronouncements on 'the picturesque interregnum between classic and romantic art . . . necessary in order to enable the imagination to form the habit of feeling through the eye'[87] suggest a kind of historical stability for the Picturesque. But even among the theorists, let alone the touring amateurs and connoisseurs, the term changes meaning as it is handed on from one to another. Gilpin's Picturesque has a decidedly classical or neoclassical foundation in its strong compositional emphasis, its respect for the *beau idéal*, and its predominantly Claudean idiom. Uvedale Price's Picturesque is little interested in composition, relishes the 'characteristic' or particularised in scenery, and favours Gainsborough and the Dutch school so disparaged by Reynolds. These two chief proponents of the Picturesque, so different in their emphases, can hardly be said to occupy an interregnum between classicism and romanticism when they partake of both. Still less can the late-eighteenth-century tourists be said to represent a consistent and self-contained phase in a period of cultural transition.

The truth is that the Picturesque phase has never really ended. We use the word as a term of appraisal for natural scenery and ancient buildings just as often as did our Georgian predecessors: the only difference is that we no longer bother about its precise meaning. Nonetheless, it still conveys the sense that what we are seeing is gratifyingly similar to the familiar images of an idealised rural beauty promoted in paintings, postcards, travelogues and calendar photos. Our use of the word signals our pleasure in recognising how closely the reality can approximate to the ideal. The persistence of the Picturesque is evident in the way our standards of beauty in natural scenery still depend very much on our perception of what can be framed: the camera viewfinder takes over the role of the Claude Glass as the means of distinguishing a fine scene. It is evident also in the skill of the modern tourist industry in promoting natural scenery as a commodity. Indeed the enormous scale of this industry now is an indication of the extent to which all of us are acquiring those habits of perception and evaluation which were developed and formulated by a leisured élite two centuries ago. It is no accident that natural scenery and ruined architecture were and still are coupled as among the chief tourist attractions and that both are now high-priority subjects for conservation. They represented for the early Picturesque tourists, as they do for their modern counterparts, a culture and an environment which are steadily disappearing, from which most of us have long been alienated, and which are now acquiring a high antique value. Picturesque theory and practice are, among other things, the idiosyncratic records of these radical changes.

# Select Bibliography of the Tours

I have included here only the travel literature consulted for the four eighteenth-century tours featured in this book. Unless otherwise stated, the place of publication is London.

Aikin, Arthur. *Journal of a Tour through North Wales and Part of Shropshire* (1797).

Anon. ('By an English Gentleman'). *A Journey to Scotland* (1699).

[A Tour through North Wales, August 1775], National Library of Wales, MS. 9280.A.

'A Tour in Scotland' (1776), National Library of Scotland, MS. 1021.

'Tour in the Summer 1776. Through Wales', National Library of Wales, MS. 2862.A.

*Northern Tour: or, Poetical Epistles* (1776).

*The Travellers. A Satire* (1778).

'Tour through N. Wales in the Year 1778', Central Library Cardiff, MS. 1.549.

*One Day's Journey to the Highlands of Scotland* (1784).

'Journal of a Tour thro' Westmoreland & Cumberland' (1786): in *The Topographer* I (1790).

'A Tour in Scotland' (1789), National Library of Scotland, MS. 1080.

*A Tour through the South of England, Wales, and Part of Ireland, made during the Summer of 1791* (1793).

'Journal of a Tour thro England and Wales, in the Months of July, August, & September 1794', British Library, Add. MS. 30,172.

'Welch Journal Aug[st] 20th 1795', British Library, Add. MS. 37,926.

*Letters describing a Tour through Part of South Wales* [in 1796] (1797).

'Sketch of a pedestrian Tour thro' parts of North and South Wales etc. Begun Sept. 3rd, 1798', National Library of Wales, MS. 4419.B.

*A Collection of Tours in Wales; or, a Display of the Beauties of Wales: selected principally from celebrated Histories and Popular Tours, with Occasional Remarks* (1799).

'A Tour through Derbyshire and the northern Counties with an Excursion to Glasgow Loch Lomond & Edinburgh' (1800), Derby Central Library, MS. 3463.

'A Journal of a Tour thro' North Wales' (1802), National Library of Wales, MS. 789.B.

*Journal of Three Years Travels through Different Parts of Great Britain in 1795, 1796, 1797* (1805).

'Notes of an Excursion from York to Edinburgh & return by a few of the Lakes in Cumberland & Westmoreland' (1817), National Library of Scotland, MS. Acc. 6793.

Baker, James. *A Picturesque Guide through Wales and the Marches* (Worcester, 1795).

Beattie, James. 'A Description of the Highlands of Scotland, and Remarks on the Second Sight of the Inhabitants': in *Annual Register* XX (1777).

Bernard, Thomas. 'A Holiday Tour' (1780): in J. B. Baker ed., *Pleasure and Pain (1780– 1818)* (1930).

Bingley, William. *A Tour round North Wales, performed During the Summer of 1798: Containing Not only the Description and Local History of the Country, but also a Sketch of the History of the Welsh Bards* (1800).

Brown, John. [Description of Vale of Keswick. ?1753]: the full 'Description' is printed in Donald Eddy, 'John Brown: "The Columbus of Keswick"', *Modern Philology* LXXIII (1976), pp. 374–84.

Buchanan, John L. *Travels in the Western Hebrides: from 1782 to 1790* (1793).

Budworth, Joseph. *A Fortnight's Ramble to the Lakes* (1792).

Byng, The Hon. John. *The Torrington Diaries*: ed. C. Bruyn Andrews (1934–8).

Catcott, A. 'Diaries of Tours made in England & Wales' (1748–74), Bristol Central Library, MS. B.6495.

Champion, Anthony. 'From a Traveller in Wales to a Friend Travelling in Scotland. August 1772': in *Miscellanies* (1801).

Clarke, James. *A Survey of the Lakes of Cumberland, Westmorland and Lancashire; together with an Account, Historical, Topographical and Descriptive, of the adjacent Country* (1787).

Clutterbuck, Robert. 'Journal of a Tour. From Cardiff, Glamorganshire, through South & North Wales. In the Summer of 1794. In company with Taylor Combe Esqre.', Central Library Cardiff, MS. 3.277.

'Journal of a Tour through the north of England & part of Scotland; In company with George Harvey & Thomas Clutterbuck Esqrs. during the Summer of 1795', Central Library Cardiff, MS. 3.277.

Clutterbuck, Thomas. 'A Tour thro' North and South Wales, with an Excursion to Dublin, from Holyhead, in the Year 1798', Central Library Cardiff, MS. 3.276.

'A Tour to the Lakes, thro' Derbyshire to Scotland in 1795', Central Library Cardiff, MS. 3.276.

Cobbold, Mrs. 'Tour in the Lake District' (1795), British Library, Add. MS. 19,203.

Cordiner, Charles. *Antiquities & Scenery of the North of Scotland, in a Series of Letters, to Thomas Pennant, Esqr.* (1780).

*Remarkable Ruins, and Romantic Prospects of North Britain. With Ancient Monuments, and Singular Subjects of Natural History* (1788).

Coxe, William. *An Historical Tour in Monmouthshire; illustrated with views by Sir R. C. Hoare, Bart.* (1801).

Cradock, Joseph. *Letters from Snowdon: Descriptive of a Tour through the Northern Counties of Wales* (1770).

    *An Account of Some of the most Romantic Parts of North Wales* (1777).

Cumberland, George. *An Attempt to Describe Hafod, and the neighbouring Scenes about the . . . Devil's Bridge, in the county of Cardigan* (1796).

Cumberland, Richard. *Odes* (1776).

Dibdin, Charles. *Observations on a Tour through almost the whole of England, and a considerable part of Scotland, in a series of letters, addressed to a large number of intelligent and respectable Friends* (1801–2).

Dick, Richard. 'Jaunt to the North Country' (1779), Mitchell Library Glasgow, MS. 89.

Diggle, Elizabeth. [Journal, 1788], Glasgow University Library, MS. Gen. 738.

Dodd, J. 'Tour' (1735), British Library, MS. 5957.

Farington, Joseph. 'Tours in Scotland in 1788 and 1792': typescript of Farington MS by James Greig, Edinburgh City Library.

Fosbroke, T. D. *The Wye Tour, or Gilpin on the Wye, with historical and archaeological additions* (Ross, 1818).

Garnett, Thomas. *Observations on a Tour through the Highlands and Part of the Western Isles of Scotland, particularly Staffa and Icolmkill: To which are added, A Description of the Falls of the Clyde, of the Country round Moffat, and an Analysis of its mineral Waters* (1800).

Gastrell, Francis. 'Journal of a Tour through Scotland in 1760', Shakespeare Centre, ER. 1/23.

Gell, William. *A Tour in the Lakes, Made in 1797*: ed. W. Rollinson (Newcastle, 1968).

Gibson, W. 'Sketch of a Two Months Tour in Scotland, performed on Horseback in the Summer of 1773', *Gentleman's Magazine*, LXII–LXIV (1792–4).

Gilpin, William. *Observations on the River Wye, and Several Parts of South Wales, etc. relative chiefly to Picturesque Beauty; made in the Summer of the Year 1770* (1782).

    *Observations relative chiefly to Picturesque Beauty, Made in the Year 1772, on Several Parts of England; particularly the Mountains, and Lakes of Cumberland, and Westmoreland* (1786).

    *Observations, relative chiefly to Picturesque Beauty, Made in the Year 1776, on Several Parts of Great Britain; particularly the High-Lands of Scotland* (1789).

    *Observations on Several Parts of the Counties of Cambridge, Norfolk, Suffolk, and Essex. Also on Several Parts of North Wales, relative chiefly to Picturesque Beauty, in two Tours, the former made in . . . 1769, the latter in . . . 1773* (1809).

Grant, Anne. *Letters from the Mountains; being the real correspondence of a Lady, between the years 1773 and 1807* (1807).

Grant, Johnson. 'A London Journal of a Three Weeks Tour, in 1797, through Derbyshire to the Lakes' in W. Mavor, *The British Tourists* (q.v.).

Gray, Thomas. 'Journal in the Lakes' (1769): in W. Mason ed., *The Poems of Mr. Gray . . .* (1775).

    'Journey into Scotland' (1764): in D. C. Tovey ed., *Gray and His Friends* (1890).

Grose, Francis. [Journey to South Wales, 1775], British Library, Add. MS. 17,398.

Hanway, Mary Anne. *A Journey to the Highlands of Scotland, with Occasional Remarks on Dr. Johnson's Tour* (1775).

Haslam, Sarah. 'Travel Journal' (1802), Wigan Public Library, Edward Hall Collection, M969, EHC 177.

Hastings, Warren. [Journal of a Tour in 1787], British Library, Add. MS. 39,889.

Heath, Charles. *The Excursion down the Wye, from Ross to Monmouth* (Monmouth, 1799).

Heron, Robert. *Observations made in a Journey through the Western Counties of Scotland in the autumn of 1792* (Perth, 1793).

Herring, Thomas. *Letters . . . to William Duncombe from the year 1728 to 1757* (1777).

Hoare, Richard Colt. 'Tour in the Summer 1797', Central Library Cardiff, MS. 3.127. 6/6.

'Tour in South Wales or rather Monmouthshire – August 1798', Central Library Cardiff, MS. 3.127. 6/6.

'Journal of a Tour in 1800', Central Library Cardiff, MS. 3.127. 5/6.

Hodgkinson, Richard. 'Memorandums of a Journey into Scotland, June 1800', Manchester Central Library, MS. L15/2/8.

Horne, T. H. *The Lakes of Lancashire, Westmoreland and Cumberland; delineated in Forty-three Engravings, from Drawings by Joseph Farington, R.A.* (1816).

Hucks, Joseph. *A Pedestrian Tour through North Wales, in a Series of Letters* (1795).

Hutchinson, William. *An Excursion to the Lakes in Westmoreland and Cumberland, August, 1773* (1774).

Ireland, Samuel. *Picturesque Views on the River Wye* (1797).

Johnson, Samuel. *A Journey to the Western Islands of Scotland* (1775).

*A Diary of a Journey into North Wales, in the Year 1774*: ed. R. Duppa (1816).

Knox, John. *A Tour through the Highlands of Scotland, and the Hebride Isles, in 1786* (1787).

Lettice, John. *Letters on a Tour through various Parts of Scotland, in the year 1792* (1794).

Loutherbourg, P. J. de. *The Romantic and Picturesque Scenery of England and Wales* (1805).

Lyttelton, Lord George. 'Description of North Wales in Letters from the Right Hon.[ble] Lord Lyttelton to his Brother Charles Lord Bishop of Carlisle' (1755), Birmingham City Library, MS. A.091/1755.

'Mr. M.' 'A Tour to South Wales, etc' (1801), National Library of Wales, MS. 1340.C.

M'Nayr, James. *A Guide from Glasgow, to some of the most Remarkable Scenes in the Highlands of Scotland and to the Falls of the Clyde* (Glasgow, 1797).

Malkin, B. H. *The Scenery, Antiquities, and Biography of South Wales* (1804).

Maton, W. G. 'A Sketch of a Tour from London to the Lakes made in the Summer of the year 1799', British Library, MS. 32,442.

Mavor, William. *The British Tourists; or, Traveller's Pocket Companion through England, Wales, Scotland and Ireland. Comprehending the most celebrated tours in the British Islands* (1798–1800).

Mawman, Joseph. *An Excursion to the Highlands of Scotland, and the English Lakes, with Recollections, Descriptions and References to Historical Facts* (1805).

Michell, J. H. *The Tour of the Duke of Somerset, and the Rev. J. H. Michell, through parts of England, Wales, and Scotland, in the year 1795* (1845).

Morgan, Mary. *A Tour to Milford Haven, in the Year 1791* (1795).

Moule, Morris. 'A Tour through the Counties of Huntingdon [etc]', Chetham's Library, Manchester, MS. Mun. A.2.34.

Murray, Sarah. *A Companion and Useful Guide to the Beauties of Scotland, to the Lakes of Westmoreland, Cumberland, and Lancashire* (1799).

Newell, R. H. *Letters on the Scenery of Wales; including a series of subjects for the pencil* (1821).

Newte, Thomas. *A Tour in England and Scotland in 1785* (1788).

    *Prospects and Observations on a Tour in England and Scotland* (1791).

Oliver, Peter. 'Journal of a Voyage to England in 1776', British Library, Egerton MS. 2673.

Pattison, Jacob. 'A Tour through part of the Highlands of Scotland in 1780', National Library of Scotland, MS. 6322.

Pennant, David. 'Tour. 1789', National Library of Wales, MS. 2523.B.

Pennant, Thomas. *A Tour in Wales, 1770* (1778).

    *A Tour in Scotland and Voyage to the Hebrides MDCCLXXII* (1774).

Percy, Thomas. 'Observanda in the Tour into Scotland, Aug. 8. 1773', British Library, Add. MS. 39,547.

Plumptre, James. 'A Journal: of a Tour through part of North Wales in the year 1792. Part 2.', Cambridge University Library, MS. Add. 5802.

    [Journal of a tour to Scotland, 1795], Cambridge University Library, MS. Add. 5808.

    'A Narrative of a Pedestrian Journey through some parts of Yorkshire, Durham and Northumberland to the Highlands of Scotland, and home by the Lakes and some parts of Wales in the Summer of the year 1799', Cambridge University Library, MS. Add. 5814–16.

Pococke, Richard. 'A Journey round Scotland to the Orkneys and through Part of England and Ireland' (1760–), British Library, Add. MS. 14,256–59.

Prichard, Will. 'A Ramble Dedicated to Mrs. Hart' (1746), Derby County Library, MS. 3379.

Radcliffe, Ann. *A Journey made in the Summer of 1794 through Holland and the Western Frontier of Germany, with a Return down the Rhine, to which are added Observations during a Tour of the Lakes in Westmorland and Cumberland* (1795).

Rees, Elizabeth. 'A Few Remarks made in an Excursion through part of the Counties of Glamorgan, Monmouth, Hereford . . . in the Year 1788', Central Library Cardiff, MS. 3.458.

Shaw, Stebbing. *A Tour, in 1787, from London, to the Western Highlands of Scotland. Including Excursions to the Lakes of Westmoreland and Cumberland* (1788).

    *A Tour to the West of England in 1788* (1789).

Skinner, John. 'Tour in South Wales, A.D. 1800', Central Library Cardiff, MS. 1.503.

    'Journal of a Tour through North Wales, in the Year 1800', Central Library Cardiff, MS. 1.503.

    'Northern Tour' (1825), British Library, Add. MS. 33,688.

Skrine, Henry. *Three Successive Tours in the North of England and great Part of Scotland* (1795).

Sotheby, William. *A Tour through Parts of Wales, Sonnets, Odes, and other Poems, with Engravings from Drawings taken on the Spot, by J. Smith* (1794).

Southey, Robert. *Letters from England: by Don Manuel Alvarez Espriella* (1807).

Stoddart, John. *Remarks on Local Scenery and Manners in Scotland during the years 1799 and 1800* (1801).

Sulivan, Richard. *Observations Made during a Tour through Parts of England, Scotland, and Wales, in 1778. In a Series of Letters* (1780).

Sykes, Christopher. 'Journal of a Tour in Wales 1796', National Library of Wales, MS. 2258.C.

Taylor, Daniell. 'Letter ... from Edenborough, Oct 7, 1710', British Library, Add. MS. 37,682.

Thrale, Hester. 'Mrs. Thrale's Tour in Wales with Dr. Johnson' (1774): in A. M. Broadley, *Dr. Johnson and Mrs. Thrale* (1910).

'Travel Book 1789. Journey to the North of England', John Rylands Library, Manchester, Eng. MS. 623.

Torbuck, John ed. *A Collection of Welsh Travels, and Memoirs of Wales* (1738).

Turner, J. M. W. 'Diary of a Tour in Wales' (1792): in John Gage ed., *Collected Correspondence of J. M. W. Turner* (Oxford, 1980).

Verdon, J. 'Journal of a Tour to North Wales & Dublin' (1699), Central Library Cardiff, MS. 4.370.

Vernon, William. 'A Journey to Wales': in *Poems on Several Occasions* (1758).

Walker, Adam. *Remarks made in a Tour from London to the Lakes of Westmoreland and Cumberland, in the Summer of MDCCXCII* (1792).

Warner, Richard. *A Walk through Wales, in August 1797* (Bath, 1798).

*A Second Walk through Wales* (Bath, 1799).

West, Thomas. *A Guide to the Lakes in Cumberland, Westmorland and Lancashire* (1778: 2nd edition, revised and enlarged, 1780).

Wigstead, Henry. *Remarks on a Tour to North and South Wales in the Year 1797* (1800).

Wilkinson, Thomas. *Tours to the British Mountains* (1824).

Willis, John. 'Tours in Ireland, Scotland, Holland etc' (1804–28), Bristol Central Library, MS. B7400.

'The Lakes and Scotland. No. 2.', Bristol Central Library, MS. B7404.

Wordsworth, Dorothy. 'A Tour made in Scotland (A.D. 1803)': in E. de Selincourt ed., *The Journals of Dorothy Wordsworth* (Connecticut, 1970).

Wordsworth, William. *A Guide through the District of the Lakes in the North of England* (5th edition, 1835).

Wraxall, Nathaniel. 'Diary' (July–September 1813), National Library of Scotland, MS. 3108.

Wright, Lucy. 'Note Book 1806', Wigan Public Library, Edward Hall Collection, M842, EHC/73.

Wyndham, Henry. *A Gentleman's Tour through Monmouthshire and Wales, in the months of June and July, 1774* (1775).

Young, Arthur. *A Six Weeks Tour through the Southern Counties of England and Wales* (1768).

*A Six Months Tour through the North of England* (1770).

# Brief Biographical Notes
## on some of the Writers and Minor Painters
### associated with the Picturesque

Sir George Beaumont (1753–1827). One of the best-known connoisseurs and patrons of the early nineteenth century: a generous friend of Constable, Hearne, Wordsworth and Coleridge and a major force in the founding of the National Gallery. Visited the Lakes with Hearne and Farington in 1778. A pupil of Alexander Cozens (and one-time colleague of J. R. Cozens), his own landscape paintings remain very much in the Claudean Picturesque manner.

William Day (1764–1807). Amateur watercolourist and enthusiastic geologist who toured Wales in 1791. Specialised in painting cliff scenery where his geological interests are fully expressed. His work is distinguished by strong pencil outlines onto which the colour is lightly washed.

Joseph Farington R.A. (1747–1821). Student of Richard Wilson. His extensive touring and wide and distinguished circle of friends are reflected in his invaluable *Diary*. His landscapes are conventional Picturesque compositions, meticulously drawn, to which ink wash or very muted colouring is added.

William Gilpin (1724–1804). Travelled extensively in England, Scotland and Wales from 1769–76. From 1777 onwards he was vicar of Boldre in the New Forest. His tour journals, illustrated with pen and wash drawings, circulated in manuscript for several years before publication and helped to promote, if not inaugurate, the fashion for Picturesque touring.

> See W. D. Templeman, *The Life and Work of William Gilpin* (1937) and C. P. Barbier, *William Gilpin: His Drawings, Teaching and Theory of the Picturesque* (1963).

Samuel Hieronymous Grimm (1733–1794). Swiss-born artist who settled in England in 1768. Contributed the drawings for Gilbert White's *Natural History and Antiquities of Selborne* (1789). Toured Wales in 1777 with Henry Wyndham. Clear pen and wash delineation with colour lightly added.

Thomas Hearne (1744–1817). An apprentice engraver and then, for three and a half years, draughtsman in the West Indies. He contributed illustrations to *The Antiquities of Great Britain* (1777–81) and was commissioned to do a number of views of Richard Payne Knight's Herefordshire estate, Downton Castle. His delicately coloured drawings influenced the topographical work of Turner and Girtin in the 1790s.

Julius Caesar Ibbetson (1759–1817). Lived for some years in the Lake District. Travelled in the East in 1787 and 1788 and made several sketching tours in Britain, including the North Wales tour (1792) with John 'Warwick' Smith and the Hon. Robert

Greville. Nicknamed the 'Berghem of England' for his rendering of British scenery in a Dutch idiom.

See R. M. Clay, *Julius Caesar Ibbetson 1759–1817* (1948).

Philippe de Loutherbourg R.A. (1740–1812). Studied at Strasburg and Paris before settling in England in 1771. Innovative set designer and scene painter at Drury Lane in the 1770s, and creator of the 'Eidophusikon' panorama. A master of the more Sublime landscape scenery, theatrically lit.

See Rudiger Joppien, *Philippe Jacques de Loutherbourg, R.A.* (1973).

Richard Payne Knight (1750–1824). Connoisseur and collector. His eclectic tastes were well expressed in the design of his Herefordshire seat at Downton, with its castle-like exterior and rooms in the classical style. His main contributions to the Picturesque debate are his didactic poem (dedicated to Uvedale Price) *The Landscape*, illustrated with 2 etchings from designs by Hearne, and his *Analytical Inquiry into the Principles of Taste* (1805).

See M. Clarke and N. Penny, *The Arrogant Connoisseur: Richard Payne Knight* (1982).

Uvedale Price (1747–1829). Writer and practitioner of Picturesque tastes in gardening, exemplified in the extensive redesigning and planting of his family estate in Herefordshire. Like Payne Knight he attacks the principles of 'Capability' Brown's landscape gardening in favour of a more rugged Picturesque aesthetic, derived from the Dutch landscape tradition and from Gainsborough (who was a friend of the family). His major work was *An Essay on the Picturesque* (1794).

Michael Angelo Rooker (1746–1801). Engraver, student of Paul Sandby, and later principal scene painter at the Haymarket Theatre. Made sketching tours throughout England and Wales, specialising in Picturesque ruins where the potentially Sublime or melancholic mood is lightened by the introduction of genre subjects.

See Patrick Conner, *Michael Angelo Rooker (1746–1801)* (1984).

Paul Sandby R.A. (1731–1809). One of the earliest and most influential watercolourists. Began his career as a draughtsman and cartographer in Scotland in the 1740s, and later became a drawing master of considerable reputation. Founder member of the Royal Academy. Painted landscapes in watercolour and gouache, and was one of the first English artists to use the aquatint process.

See Luke Herrmann, *Paul and Thomas Sandby* (1986).

John 'Warwick' Smith (1749–1831). Student of Gilpin's father and brother (Sawrey), and later under the patronage of the Earl of Warwick. An Associate of the Old Society of Painters in Watercolours. Travelled extensively in Britain and Europe. Landscape watercolours inclined to be formulaic in composition but quite richly lit.

Francis Towne (1740–1816). Undertook most of the recognised Picturesque tours in Britain, emphasising in many of his paintings that they were 'on the spot' records of the views chosen. He staked his reputation on his oils; but it is now his watercolours which are highly valued. These are highly distinctive, delicate pen drawings with flat colour washes of deceptive simplicity and considerable beauty.

See A. Bury, *Francis Towne* (1962).

John Varley (1778–1842). Popular drawing master, whose *Treatise* (1816–21) on landscape painting was widely respected. His pupils included Linnell and David Cox, and through the former he was introduced into the Blake circle. He made several tours to Wales (at least one in the company of his painter brother Cornelius), and many of his later idealised landscape compositions are based on Welsh scenery.

See C. M. Kauffmann, *John Varley (1778–1842)* (1984).

Thomas West (c.1720–1779). Antiquarian and topographer. As a Jesuit chaplain in Cumbria he could indulge his interests in the local ancient monuments (*The Antiquities of Furness*, 1774) and in the scenery of the Lake District. His *Guide to the Lakes* (1778) was dedicated to the 'Lovers of Landscape Studies', for whom he established specific viewpoints or Stations on the perimeters of the lakes. The *Guide* was, for several decades, highly influential in determining the way tourists registered the scenery of the Lake District.

# Notes and References

## LIST OF ABBREVIATIONS

Gilpin, *Cambridge*     William Gilpin, *Observations on Several Parts of the Counties of Cambridge, Norfolk, Suffolk, and Essex. Also on Several Parts of North Wales, relative chiefly to Picturesque Beauty, in two Tours, the former made in* [. . .] *1769, the latter in* [. . .] *1773* (1809).

Gilpin, *Forest Scenery*     William Gilpin, *Remarks on Forest Scenery, and other Woodland Views (relative chiefly to Picturesque Beauty), illustrated by the Scenes of New-Forest in Hampshire* (1791), 2 vols.

Gilpin, *High-Lands*     William Gilpin, *Observations, relative chiefly to Picturesque Beauty, Made in the Year 1776, on Several Parts of Great Britain; particularly the High-Lands of Scotland* (1789), 2 vols.

Gilpin, *Lakes*     William Gilpin, *Observations relative chiefly to Picturesque Beauty, made in the Year 1772, on Several Parts of England; particularly the Mountains, and Lakes of Cumberland and Westmoreland* (1786), 2 vols.

Gilpin, *Three Essays*     William Gilpin, *Three Essays: – on Picturesque Beauty; – on Picturesque Travel; and, on Sketching Landscape: to which is added a Poem, on Landscape Painting* (1792).

Gilpin, *Two Essays*     William Gilpin, *Two Essays: one on the Author's Mode of executing rough Sketches; the other on the Principles on which they are composed. To these are added, three plates of figures by S. Gilpin* (1804).

Gilpin, *Wye*     William Gilpin, *Observations on the River Wye, and Several Parts of South Wales, etc. relative chiefly to Picturesque Beauty; made in the Summer of the Year 1770* (1782).

BL     The British Library.

Note: In the following references the place of publication, unless otherwise stated, is London.

## Preface

1. Christopher Hussey, *The Picturesque : Studies in a Point of View* (1927), p. 4.
2. John Dixon Hunt, 'Ut Pictura Poesis, Ut Pictura Hortus and the Picturesque', *Word and Image* I (1985), i, 102.
3. A starting point for this approach might be the undeveloped comments by Leslie Parris in the 1973 Tate Gallery exhibition catalogue *Landscape in Britain, c. 1750–1850* (p. 58). He describes the Picturesque as 'the building into experience of the countryside of a comfortable myth . . . the gypsy could then be an interesting piece of local colour rather than a peripatetic threat to the *status quo* . . . It was a holding operation, by and for the squirearchy which had lost ground and continued to lose ground in the dynamic of country life'.

## Chapter 1

1. Richard Warner, *A Walk through Wales, in August 1797* (1799), p. 232.
2. Anon., *Northern Tour: or, Poetical Epistles* (1776), p. 14.
3. Archibald Alison, *Essays on the Nature and Principles of Taste* (Edinburgh, 1790), p. 45.
4. Richard Payne Knight, *An Analytical Inquiry into the Principles of Taste* (1805), p. 150.
5. *The Prose of John Clare*, ed. J. W. and Anne Tibble (1951), pp. 174–5.
6. Mary Anne Hanway, *A Journey to the Highlands of Scotland* (1775), p. 120.
7. Alexander Pope, *A Discourse on Pastoral Poetry* (1709). This and all subsequent quotations from Pope (unless otherwise stated) are taken from the one-volume Twickenham Edition of *The Poems of Alexander Pope*, edited by John Butt (1963: repr. 1970).
8. Gilpin, *High-Lands*, II, pp. 11–12.
9. Joseph Mawman, *An Excursion to the Highlands of Scotland, and the English Lakes, with Recollections, Descriptions and References to Historical Facts* (1805), p. 136.
10. For an excellent and very full survey of this tradition see Maren-Sofie Røstvig, *The Happy Man: Studies in the Metamorphosis of a Classical Ideal 1600–1700*

(Oxford, 1954). A second volume takes the study up to 1760.
11. In Abraham Cowley, 'Of Agriculture', in *Discourses by Way of Essays in Verse and Prose* (1668).
12. On Pope, the theme of retirement and the Twickenham garden, see Maynard Mack, *The Garden and the City* (Toronto, 1969), esp. Chs. 1–3.
13. William Wordsworth, *Guide to the Lakes* (5th ed. 1835: edited by E. de Selincourt, Oxford, 1906), p. 74.
14. William Vernon, 'The Cottage', in *Poems on Several Occasions* (1758).
15. William Marshall, *Planting and Ornamental Gardening* (1785), p. 611. See also Gilpin's discussion of the 'artificial cottage' in *Western Parts*, pp. 308–11.
16. Richard Payne Knight, *The Landscape* (1794), II, ll. 288–93.
17. John Dryden, *Virgil's Georgics* (1697), I, ll. 183–6.
18. Joseph Warton, *An Essay on the Genius and Writings of Pope* (1756: 4th ed. 1782), II, p. 185fn.
19. James Thomson, Preface to *Winter* (1726). This and all subsequent quotations from Thomson are taken from *The Poems of James Thomson*, ed. J. L. Robertson (Oxford, 1908: repr. 1963).
20. William Mason, *The English Garden* (1772–81): see 'General Postscript', p. 53.
21. John Aikin, *Letters from a Father to his Son* (2nd ed. 1794), pp. 148–9.
22. The letter to Mallet is published in *Miscellanies of the Philobiblion Society*, IV (1857–8), 20.
23. Thomas Gray, 'The Progress of Poesy', ll. 77–82. This and all subsequent quotations from Gray's poetry are taken from *Gray and Collins: Poetical Works*, ed. Roger Lonsdale (Oxford, 1977).
24. For a full discussion of this controversy see J. E. Congleton, *Theories of Pastoral Poetry 1684–1798* (New York, 1952).
25. They nonetheless won some important victories: e.g. an altogether deeper understanding of Greek poetry came with the end of the eighteenth century: see Gilbert Highet, *The Classical Tradition* (Oxford, 1949), esp. pp. 261–88.

26. A most stimulating essay on the theme of cultural naturalisation is Geoffrey Hartman's 'Genius Loci' in his *Beyond Formalism* (New Haven, 1970), pp. 311–336.

27. John Milton, *L'Allegro*, ll. 57–82. This and all subsequent quotations from Milton's poetry are taken from *The Poetical Works of John Milton*, ed. H. C. Beeching (Oxford, 1925).

28. The following statistics are given in R. D. Havens, *The Influence of Milton on English Poetry* (Harvard, 1922), pp. 669–679.

29. Sir Joshua Reynolds, *Discourses on Art*, ed. Robert Wark (1959: Collier, 1966), p. 212. Hereafter abbreviated to *Discourses*.

30. Richard Payne Knight, *The Landscape* (1794), II, ll. 284–6.

31. See Jerrold Ziff, 'J. M. W. Turner on Poetry and Painting', *Studies in Romanticism* III (1964), 199.

32. The first version of *Coopers Hill* was published in August 1642, a few days before civil war was declared. The final version appeared in 1668. This is the version printed in Charles Peake's *Poetry of the Landscape and the Night* (1967), from which my quotations are taken. For two interesting discussions of the moral, political and philosophical dimensions of this poem see Earl Wasserman, *The Subtler Language* (Baltimore, 1959) and James Turner, *The Politics of Landscape* (Oxford, 1979).

33. *Coopers Hill*, ll. 42–6, 49–50.

34. *Ibid.*, ll. 47–8.

35. *Windsor-Forest*, l. 270.

36. *Ibid.*, l. 159.

37. *Ibid.*, ll. 361–2.

38. *Ibid.*, ll. 225–30.

39. *Summer*, ll. 1433–5.

40. David Solkin, *Richard Wilson: The Landscape of Reaction* (1982), pp. 78–84.

41. *Summer*, ll. 1438–9 and see fns.

42. Hussey, *op. cit.*, p. 18.

43. Gilpin, *Lakes*, I, p. 5.

44. *Paradise Lost*, IV, l. 247.

45. *Ibid.*, IX, ll. 115–17.

46. *Ibid.*, IV, ll. 241–6.

47. *Windsor-Forest*, ll. 13–16.

48. *Coopers Hill*, ll. 211–12, 227–8.

49. Anthony Ashley Cooper, 3rd Earl of Shaftesbury, *Characteristics* (1711), Part I, Sect. 3.

50. Earl Wasserman, *The Subtler Language* (Baltimore, 1959).

51. *Windsor-Forest*, ll. 17–24.

52. Solkin, *op. cit.*, pp. 66–74.

53. Michael Rosenthal, *Constable: The Painter and his Landscape* (New Haven, 1983), p. 52.

54. Arline Meyer, *John Wootton, 1682–1764: Landscapes and Sporting Art in Early Georgian England* (1984), pp. 25–6.

55. Joseph Warton, 'The Enthusiast, or the Lover of Nature', ll. 29–38: in E. Partridge ed., *The Three Wartons: A Choice of their Verse* (1927).

56. *Spring*, ll. 950–62.

57. John Barrell, *The Idea of Landscape and the Sense of Place, 1730–1840* (Cambridge, 1972): the particular discussion of this passage is on pp. 12–20.

## Chapter 2

1. Horace Walpole, *The Anecdotes of Painting in England* (1762), I, p. xii.

2. *Ibid.* (4th ed. 1786), IV, pp. 309–10.

3. *Ibid.*, p. 140.

4. Gilpin, *Cambridge*, p. 38.

5. *The Letters of Thomas Gainsborough*, ed. M. Woodall (1963), p. 115: hereafter abbreviated to *Gainsborough: Letters*.

6. Quoted in John Hayes, *Thomas Gainsborough* (Tate Gallery, 1980), p. 27.

7. *Monthly Review* XVIII (1758), p. 278.

8. Gilpin, *Three Essays* (1792: 2nd ed. 1794), pp. 77, 137.

9. John Aikin, *Essay on the Application of Natural History to Poetry* (Warrington, 1777), p. 58.

10. Gilpin, *Lakes*, II, p. 44.

11. Aikin, *op. cit.*, p. 57.

12. *Gainsborough: Letters*, p. 99. For the comments on Wilson's figures see J. Greig ed., *The Farington Diaries*, V (1925), p. 183.

13. *Discourses*, p. 66.

14. See Helen Langdon, 'Salvator Rosa and Claude', and John Sunderland, 'The Legend and Influence of Salvator Rosa in England in the Eighteenth Century': *Burlington Magazine* CXV (1973), pp. 779–88; see also Anne French, *Gaspard Dughet,*

*called Gaspar Poussin, 1615–75* (1980), pp. 5–31.

15. Quoted in E. W. Manwaring, *Italian Landscape in Eighteenth Century England* (New York, 1925), p. 94: hereafter abbreviated to *Manwaring*.

16. See C. R. Leslie, *Memoirs of the Life of John Constable* (1843: ed. J. Mayne, 1951), p. 114.

17. William Holman Hunt, *Pre Raphaelitism and the Pre Raphaelite Brotherhood* (1913), p. 19.

18. Gilpin, *Two Essays*, p. 14.

19. [Joseph Pott], *An Essay on Landscape Painting* (1782), p. 67.

20. William Mason, *The English Garden* (1772–81), I, ll. 187–93.

21. Joseph Spence, *Observations, Anecdotes, and Characters of Books and Men*, ed. J. M. Osborn (Oxford, 1966), pp. 410–11, 427: hereafter abbreviated to *Spence*.

22. Quoted in Stuart Piggott, *Ruins in a Landscape* (Edinburgh, 1976), p. 122.

23. Gilpin, *Forest Scenery*, II, p. 227.

24. *Spence*, p. 649.

25. See James Holloway and Lindsay Errington, *The Discovery of Scotland* (Edinburgh, 1978), p. 26.

26. See Sybil Rosenfeld, *Georgian Scene Painters and Scene Painting* (Cambridge, 1981).

27. James Clarke, *Survey of the Lakes* (1787: 2nd ed. 1789), p. 27.

28. R. H. Newell, *Letters on the Scenery of Wales* (1821), p. 50.

29. The illustrations face pp. 18 and 19 in Gilpin, *Three Essays*.

30. Gilpin, *Western Parts*, p. 75.

31. Gilpin, *Two Essays*, p. 33.

32. John Stoddart, *Remarks on Local Scenery & Manners in Scotland during the Years 1799 and 1800* (1801), I, p. 5.

33. W. H. Craig, *An Essay on the Study of Nature in Drawing Landscape* (1793), p. 9.

34. Quoted in *Manwaring*, p. 89.

35. Du Fresnay, *The Art of Painting*, translated by William Marsh with Notes by Joshua Reynolds (1783), p. 68.

36. John Wolcot ('Peter Pindar'), 'Advice to Landscape Painters', in R. Chambers ed., *Cyclopaedia of English Literature* (Edinburgh, 1844), II, p. 298.

37. John Hayes, *op. cit.*, p. 25.

38. R. H. Newell, *op. cit.*, p. 147.

39. William Marshall, *Planting and Gardening* (1785), p. 604.

40. *Gainsborough: Letters*, p. 87.

41. See J. L. Roget, *A History of the 'Old Water-Colour' Society* (1891), I, p. 33.

42. [Joseph Pott], *op. cit.*, pp. 62–3.

43. John Byng, 'A Tour to North Wales: 1793', in *The Torrington Diaries*, ed. C. Bruyn Andrews (1936), III, p. 254: hereafter abbreviated to *Torrington Diaries*.

44. *The English Garden*, IV, ll. 410–12.

45. Richard Payne Knight, *The Landscape* (1794), II, ll. 284–5.

46. [Joseph Pott], *op. cit.*, pp. 58–9.

47. Bernard Denvir, 'Regency Painting', in *English Painting and Sculpture: Tudor-Early Victorian* (1962), ed. L. G. G. Ramsay, p. 93.

48. See William Sandby, *Thomas and Paul Sandby: Royal Academicians* (1892), pp. 114–15.

49. [Joseph Pott], *op. cit.*, pp. 76–7.

50. J. L. Roget, *op. cit.*, p. 23.

51. Gilpin, *Two Essays*, p. 25.

52. Quoted in John Gage, *Colour in Turner: Poetry and Truth* (1969), p. 28.

## Chapter 3

1. *The Letters of Mrs. Elizabeth Montagu* (1813), III, pp. 235–6.

2. *The Spectator*, 27 June 1712.

3. *Ibid.*, 25 June 1712.

4. Samuel Rogers quoted in C. P. Barbier, *Samuel Rogers and William Gilpin: Their Friendship and Correspondence* (Oxford, 1959), p. 22.

5. Richard Payne Knight, *Analytical Inquiry*, p. 147.

6. Ronald Paulson, *Emblem and Expression: Meaning in English Art of the Eighteenth Century* (1975), p. 85.

7. See John D. Scheffar, 'The Idea of Decline in Literature and the Fine Arts in Eighteenth-Century England' in *Modern Philology* XXXIV (1936–7), pp. 155–78; and W. J. Bate, 'The English Poet and the Burden of the Past, 1660–1820', in *Aspects of the Eighteenth Century*, ed. E. R. Wasserman (1965), pp. 245–64.

8. See E. N. Hooker, 'The Discussion of Taste, from 1750 to 1770' in *PMLA* XLIV (1934), pp. 577–92.

9. David Solkin, *op. cit.*, Chapter II. See also Laurence Goldstein, *Ruins and Empire* (Pittsburgh, 1979), esp. Chs. 1–4.

10. Charles Heath, *The Excursion down the Wye* (1799): the book has no pagination.

11. C. A. Moore, *Backgrounds of English Literature, 1700–1760* (1953), p. 232.

12. Robert Aubin, *Topographical Poetry in XVIII-Century England* (New York, 1966), p. 180.

13. David Hartley, *Observations on Man, His Frame, His Duty, and His Expectations* (1749), I, p. 419.

14. Gilpin, *Three Essays*, pp. 49–50.

15. John Ruskin, *Praeterita* (1899: Hart-Davis, 1949), p. 103.

16. John Aikin, *Letters from a Father to his Son, on Various Topics, Relative to Literature and the Conduct of Life* (2nd ed., 1794), p. 263.

17. Berkeley, 'Dialogue II' (1713): *The Works of George Berkeley D.D.*, ed. A. C. Fraser (Oxford, 1871), I, p. 302.

18. Quoted in *The Genius of the Place* (1975), ed. John Dixon Hunt and Peter Willis, p. 124: hereafter abbreviated to *Genius of the Place*.

19. Barbara Maria Stafford, 'Toward Romantic Landscape Perception: Illustrated Travels and the Rise of "Singularity" as an Aesthetic Category', *Art Quarterly*, NS I (1977), pp. 89–124.

20. John Aikin, *Letters from a Father to his Son*, pp. 269–70: the passage is quoted in Patrick Conner, *Michael Angelo Rooker (1746–1801)* (1984), which has an excellent discussion of the attitudes to ruins in this period on pp. 62–85.

21. Vanbrugh's letter of 11 June 1709 is printed in *Genius of the Place*, pp. 120–1.

22. Quoted in Goldstein, *op. cit.*, p. 36.

23. R. Ginsberg, 'The Aesthetics of Ruins', *The Bucknell Review* XVIII (1970), pp. 89–102.

24. *Grongar Hill*, ll. 84–92.

25. Richard Hurd, *Moral and Political Dialogues; with Letters on Chivalry and Romance* (4th ed., 1771), I, p. 153.

26. Uvedale Price, *Essay on the Picturesque* II (1798), p. 301.

27. William Shenstone, 'The Ruined Abbey; or, the Effects of Superstition', ll. 344–53. The text is from George Gilfillan's *The Poetical Works of William Shenstone* (Edinburgh, 1854).

28. See Margaret Aston, 'English Ruins and English History: The Dissolution and the Sense of the Past', *Journal of Warburg and Courtauld Institute* XXXVI (1973), pp. 231–55.

29. William Shenstone, 'Unconnected Thoughts on Gardening', first published in Dodsley's two-volume *The Works in Verse and Prose, of William Shenstone Esq.* (1764). The text is reprinted in *Genius of the Place*. Both the 'Thoughts' and Gilpin's *Dialogue* are of modest length, so I have not burdened the text with reference numbers for the many quotations from these two works.

30. [William Gilpin], *A Dialogue upon the Gardens of the Right Honourable the Lord Viscount Cobham at Stow in Buckinghamshire* (1748), *passim*.

31. 'Mr. M.', 'A Tour to South Wales, etc.' (1801): National Library of Wales, MS. 1340 C, f. 120.

32. Gilpin, *Lakes* II, pp. 187–8.

33. John Aikin, *Letters from a Father to his Son*, p. 266.

34. Thomas Whately, *Observations on Modern Gardening* (1770), pp. 119–20.

35. Solkin, *op. cit.*, pp. 109–10.

36. See David Watkin, *Thomas Hope (1769–1831) and the Neo-Classical Idea* (1968), pp. 148–51.

37. *Spence*, p. 416.

38. *Anecdotes* IV (1786), p. 309.

39. *Spence*, pp. 423, 252.

40. *Ibid.*, p. 413.

41. *Ibid.*, pp. 418, 1739.

42. The 'Description' was published in Dodsley's 1764 edition of Shenstone's *Works*.

43. Gilpin, *Three Essays*, p. 57.

44. See *Genius of the Place*, p. 178.

45. *Grongar Hill*, ll. 99–102.

46. On what he calls 'the victory of visualism' and the waning of the old iconography, see R. Paulson, *op. cit.*, pp. 48–57.

47. Gilpin, *Observations on the Coasts of Hampshire, Sussex, and Kent, Relative chiefly to Picturesque Beauty: made in the Summer of the Year 1774* (1804), p. 61.

48. John Stoddart, *op. cit.*, I, p. 2.

49. Burke, *Enquiry* (1757: rev. 1759), p. 72.

50. Letter of 3 July 1770: quoted in C. P. Barbier, *William Gilpin: His Drawings, Teaching, and Theory of the Picturesque* (Oxford, 1963), p. 50.

51. Gilpin, *An Essay upon Prints* (1768), p. x.

52. Letter to Messrs. T. Cadell and W. Davies: 2 August 1802. The letter was shown to me by courtesy of the Fry Gallery, London.

53. For the reasons mentioned above (see ref. 29) I have not given reference numbers for quotations from this text. The correspondence between Gilpin and Reynolds is reproduced at the end of the essay 'On Picturesque Beauty'.

54. *An Essay on the Picturesque* appeared in 1794. In 1795 Price published his retaliatory *A Letter to H. Repton*, intended as a supplement to the *Essay*. In 1798 his *Essays on the Picturesque* was published as 'Volume II' to the 1794 volume. Repton had disagreed with Price's arguments about the affinity between painting and gardening.

55. Most of the following argument is summarized from Chapter III of the *Essay*.

56. The Price–Repton–Knight controversies are traced in Walter Hipple, *The Beautiful, the Sublime, and the Picturesque in Eighteenth-Century British Aesthetic Theory* (Illinois, 1957), pp. 224–83.

57. Goldsmith, *The Traveller; or, a Prospect of Society* (1764), ll. 159–64: in George Gilfillan's edition of *The Poetical Works of Goldsmith, Collins, T. Warton* (1854).

58. See Patrick Conner, *op. cit.*, esp. the section 'Ruin and Haystack', pp. 74–85.

59. *Discourses*, p. 45.

60. William Mason ed., *The Poems of Mr. Gray. To which are prefixed Memoirs of his Life and Writings* (1775), p. 360n.

61. R. Paulson, *op. cit.*, p. 22.

62. B. Malkin, *The Scenery, Antiquities, and Biography of South Wales* (1804), p. 344.

63. M. Girouard, *Life in the English Country House* (Yale, 1978: Penguin, 1980), p. 214.

64. *Spence*, p. 426.

65. Gilpin, *Three Essays*, p. 127.

66. Gilpin, *Forest Scenery*, II, p. 199.

67. James Turner, *op. cit.*, p. 5.

68. Gilpin, *Forest Scenery*, I, p. 79. There is an interesting discussion of these changing tastes in John Barrell's chapter on the landscape of agricultural improvement, in his *The Idea of Landscape and the Sense of Place*.

69. *The Prelude* (1850), I, l. 89. All quotations from Wordsworth's poetry are taken from *Poetical Works*, ed. E. de Selincourt and Helen Darbishire (Oxford, 1940–49), the 5-volume edition and the single-volume *Prelude*.

70. Gilpin, *Forest Scenery*, II, p. 166.

71. Gilpin, *Lakes*, II, p. 44.

72. Price, *Essay on the Picturesque* (1796), I, p. 40n.

73. *Ibid.*, p. 39n.

74. Price, *An Essay on the Picturesque* (1794), pp. 28–9. The implications of this analogy have been much debated in recent years. See e.g. J. Barrell, *The Dark Side of the Landscape* (Cambridge, 1980), esp. pp. 22–23, and D. Solkin, *op. cit.*, esp. pp. 32–4.

75. Gilpin, *High-Lands*, I, p. 49.

76. John Clare, 'Shadows of Taste', ll. 141–2: *Clare: Selected Poems and Prose*, ed. E. Robinson and G. Summerfield (Oxford, 1966).

77. *The Excursion*, Book VIII, ll. 95–111.

78. William Marshall, *A Review of the Landscape* (1795), pp. 255–6. 'The Landscape' in the title refers to Richard Payne Knight's didactic poem published in 1794.

## Chapter 4

1. James Plumptre, 'A Narrative of a Pedestrian Journey through some parts of Yorkshire, Durham and Northumberland to the Highlands of Scotland, and home by the Lakes and some parts of Wales in the summer of the year 1799': 3 vols. Cambridge University Library MS. Add 5814, see ff. 35–6. Hereafter abbreviated to 'James Plumptre, "Narrative"'.

2. William Marshall, *A Review of the Landscape* (1795), p. 255.

3. Gilpin, *Three Essays*, p. 48.

4. A. Walker, *Remarks made in a Tour from London to the Lakes of Westmoreland and Cumberland, in the Summer of M, DCCXCI* (1792), p. 63.

5. William Mason, *The Poems of Mr. Gray to which are prefixed Memoirs of His Life and Writings* (1775), p. 352n.

6. Norman Nicholson, *The Lakers* (1955), pp. 53–4.

7. Gilpin, *High-Lands*, I, p. 124.

8. Letter to Warton, 1 October 1769: Paget Toynbee and Leonard Whibley ed., *Correspondence of Thomas Gray* (Oxford, 1935), p. 1079. This edition is hereafter abbreviated to *Gray: Correspondence*.

9. Jean Hagstrum, *The Sister Arts* (Chicago, 1958), pp. 141–2. There is also an interesting discussion of the Claude Glass in John Dixon Hunt's 'Picturesque Mirrors and the Ruins of the Past', *Art History* IV (1981), pp. 254–70.

10. Gilpin, *Forest Scenery*, II, p. 225.

11. *Ibid.*

12. T. D. Fosbroke, *The Wye Tour* (1818), p. 83.

13. S. T. Coleridge, letter to Humphry Davy, 25 July 1800: E. L. Griggs ed., *The Letters of Samuel Taylor Coleridge* (1956), I, p. 342. This edition is hereafter abbreviated to *Coleridge: Letters*.

14. Letter to George Dyer, 10 March 1795: *Coleridge: Letters*, I, p. 154.

15. Christopher Wordsworth, *Memoirs of William Wordsworth* (1851), II, p. 477.

16. S. T. Coleridge, *Biographia Literaria* (1817), Chapter XIV.

17. Quoted in S. Piggott, *Ruins in a Landscape* (Edinburgh, 1976), pp. 124–5.

18. Anonymous review in *The Topographer* I, iii (June 1789), p. 164.

19. *Torrington Diaries*, I, p. 69.

20. *Ibid.*, p. 115.

21. *Topographer*, I, iii (June 1789), p. 163.

22. J. Aikin, *An Essay on the Application of Natural History to Poetry* (1777), p. 5.

23. Thomas Bernard, 'A Holiday Tour' (1780); in J. Bernard Parker ed., *Pleasure and Pain (1780–1818)* (1930), p. 31.

24. Thomas Percy, 'Observanda in the Tour into Scotland, Aug. 8. 1773', BL. MS. Add. 39,547, f. 19.

25. Robert Heron, *Observations made in A Journey through the Western Counties of Scotland in the autumn of 1792* (1793), I, pp. 164–5.

26. W. G. Maton, 'A Sketch of a Tour from London to the Lakes made in the Summer of the year 1799', BL. MS. 32442, I, f. 59.

27. *Letters from ... Dr. Thomas Herring ... to William Duncombe* (1777), pp. 45–6.

28. William Bingley, *A Tour around North Wales* (1800), p. viii.

29. Samuel Ireland, *Picturesque Views on the River Wye* (1797), p. ix.

30. Charles Dibdin, *Observations on a Tour through almost the whole of England, and a considerable part of Scotland, in a series of letters, Addressed to a large number of intelligent and respectable Friends* (1802), I, p. 13.

31. Thomas Clutterbuck, 'A Tour thro' North, and South Wales, with an Excursion to Dublin, from Holyhead, in the Year 1798', Central Library Cardiff, MS. 3.276.

32. Warren Hastings, [Journal of a Tour in 1787], BL. Add. MS. 39,889, f. 17.

33. J. Grant, 'Journal of a Three Weeks Tour, in 1797, Through Derbyshire to the Lakes', in Mavor's *The British Tourists*, IV, p. 261.

34. William Sanderson, *Graphice* (1658), p. 70.

35. *Grongar Hill*, ll. 57–79.

36. The discussion takes place in Gilpin, *Wye*, pp. 60–2.

37. Letter to Palgrave, 6 September 1758: *Gray: Correspondence*, p. 587.

38. Thomas Newte, *A Tour in England and Scotland in 1785* (1788), pp. 2–3.

39. Gilpin, *Wye*, p. 2.

40. Joseph Budworth, *A Fortnight's Ramble to the Lakes* (1792), pp. 42–3.

41. Gilpin, *Three Essays*, p. 64.

42. Gilpin, *High-Lands*, p. v.

43. Gilpin, *Three Essays*, pp. 107–8.

44. Quoted in Peter Bicknell and Robert Woof, *The Discovery of the Lake District 1750–1810* (Newcastle, 1982), p. 40.

45. *Gainsborough: Letters*, p. 125.

46. Anon, 'A Tour in Scotland' (1789), National Library of Scotland MS. 1080, f. 2.

47. Samuel Brewer, 'Journal of a Tour from Dockwray Hall in Cumberland to London' (1691), Central Library Cardiff, MS. 3.24. Praef. f. 1.

48. Mary Anne Hanway, *A Journey to the Highlands of Scotland* (1775), p. viii.

49. Joseph Budworth, *op. cit.*, p. vi.

## Chapter 5

Frequent reference is made in this chapter to the following tour books which do not feature in these Notes. The authors of quotations from these books are always identified in the text and it would not be difficult for the reader to track down particular references. The full titles are listed separately here. The aim is to avoid a lot of repetitive annotation.

William Gilpin: *Observations on the River Wye, and Several Parts of South Wales, etc. relative chiefly to Picturesque Beauty; Made in the Summer of the Year 1770* (1782).

Samuel Ireland: *Picturesque Views on the River Wye* (1797).

William Coxe: *An Historical Tour in Monmouthshire; illustrated with views by Sir R. C. Hoare, Bart.* (1801).

John Byng: 'Tour to the West, 1781', in *The Torrington Diaries* ed. C. Bruyn Andrews (1934), I, 3–60.

Stebbing Shaw: *A Tour to the West of England in 1788* (1789).

T. D. Fosbroke: *The Wye Tour* (1818).

Charles Heath: *The Excursion down the Wye from Ross to Monmouth* (1799).

1. Gilpin, *Lakes*, I, pp. 7–8.
2. See *The Letters of William and Dorothy Wordsworth* ed. E. de Selincourt (2nd ed., rev. C. L. Shaver, Oxford, 1967), I, p. 222n; and Mary Moorman, *William Wordsworth: The Early Years, 1770–1803* (Oxford, 1957), p. 402.
3. Gilpin, *Wye* (2nd edition, 1789), p. ix.
4. Letter 24 August 1770: *Gray: Correspondence*, p. 1144.
5. Letter 3 July 1770: quoted in C. P. Barbier, *William Gilpin: His Drawings, Teaching, and Theory of the Picturesque* (Oxford, 1963), p. 50.
6. Esther Moir, *The Discovery of Britain* (1964), p. 125.
7. 'Mr. M.', 'A Tour to South Wales, etc.' (1801), National Library of Wales, MS. 1340. C., f. 46.
8. Quoted in P. W. Clayden, *The Early Life of Samuel Rogers* (1887), pp. 179–80.
9. *Ibid.*, p. 180.
10. The descriptions quoted here are from pp. 108–10 of the 3rd edition (1771) of *Observations*.

11. Sneyd Davies, 'A Voyage to *Tintern Abbey* in *Monmouthshire*, from *Whitminster* in *Gloucestershire*. Aug. 1742', in G. Harding, *Biographical Memoirs of the Revd. Sneyd Davies, D.D.* (1816), pp. 117–18.
12. Jeremiah Milles, 'A Journey from London to Holy Head in 1742', BL. Add. MS. 15,776, f. 134.
13. Francis Grose, *The Antiquities of England and Wales* (1773–87), II: (no pagination).
14. Lucy Wright, 'Note Book 1806', Wigan Public Library, Edward Hall Collection, M842 EHC/73, f. 61.
15. 'Sketch of a pedestrian Tour, thro' parts of North and South Wales etc. Begun Sept. 3rd, 1798. By GN D.J. J.R.P.', National Library of Wales, MS. 4419 B.
16. John Skinner, 'Journal of a Tour through North Wales, in the Year 1800', Central Library Cardiff, MS. 1.503.
17. Richard Colt Hoare, 'Tour in South Wales or rather Monmouthshire – August 1798', Central Library Cardiff, MS. 3.127.6/6, ff. 131–2.
18. See Rudiger Joppien, 'A Visitor to a

Ruined Churchyard – a newly discovered painting by P. J. de Loutherbourg', *Burlington Magazine* CXVIII (1976), esp. pp. 294–5.

19. Francis Grose, *op. cit.*

20. Francis Grose, [Journey to South Wales] (1775), BL. Add. MS. 17,398, f. 63.

21. See P. W. Clayden, *op. cit.*, pp. 199–200.

22. 'Sketch of a pedestrian Tour': see above ref. 15.

23. Grose, [Journey to South Wales], f. 95.

24. The poem is printed in Heath's *Excursion*.

25. James Baker, *Picturesque Guide through Wales and the Marches* (1795), I, p. 31.

26. For the account of Morris's career and the development of Piercefield see Ivor Waters, *The Unfortunate Valentine Morris* (Chepstow, 1964).

27. Arthur Young, *A Six Weeks Tour through the Southern Counties of England and Wales* (1768), p. 136.

28. *Ibid.*, p. 138.

29. *Ibid.*

# Chapter 6

Welsh tour books omitted from the following Notes:

William Gilpin: *Observations on Several Parts of the Counties of Cambridge, Norfolk, Suffolk, and Essex. Also on Several Parts of North Wales, relative chiefly to Picturesque Beauty, in two tours, the former made in [. . .] 1769, the latter in [. . .] 1773* (1809).

Joseph Cradock: *Letters from Snowdon: Descriptive of a Tour through the Northern Counties of Wales* (1770).

George Lyttelton: *Account of a Journey into Wales*. A manuscript 'Description of North Wales in Letters from the Right Hon.^ble Lord Lyttelton to his Brother Charles Lord Bishop of Carlisle', dated 1755, is in the Birmingham City Library (MS. A 091/1755). I have used the version of the *Account* printed in a 1781 edition of Henry Wyndham's *Gentleman's Tour*.

J. Hucks: *A Pedestrian Tour through North Wales, in a Series of Letters* (1795).

John Byng: 'A Tour to North Wales: 1784', in *The Torrington Diaries*, ed. C. Bruyn Andrews (1934), I, 115–98.

1. Henry Wyndham, *A Gentleman's Tour through Monmouthshire and Wales, in the months of June and July, 1774* (1775), p. ii.

2. Anon, 'Tour in the Summer 1776. Through Wales', National Library of Wales MS. 2862.A., f. 37.

3. Anon, 'A Trip to North Wales', in John Torbuck, *A Collection of Welsh Travels, and Memoirs of Wales* (1738), pp. 4–5.

4. Quoted in M. H. Nicolson, *Mountain Gloom and Mountain Glory* (Cornell, 1959: Norton Ed., 1963): see Chapters 5 and 6 for a full discussion of Burnet and his influence.

5. *Letters from . . . Dr. Thomas Herring . . . to William Duncombe . . . 1728 to 1757* (1777), pp. 39–40.

6. William Vernon, 'A Journey to Wales', in *Poems on Several Occasions* (1758), p. 12.

7. David Solkin, *op. cit.*, pp. 100–3.

8. Letter 8 September 1800: *Coleridge: Letters*, I, p. 620.

9. Anthony Champion, 'From a Traveller in Wales to a Friend Travelling in Scotland. August 1772', in *Miscellanies* (1801), pp. 79–80.

10. Letter 16 August 1774: R. Duppa ed., *A Diary of a Journey into North Wales, in the year 1774; by Samuel Johnson, LL.D.* (1816), p. 93.

11. Anon, *A Tour through the South of England, Wales, and Part of Ireland, made during the Summer of 1791* (1793), pp. 273–4.

12. *The Gentleman's Magazine* XXXVIII (1768), p. 6.

13. John Wolcot ('Peter Pindar'), 'Advice to

Landscape Painters' in *Cyclopaedia of English Literature* (1844) ed. R. Chambers, II, p. 298.

14. Peter Hughes, 'Paul Sandby and Sir Watkin Williams-Wynn', *Burlington Magazine* CXIV (1972), pp. 459–66.

15. Anon, 'Welch Journal Aug^st 20th 1795', BL. MS. Add. 37,926, ff. 143, 152.

16. Donald Moore, *Moses Griffith 1747–1819* (Caernarvon, 1979), p. 18.

17. J. M. W. Turner, 'Diary of a Tour in Wales' (1792), printed in John Gage ed., *Collected Correspondence of J. M. W. Turner* (Oxford, 1980), p. 13.

18. Anon, [A Tour through North Wales: August 1775], National Library of Wales MS. 9280.A.

19. Henry Wigstead, *Remarks on a Tour to North and South Wales in the Year 1797* (1800), p. 17.

20. Robert Clutterbuck, 'Journal of a Tour. From Cardiff, Glamorganshire, through South & North Wales. In the Summer of 1794. In Company with Taylor Combe Esqte.', Central Library, Cardiff MS. 3.277.

21. *Coleridge: Letters*, I, p. 91.

22. Anon, 'Welch Journal' (see above ref. 15), ff. 155–6.

23. James Plumptre, 'A Journal: of a Tour through part of North Wales in the year 1792. Part 2', Cambridge University Library MS. Add. 5802, f. 6.

24. Richard Colt Hoare, 'Tour in the Summer 1797', Central Library, Cardiff MS. 3.127. 6/6, f. 66.

25. Anon, 'Welch Journal' (see above ref. 15), f. 133.

26. Peter Oliver, 'Journal of a Voyage to England', BL. Egerton MS. 2673, f. 124.

27. John Stoddart, *op. cit.*, I, p. 199.

28. Anon, 'Tour through N. Wales in the Year 1778', Central Library, Cardiff MS. 1.549.

29. Richard Colt Hoare, 'Journal of a Tour in 1800', Central Library, Cardiff MS.3.127. 5/6, ff. 84–5.

30. 'Mrs. Thrale's Tour in Wales with Dr. Johnson' (1774) in A. M. Broadley, *Dr. Johnson and Mrs Thrale* (1910), p. 186.

31. *Coleridge: Letters*, I, pp. 51–2.

32. *Ibid.*, p. 51.

33. Letter to William Gilpin, 12 January 1801: in C. P. Barbier, *Samuel Rogers and William Gilpin: Their Friendship and Correspondence* (1959), p. 56.

34. Turner, *op. cit.*, p. 15.

35. P. J. de Loutherbourg, *The Romantic and Picturesque Scenery of England and Wales* (1805): no pagination. The account of the de Loutherbourgs' visit faces the engraving based on the watercolour.

36. Letter 24 or 31 May 1757: *Gray: Correspondence*, p. 502.

37. Letter 24 March 1758: *Gray: Correspondence*, p. 568. See also Joseph Warton, *Essay on the Genius and Writings of Pope* (1756), p. 7.

38. See David Solkin, *op. cit.*, pp. 86–7.

39. Quoted in Solkin, *op. cit.*, p. 96. There is an interesting discussion of the cult of the Bard in relation to the wider literary context in John Dixon Hunt, *The Figure in the Landscape* (Baltimore, 1976), Chapter 4.

40. Quoted in John Dixon Hunt, *op. cit.*, p. 146.

41. Letter to William Gilpin, 21 December 1799: in Barbier, *op. cit.*, p. 52. Sandby designated his painting of the Bard 'An Historical Landskip': see *Gray: Correspondence*, p. 705, fn. 16.

42. Mrs Elizabeth Montagu in a letter to Benjamin Stillingfleet, 22 October 1758: in *The Letters of Mrs. Elizabeth Montagu* (1809), IV, p. 112.

43. Anon, 'Welch Journal' (see above ref. 15).

44. Mrs [Mary] Morgan, *A Tour to Milford Haven, in the Year 1791* (1795), p. 318.

45. Herring, *op. cit.*, pp. 48–9.

46. Quoted in P. W. Clayden, *The Early Life of Samuel Rogers* (1881), pp. 202–3.

47. *Summer*, ll. 1162–5.

48. Quoted in John Julius Norwich, *A Christmas Cracker* (1980), p. 67.

49. Richard Colt Hoare, *op. cit.* (see above ref. 29), f. 125.

50. See Isaac Williams, *Welsh Topographical Prints* (Aberystwyth, 1926).

51. Anon, 'Tour in the Summer 1776. Through Wales', National Library of Wales MS. 2862.A., ff. 55–6.

52. Richard Warner, *A Walk through Wales, in August 1797* (1798), p. 137.

53. Solkin, *op. cit.*, pp. 92–3.
54. These lines, assumed to be Turner's own composition, appeared in the Royal Academy catalogue for the 1800 exhibition.
55. Thomas Pennant, *A Tour in Wales, 1770* (1778), II, p. 181.
56. *Ibid.*, p. 164.
57. William Sotheby, *A Tour through Parts of Wales* (1794), p. 35.
58. *The Prelude* (1805–6) XIII, ll. 33–59. See also the variant versions of this episode in the notes on pp. 482–4 of the de Selincourt edition.
59. Anon, 'Tour of Caernarvonshire and Anglesea', in *A Collection of Tours in Wales* (1799), p. 35.
60. Robert Clutterbuck, 'Journal' (see above ref. 20).
61. Henry Wyndham, *op. cit.*, p. 137.
62. Richard Warner, *op. cit.*, p. 119.
63. Joseph Cradock, *An Account of Some of the most Romantic Parts of North Wales* (1777), pp. 44–5.
64. Henry Wyndham, *op. cit.*, p. 132.
65. John Skinner, 'Journal of a Tour through North Wales, in the Year 1800', Central Library, Cardiff MS. 1.503.
66. *Ibid.*
67. Arthur Aiken, *Journal of a Tour through North Wales and Part of Shropshire* (1797), pp. 61–2.
68. William Bingley, *A Tour round North Wales, performed During the Summer of 1798* (1800), I, p. 465.
69. Thomas Clutterbuck, 'A Tour thro' North and South Wales, with an Excursion to Dublin, from Holyhead, in the Year 1798', Central Library, Cardiff MS. 3.276.
70. Richard Warner, *op. cit.*, p. 93.
71. Richard Rolt, *Cambria. A Poem in Three Books* (1749), p. 47.
72. Anon, 'A Journal of a Tour thro' North Wales' (1802), National Library of Wales MS. 789.B, f. 19.
73. Anon, 'A Trip to North Wales' (see above ref. 3), p. 7.
74. 'Mr. M.', 'A Tour to South Wales, etc.' (1801), National Library of Wales MS. 1340.C.
75. R. H. Newell, *Letters on the Scenery of Wales* (1821), p. 105.
76. Much of the following account of Hafod is drawn from Elizabeth Inglis-Jones, *Peacocks in Paradise* (1950) and from George Cumberland's *An Attempt to Describe Hafod* (1796).
77. Benjamin Malkin, *The Scenery, Antiquities, and Biography of South Wales* (1804), p. 341.
78. *Ibid.*, pp. 344–5.
79. Anon, *A Tour through the South of England, Wales, and Part of Ireland, made during the Summer of 1791* (1793), p. 266.
80. Anon, 'Journey through N. Wales in the Year 1778', Central Library, Cardiff MS. 1.549.
81. Anon, *A Tour* (see above ref. 79), pp. 260–1.
82. Richard Warner, *A Second Walk through Wales* (1799), p. 157.
83. 'Mr. M.', 'A Tour' (see above ref. 74), f. 140.
84. Richard Warner, *op. cit.*, pp. 179–89.

## Chapter 7

Lakes tour books omitted from the following Notes:

William Gilpin: *Observations relative chiefly to Picturesque Beauty, Made in the Year 1772, on Several Parts of England; particularly the Mountains, and Lakes of Cumberland, and Westmoreland* (1786).

Joseph Budworth: *A Fortnight's Ramble to the Lakes in Westmorland, Lancashire and Cumberland, by a Rambler* (1792).

William Hutchinson: *An Excursion to the Lakes in Westmoreland and Cumberland, August 1773* (1774).

*Notes and references*   Johnson Grant: 'A London Journal of a Three Weeks Tour, in 1797, through Derby-shire to the Lakes', in W. Mavor, *The British Tourists* (1798–1800), IV, pp. 219–92.

Ann Radcliffe: *A Journey made in the Summer of 1794 through Holland and the Western Frontier of Germany, with a Return down the Rhine, to which are added Observations during a Tour of the Lakes in Westmoreland and Cumberland* (1795).

James Clarke: *A Survey of the Lakes of Cumberland, Westmorland and Lancashire; together with an Account, Historical, Topographical and Descriptive, of the adjacent Country* (1787).

[Robert Southey]: *Letters from England: by Don Manuel Alvarez Espriella* (1807).

Thomas West: *A Guide to the Lakes in Cumberland, Westmorland and Lancashire* (1778). I have used the 2nd edition, 1780, enlarged and edited by W. Cockin.

1. H. L. Piozzi, 'Journey through the North of England & Part of Scotland, Wales etc.' (1789), John Rylands Library Eng. MS. 623, f. 167.

2. Richard Cumberland, Dedication of *Ode to the Sun* (1776).

3. *Ibid.*

4. Wordsworth, Letter to the Editor of the *Morning Post*, 9 December 1844: reprinted in de Selincourt's edition of Wordsworth's *Guide to the Lakes* (Oxford, 1906: repr. 1970), p. 150.

5. 'The Brothers', ll. 1–5. All quotations from Wordsworth's poetry are taken from the 5 volume *The Poetical Works of William Wordsworth*, ed. E. de Selincourt and Helen Darbishire (Oxford, 1940–49).

6. *The Gentleman's Magazine*, XXII (1752), p. 518.

7. Defoe, quoted in N. Nicholson, *The Lake District* (1978), p. 25.

8. Morris Moule, 'A Tour through the Counties of Huntingdon etc.' (1792), Chetham's Library, Manchester, MS. Mun. A.2.34, f. 57.

9. Letter 1–5 August 1802: *Coleridge: Letters*, II, p. 450.

10. 'The Brothers', ll. 6–10.

11. Letter 6 September 1758: *Gray: Correspondence*, p. 587.

12. Coleridge, November 1799: in K. Coburn ed., *The Notebooks of Samuel Taylor Coleridge* (1957), I, pp. 548–9. Hereafter abbreviated to *Coleridge: Notebooks*.

13. Arthur Young, *A Six Months Tour through the North of England* (1770).

14. William Wordsworth, *Vale of Esthwaite*, ll.75–6.

15. Stebbing Shaw, *A Tour, in 1787, from London, to the Western Highlands of Scotland. Including Excursions to the Lakes of Westmoreland and Cumberland* (1788), p. 67.

16. Young, *op. cit.*, III, p. 187.

17. William Gell, *A Tour in the Lakes, Made in 1797*, ed. William Rollinson (Newcastle-upon-Tyne, 1968), p. 11.

18. T. H. Horne, *The Lakes of Lancashire, Westmoreland and Cumberland; delineated in Forty-three Engravings, from Drawings by Joseph Farington, R.A.* (1816), p. 11.

19. This famous anecdote is in Clarke's *Survey*, p. 143 and Grant's *Journal*, p. 256.

20. See Robert Woof and Peter Bicknell, *The Discovery of the Lake District 1750–1810* (1982), pp. 43–4.

21. William Green, *A Description of Sixty Studies from Nature* (1810), p. 19.

22. Stebbing Shaw, *op. cit.*, p. 68.

23. See John Murdoch, *The Discovery of the Lake District* (1984), p. 31.

24. James Plumptre, 'Narrative', Cambridge University Library MS. Add. 5815, f. 288.

25. W. G. Maton, 'A Sketch of a Tour from London to the Lakes made in the Summer of the year 1799', BL. MS. 32, 442, 1, f. 30.

26. John Dyer, *Grongar Hill*, ll. 121–6.

27. Thomas Pennant, *A Tour in Scotland [. . .] 1772* (1774), II, p. 36.

28. Plumptre, *op. cit.*, ff. 274–6.

29. Wordsworth, *Guide to the Lakes*, pp. 11–12.

30. Joseph Mawman, *An Excursion to the Highlands of Scotland, and the English Lakes* (1805), p. 235.

31. William Mason ed., *The Poems of Mr. Gray*.

*To which are prefixed Memoirs of his Life and Writings* (1775), p. 366n.

32. Mrs Cobbold, 'Tour in the Lake District', 1795 BL. Add. MS. 19, 203.

33. Anon, 'Journal of a Tour thro' Westmoreland & Cumberland' in 1786, *Topographer* I (1790), p. xv.

34. See Blake Tyson, 'The Rydal Grotto, Westmoreland 1668–9', *Transactions of the Ancient Monuments Society*, New Series 24 (1980).

35. William Wordsworth, *An Evening Walk*, ll. 66–71 (from 1849 version). The 'listless swain' detail was added in 1794.

36. Anon, 'Notes of an Excursion from York to Edinburgh & return by a few of the Lakes in Cumberland & Westmoreland' (1817), National Library of Scotland MS. Acc. 6793.

37. The Red Bank identification is made in Robert Woof and Peter Bicknell, *The Discovery of the Lake District*, pp. 9–11.

38. William Wordsworth, 'Home at Grasmere', ll. 19–21.

39. Letter 3 January 1770: *Gray: Correspondence*, pp. 1098–9.

40. W. G. Maton, *op. cit.*, f. 37.

41. William Wordsworth (see n. 4 above), pp. 162–3.

42. There are many descriptions of Mary. She features in William Gell's *Tour in the Lakes* and Grant's *Three Weeks Tour*. Richard Colt Hoare saw her in 1800 and thought she resembled a fine Italian beauty both in countenance and in the way she dressed her hair (see n. 44 below): her career is summarized by Norman Nicholson in *The Lakers* (1955).

43. Again, there are many accounts of these legendary figures. Budworth's is one of the best. There is also quite a detailed description in Stebbing Shaw, *op. cit.*, pp. 76–9.

44. Richard Colt Hoare, 'Journal of a Tour in 1800', Central Library, Cardiff MS. 3.127. 5/6, ff. 95–6.

45. There are descriptions of Crosthwaite's Museum by Grant, William Gell, Sarah Murray (in her *Companion and Useful Guide*, 1799) and Mrs Cobbold.

46. There is a set of musical stones in the charming Ruskin Museum at Coniston.

47. David Pennant, 'Tour. 1789', National Library of Wales MS. 2523 B., f. 30.

48. Brown's *Description* of Keswick from which this quotation comes is reprinted in full in Donald D. Eddy, 'John Brown: "The Columbus of Keswick"', *Modern Philology* LXXIII (1976), pp. 574–584.

49. It is first referred to in a review article 'Books publish'd in December' (1754) in *The Gentleman's Magazine*, XXIV, p. 581. My quotations from the poem come from the extract printed in the Addenda to the second edition of West's *Guide*.

50. Arthur Young, *op. cit.*, p. 155.

51. Thomas Pennant, *op. cit.*, p. 40.

52. Arthur Young, *op. cit.*, pp. 155–6.

53. Gilpin's discussion of possible improvements to the Derwentwater scenery appears in *High-Lands*, II, pp. 159–72.

54. John Leland, *The Itinerary*, ed. Lucy Toulmin Smith (1964), V, p. 54.

55. William Wordsworth, *Guide to the Lakes*, p. 71.

56. Elizabeth Diggle, [Journal] 1788, Glasgow University Library MS. Gen. 738.

57. Morris Moule, *op. cit.*, f. 54.

58. Letter November 1769: *Gray: Correspondence*, pp. 1089–90.

59. See e.g. Peter Bicknell, *Beauty, Horror and Immensity* (Cambridge, 1981), p. 75.

60. Morris Moule, *op. cit.*, f. 55.

61. Letter November 1769: *Gray: Correspondence*, p. 1090.

62. William Maton, *op. cit.*, ff. 51–2.

63. William Gell, *op. cit.*, p. 16.

64. Sarah Murray, *A Companion and Useful Guide to the Beauties of Scotland, to the Lakes of Westmoreland, Cumberland, and Lancashire* (1799), p. 21.

65. *Coleridge: Notebooks*, I, p. 542.

66. T. H. Horne, *op. cit.*, p. 42.

67. William Maton, *op. cit.*, f. 46.

68. *Ibid.*, ff. 47–8.

69. Stebbing Shaw, *op. cit.*, pp. 89–90.

70. Letter November 1769: *Gray: Correspondence*, p. 1088.

71. Anon, 'Journal of a Tour thro' Westmoreland & Cumberland', *Topographer* I, (June 1790), p. xv.

72. T. H. Horne, *op. cit.*, pp. 43–4.

73. See Radcliffe, *op. cit.*, p. 465; Budworth, *op. cit.*, pp. 177–8; Henry Skrine, *Three Successive Tours* (1795), p. 25.

74. Thomas Bernard, 'A Holiday Tour' (1780): printed in *Pleasure and Pain (1780–1818)*, ed. J. Bernard Baker (1930), p. 20.

# Chapter 8

Highlands tour books omitted from the following Notes:

William Gilpin: *Observations, relative chiefly to Picturesque Beauty, Made in the Year 1776, on Several Parts of Great Britain; particularly the High-Lands of Scotland* (1789) 2 vols.

Samuel Johnson: *Journey to the Western Islands of Scotland* (1775).

Robert Heron: *Observations made in a Journey through the Western Counties of Scotland in the autumn of 1792* (1793) 2 vols.

[Mary Anne Hanway]: *A Journey to the Highlands of Scotland, with Occasional Remarks on Dr. Johnson's Tour* (1775).

W. Gibson: 'Sketch of a Two Months Tour in Scotland, performed on Horseback in the Summer of 1773', *Gentleman's Magazine* LXII–LXIV (1792–4).

John Stoddart: *Remarks on Local Scenery and Manners in Scotland during the years 1799 and 1800* (1801) 2 vols.

Elizabeth Diggle: [1788 tour journal in a series of letters to her sister at Broadstairs, Kent], Glasgow University Library, MS General 738.

Dorothy Wordsworth: 'A Tour made in Scotland (A.D. 1803)': in *The Journals of Dorothy Wordsworth*, ed. E. de Selincourt (Connecticut, 1970).

1. Letter 26 September 1753: K. C. Balderston ed., *Collected Letters of Oliver Goldsmith* (Cambridge, 1928), pp. 9–10.

2. *A Journey to Scotland*, 'by an English Gentleman' (1699), p. 13.

3. John Knox, *A Tour through the Highlands of Scotland, and the Hebride Isles, in 1786* (1787), p. lxvi.

4. See P. W. Clayden, *The Early Life of Samuel Rogers* (1887), p. 105.

5. John Lettice, *Letters on a Tour through various Parts of Scotland, in the year 1792* (1794), p. iv.

6. Henry Skrine, *Three Successive Tours in the North of England and Great Part of Scotland; interspersed with Descriptions of the Scenes they Presented, and Occasional Observations on the State of Society and the Manners and Customs of the People* (1795), p. 21.

7. Hester Lynch Piozzi, 'Travel Book 1789. Journey to the North of England', John Rylands Library, Manchester, Eng. MSS. 623, f. 9a.

8. Entry for 6 February 1802: J. Greig ed., *The Farington Diary* (1922), I, p. 340.

9. John Dalrymple, *An Essay on Landscape Gardening* [written c.1750] (1823), p. 7.

10. Letter c. September 1765: *Gray: Correspondence*, p. 894.

11. *Ibid.*, p. 899.

12. Nathaniel Wraxall, 'Diary' [July–September 1813], National Library of Scotland, MS. 3108, f. 14.

13. *A Journey to Scotland*, 'by an English Gentleman' (1699), p. 3.

14. Anon., 'Scotland Characterised': *The Harleian Miscellany* VII (1746), pp. 357–8.

15. Quoted in James Holloway and Lindsay Errington, *The Discovery of Scotland* (Edinburgh, 1978), p. 63. Much use is made in this chapter of the excellent catalogue essays in this book, mainly by James Holloway, on the early depictions of Scottish landscapes: references hereafter are abbreviated to *Discovery of Scotland*.

16. Thomas Garnett, *Observations on a Tour through the Highlands and Part of the Western Isles of Scotland, particularly Staffa and Icolmkill: To which are added, A Description of the Falls of the Clyde, of the Country round Moffat, and an Analysis of its mineral Waters* (1800), I, p. 109.

17. Anon., 'To General Wade', in *Scottish Descriptive Poems* (1803), pp. 154–5.

18. Anon., 'A Description of *Scotland*, in a Letter from an Officer in the Army, to his Friend in London', in *A Journey to Scotland* (1699), p. 13.

19. Piozzi, *op. cit.*, f. 9.

20. Joseph Mawman, *An Excursion to the Highlands of Scotland, and the English Lakes, with Recollections, Descriptions and References to Historical Facts* (1805), p. 170.

21. James Beattie, 'On Poetry and Music, as they affect the Mind' (1762), in James Beattie, *Essays* (Edinburgh, 1776), pp. 479–83.

22. Anne Grant, *Letters from the Mountains* (1807), I, p. 12.

23. Quoted in Samuel Monk, *The Sublime* (Michigan, 1960), p. 213.

24. *The Works of Ossian, the Son of Fingal*, 'Translated from the Gaelic Language by James Macpherson' (1765), II, pp. 314–16.

25. *The Letters of Mrs. Elizabeth Montagu* (1809), IV, p. 319.

26. *The Works of Ossian*, II, p. 409.

27. *Ibid.*, I, pp. 179–80.

28. Anon., *One Day's Journey to the Highlands of Scotland* (1784).

29. [J. H. Michell], *The Tour of the Duke of Somerset, and the Rev. J. H. Michell, through parts of England, Wales, and Scotland, in the year 1795* (1845), p. 148.

30. John Stoddart, *op. cit.*, II, pp. 4–5.

31. James Plumptre, 'Narrative', f. 60.

32. J. de Lancey Ferguson ed., *The Letters of Robert Burns* (Oxford, 1931), I, pp. 132–3.

33. 'Sadlers Wells Vol. 2, 1787–1795': a collection of press cuttings, songs, posters etc in the British Library.

34. Knox, *op. cit.*, p. 9.

35. Skrine, *op. cit.* (2nd ed., 1813), p. 34.

36. Thomas Pennant, *A Tour in Scotland and Voyage to the Hebrides MDCCLXXII* (1774).

37. Quoted in *Discovery of Scotland*, p. 71.

38. *Ibid.*, p. 76.

39. Letter c. 30 September 1765: *Gray: Correspondence*, p. 888.

40. Joseph Farington, 'Tours in Scotland in 1788 and 1792': typescript of the Farington MSS by James Greig, Edinburgh City Library, pp. 18–23.

41. Morris Moule, *op. cit.*, f. 24.

42. Anthony Champion, 'A Fragment. 1771', in *Miscellanies* (1801), p. 67.

43. Wraxall, *op. cit.*, f. 56.

44. *Ibid.*, f. 29.

45. James Plumptre, [Journal of a tour to Scotland], 1795, Cambridge University Library, MS Add. 5808, f. 5. Hereafter abbreviated to 'Plumptre, *Scotland* (1795)'.

46. Skrine, *op. cit.*, p. 71.

47. Lettice, *op. cit.*, p. 474.

48. Sarah Murray, *A Companion and Useful Guide to the Beauties of Scotland* (1799), I, pp. 137–8.

49. *Ibid.*, p. 132.

50. Plumptre, *Scotland* (1795), f. 12.

51. *Ibid.*, f. 3.

52. Thomas Newte, *Prospects and Observations on a Tour in England and Scotland* (1791), p. 154.

53. John Skinner, 'Northern Tour' (1825), BL. Add. MS. 33,688, ff. 80–2.

54. Plumptre, 'Narrative', f. 338.

55. James M'Nayr, *A Guide from Glasgow, to some of the most Remarkable Scenes in the Highlands of Scotland and to the Falls of the Clyde* (Glasgow, 1797), p. 98.

56. Warren Hastings, [Journal of a Tour], 1787, BL. Add. MS. 39,889, f. 13.

57. Richard Dick, 'Jaunt to the North Country' (1779), Mitchell Library, Glasgow, MS. 89.

58. *Discovery of Scotland*, p. 37.

59. Robert Burns, 'The Humble Petition of Bruar Water to the Noble Duke of Athole', *Burns: Poems and Songs*, ed. J. Kinsley (Oxford, 1969), p. 283.

60. R. Chambers ed., *The Life and Works of Robert Burns* (1856), II, p. 120.

61. Robert Burns, 'Written with a Pencil over the Chimney-piece, in the Parlour of the Inn at Kenmore, Taymouth', in Kinsley ed., *op. cit.*, p. 279.

*Notes and references*

62. Murray, *op. cit.*, pp. 316–17.
63. Plumptre, 'Narrative' (1799), ff. 53–4.
64. Richard Sulivan, *Observations Made during a Tour through Parts of England, Scotland, and Wales, in 1778. In a Series of Letters* (1780), p. 221.
65. M'Nayr, *op. cit.*, pp. 134–5.
66. Murray, *op. cit.*, pp. 345–6.
67. See Barbara Maria Stafford's article cited above, Part One, Ch. 3, fn. 19.
68. On Fingal's Cave and the 'organic' architecture debates see Geoffrey Grigson, 'Fingal's Cave', *Architectural Review* CIV (1948), pp. 51–4; and John Summerson, 'The Vision of J. M. Gandy', in Summerson's *Heavenly Mansions* (1949).
69. Lettice, *op. cit.*, p. 305.
70. Tobias Smollett, 'Ode to Leven-Water', in Smollett's *Humphry Clinker* (1771).
71. Garnett, *op. cit.,* I, p. 29.
72. Thomas Wilkinson, *Tours to the British Mountains* (1824), p. 12.
73. Newte, *op. cit.*, p. 74.
74. *Ibid.*, p. 77.
75. Piozzi, *op. cit.*, f. 12.
76. Garnett, *op. cit.*, I, p. 61.
77. Anne Grant, *op. cit.*, I, p. 3.
78. Jacob Pattison, 'A Tour through part of the Highlands of Scotland in 1780', National Library of Scotland, MS. 6322, f. 5.
79. Robert Clutterbuck, 'Journal of a Tour through the north of England [etc]' (1795), Central Library, Cardiff MS. 3. 277.
80. See also James Holloway's chapter 'The Falls of Clyde' in *Discovery of Scotland*.
81. Murray, *op. cit.*, p. 389.
82. Quoted in *Discovery of Scotland*, p. 47.
83. *Ibid.*
84. F. E. Hardy, *The Life of Thomas Hardy* (London & New York, 1965), p. 216.
85. Letter 11 February 1845: M. House and G. Storey eds., *The Letters of Charles Dickens*, IV (Oxford, 1977), p. 266.
86. Letter September 1789: W. S. Lewis ed., *Horace Walpole's Correspondence* (Oxford, 1961), XXXI, ii, p. 320.
87. Christopher Hussey, *The Picturesque* (1927), p. 4.

# Index

(Numbers in italics refer to illustration pages)